Assembling Health Rights in Global Context

What do we mean when we talk about rights in relation to health? Where does the language of health rights come from and what are the implications of using such a discourse?

During the last 20 years there have been an increasing number of initiatives and efforts – for instance in relation to HIV/AIDS – that draw on the language, institutions and procedures of human rights in the field of global health. This book explores the historical, cultural and social context of public health activists' increasing use of rights discourse and examines the problems it can entail in practice.

Structured around three interlinked themes, this book begins by looking at what health as a right means for our understandings of citizenship and political subjectivities. It then goes on to consider how and why some health problems came to be framed as human rights issues. The final part of the book investigates what happens when health rights are put into practice – how these are implemented, realized, cited, ignored and resisted.

Assembling Health Rights in Global Context provides an in-depth discussion of the historical, anthropological, social and political context of rights in health and develops much needed critical perspectives on the human rights approach to global health. It will be of interest to scholars of public health and human rights within health care as well as sociology and anthropology.

Alex Mold is Lecturer in History in the Centre for History and Public Health, London School of Hygiene and Tropical Medicine, UK.

David Reubi is a Lecturer in the School of Geography, Queen Mary, University of London, UK.

Routledge Studies in Public Health

Available titles include:

Planning in Health Promotion Work
Roar Amdam

Alcohol, Tobacco and Obesity
Morality, mortality and the new
public health
*Edited by Kirsten Bell, Amy Salmon
and Darlene McNaughton*

Population Mental Health
Evidence, policy, and public
health practice
*Edited by Neal Cohen and
Sandro Galea*

**International Perspectives on Public
Health and Palliative Care**
*Edited by Libby Sallnow,
Suresh Kumar and Allan Kellehear*

**Organisational Capacity Building in
Health Systems**
Niyi Awofeso

**Health and Health Promotion in
Prisons**
Michael Ross

Global Health Disputes and Disparities
A Critical appraisal of international
law and population health
Dru Bhattacharya

**Gender-based Violence and
Public Health**
International perspectives on
budgets and policies
Edited by Keerty Nakray

**Assembling Health Rights in
Global Context**
Genealogies and Anthropologies
Edited by Alex Mold and David Reubi

Forthcoming titles:

**Empowerment, Health Promotion
and Young People**
A Critical Approach
Grace Spencer

**Globalization, Environmental Health
and Social Justice**
R. Scott Frey

Assembling Health Rights in Global Context

Genealogies and Anthropologies

Edited by
Alex Mold and David Reubi

Routledge
Taylor & Francis Group

LONDON AND NEW YORK

First published 2013
by Routledge
Published 2014 by Routledge
2 Park Square, Milton Park, Abingdon, Oxfordshire OX14 4RN

Simultaneously published in the USA and Canada
by Routledge
711 Third Avenue, New York, NY 10017

Routledge is an imprint of the Taylor and Francis Group, an informa business

First issued in paperback 2015

British Library Cataloguing in Publication Data
A catalogue record for this book is available from the British Library

Library of Congress Cataloging in Publication Data
Assembling health rights in global context : genealogies and anthropologies /
edited by Alex Mold and David Reubi.
p. ; cm. – (Routledge studies in public health)
Includes bibliographical references.
I. Mold, Alex. II. Reubi, David. III. Series: Routledge studies in public health.
[DNLM: 1. World Health–history. 2. Bioethical Issues–history. 3. Health
Policy–history. 4. History, 20th Century. 5. History, 21st Century. 6. Human
Rights–history. WA 11.1]
174.2–dc23
2013000794

ISBN 978-0-415-53011-8 (hbk)
ISBN 978-1-138-96028-2 (pbk)
ISBN 978-0-203-75837-3 (ebk)

Typeset in Sabon
by Taylor & Francis Books

Contents

Notes on contributors

Dominique P. Béhague is Associate Professor in the Departments of Medicine, Health & Society and Anthropology at Vanderbilt University; Senior Lecturer in the Department of Social Science, Health and Medicine at King's College London; and Honorary Lecturer at the London School of Hygiene and Tropical Medicine.

Beatrix Hoffman is Professor of History at Northern Illinois University (USA) and author of *Health Care for Some: Rights and Rationing in the United States since 1930* (University of Chicago Press, 2012)

Marion A. Hulverscheidt is a guest researcher at the Berlin Museum of Medical History at the Charité and at the German Institute for Tropical and Subtropical Agriculture in Witzenhausen. She teaches philosophy of science at the University of Kassel, Germany.

Christos Lynteris is an Andrew Mellon & Isaac Newton Interdisciplinary Postdoctoral Research Fellow at the Centre for Research in the Arts, Social Sciences and Humanities of the University of Cambridge, UK.

Benjamin Mason Meier is Assistant Professor of Global Health Policy in the Department of Public Policy, University of North Carolina at Chapel Hill, USA.

Alex Mold is Lecturer in History in the Centre for History and Public Health, London School of Hygiene and Tropical Medicine, UK.

David Reubi is a Lecturer in the School of Geography at Queen Mary, University of London, UK.

Jane K. Seymour is Wellcome Library Research Fellow at the Centre for History and Public Health, London School of Hygiene and Tropical Medicine, UK.

Katerini T. Storeng is a postdoctoral fellow in medical anthropology in the Centre for Development and the Environment, University of Oslo, Norway, and honorary lecturer at the London School of Hygiene and Tropical Medicine, UK.

Hannah Waterson has recently been awarded a PhD in Japanese studies from the University of Manchester, UK.

Jarrett Zigon is Associate Professor in the Department of Anthropology and Sociology at the University of Amsterdam, the Netherlands.

Acknowledgements

This collection is based on a selection of papers given at a conference on health rights in global historical perspective at the London School of Hygiene and Tropical Medicine in February 2011. We would like to thank all conference participants for their contributions, and particularly Kirsten Gray, Minna Harjula, Marieke van Eijk, Summer Wood, Nicole Baur, Nancy Tomes, Noemi Tousignant, Adrian Viens, Maureen Lux, Glen O'Hara, Nato Pitskhelauri, Nino Chikhladze, Elene Pitskhelauri, Gayle Davis, Linda Bryder, Virginia Berridge, Susanne MacGregor, Anne Hardy, Martin Gorsky and John Manton. We are also grateful to the Wellcome Trust, which provided a conference grant to support the conference. In addition, we would like to thank Serge Reubi for his advice on nineteenth-century anthropology and the anonymous reviewers of the book proposal for their insightful comments. We would also like to acknowledge Grace McInnes and James Watson at Routledge for their help in seeing this book through to publication.

Introduction

Global assemblages of virtue and vitality: genealogies and anthropologies of rights and health

David Reubi and Alex Mold

This book explores some of the assemblages of virtue and vitality where the political and moral language of rights are brought together and combine with the knowledges and practices of biomedicine and health. Over the last hundred years or so, rights, health and medicine have been repeatedly associated and assembled in a variety of ways and forms. The concepts of social rights, solidarity and citizenship developed by T. H. Marshall (1992) and others, for example, dominated how medical care was administered in most Western democracies up until the 1970s (Seymour, this volume; Dean 2010; Miller and Rose 2008; Burchell, Gordon and Miller 1991; Collini 1979). According to these social liberal theories of rule, the nation's citizenry had a social right to access medical care made available through the welfare state (Reubi 2012a; Bolton 2008). Another example is the way in which bioethical notions of individual rights and autonomy have progressively informed the practice of medicine and research across the globe from the late 1970s onwards, displacing the social liberal assemblage of virtue and vitality (Mold 2011; Wilson 2011; Reubi 2010a; Stevens 2000). For bioethical philosophies of government, doctors and medical scientists have to respect the right of patients and research subjects to decide freely whether or not they want to undergo particular treatments and experiments (Fox and Swazey 2008; Sunder Rajan 2007; Jasanoff 2005; Tutton and Corrigan 2004). Another more recent example of the combination of rights and health has been the increasing prominence of human rights in the field of global public health (Reubi 2011). Indeed, from HIV/AIDS and access to medicines to sexual and reproductive health, human rights concepts such as the principle of non-discrimination and the right to health have come to play a significant role in the regulation of health (Hulverscheidt, this volume; Waterson, this volume; Zigon 2011; Nguyen 2010; Petryna 2009; Robins 2008; Biehl 2007).

This collection of essays brings together historians, anthropologists, lawyers and sociologists to explore some of these and other assemblages of virtue and vitality. The aim of these pieces is not to outline and defend a specific rights framework for biomedicine and health. Indeed, there are already sizeable bodies of literature doing exactly that, including the work of Jonathan Mann, Paul Farmer, Paul Hunt and others, which advance a human rights-based approach to global health (e.g. Schrecker, Chapman, Labonte and De Vogli 2010; Farmer 2004; Hunt 2003; Mann *et al.* 1999). Instead, the authors in this collection take a social constructivist and critical approach to examine three different aspects of health rights assemblages. First, they look at the ways in which these assemblages are made. For example, in her chapter, Marion Hulverscheidt analyses the way in which female genital mutilation became framed as both a medical issue and a human rights problem in global health policy in the late twentieth century. Similarly, Hannah Waterson examines how, influenced by international models, AIDS became understood as a human rights issue in Japan over the last 10 decades. Second, the chapters in this collection also study the problems inherent to assemblages of virtue and vitality. So, in her chapter, Beatrix Hoffman shows how immigrants to the USA have their access to health care curtailed because of the national nature of the right to health in that country. Likewise, Katerini Storeng and Dominique Béhague suggest that the way in which evidence-based advocacy has reconfigured human rights dis- courses in relation to maternal health has severely limited the possibility of making claims purely based on social justice arguments. Third, the studies found in this collection also examine the influence health rights assemblages have on identities and understandings of citizenship. For example, in her chap- ter, Jane Seymour examines the social liberal understanding of the citizen in relation to health that existed in the UK in the inter-war period. Likewise, Jarrett Zigon explores how the Russian Orthodox Church's drug rehabilitation programmes, which are based on a very particular reading of human rights, seek to transform participants through practices such as confessions, daily manual labour and talk therapy.

In this three-part introduction, we set the scene for the studies of health rights assemblages carried out in these chapters. In the first part, we sketch a possible genealogy of health rights over the last two centuries. Arguing against a celebratory history, we suggest that one of the first combinations of health and rights was the social liberal assemblage articulated around social rights, solidarity and the welfare state. Thereafter, the language of human rights and bioethics, both developed after and to some extent in reaction to World War Two, progressively replaced the language of social rights. This was especially the case after the 1970s, with the rise of bioethical notions of indivi- dual autonomy, and after the 1980s, with the rise of human rights talk of non-discrimination against HIV/AIDS patients. In the second part, we explore some of the questions, approaches and concepts articulated in the growing anthropological, sociological and political science literature on health rights assemblages. We start by introducing the concept of assemblage or apparatus of virtue and vitality. We then outline the importance of transna- tional expert and advocacy networks in the making of health rights appara- tuses, survey some of the problems and difficulties inherent to health rights and discuss the notion of subjectivity in relation to health rights. In the third and last part, we summarize the different chapters that make up this collection.

Genealogies of health rights

In the West, the language of rights has been applied to health since at least the eighteenth century. Although the right to health was not included in the French revolutionaries' Declaration of the Rights of Man and Citizen in 1789, it was added to the list of the state's obligations to its citizens by the Constituent Assembly in 1791 (Porter 1999: 57). For historians such as Lynn Hunt, this period saw the 'invention' of human rights, that is rights that were seen as being natural, equal and universal (Hunt 2007: 20). Although some commentators locate the origin of human rights prior to the Enlightenment (see, for example, Ishay, 2004) the danger, as Kenneth Cmiel noted, is that 'The expansive approach can wind up equating "human rights" with anything "good". Buddha and Jesus now become human rights activists' (Cmiel, 2004: 119). There has been a tendency to point to a seemingly inevitable 'rise and rise' of human rights (Sellars 2002) over the course of history, when, as more nuanced accounts demonstrate (such as Moyn 2010), human rights discourses have actually waxed and waned.

Indeed, the meaning of rights in general, and in the context of health in particular, has changed considerably over time. The birth of human rights is often located in the eighteenth century as it was in this period that rights were conceived of as being universal, applying equally to all men regardless of status – although not to women or ethnic minorities. Yet, most commentators suggest that from the close of the eighteenth century until the end of World War Two, human rights disappeared from Western political discourses (Hoffmann 2010; Hunt 2007). Rights talk, however, did not go away. Rights remained fundamental to politics, but the nature of the rights being demanded changed. In the nineteenth century, the focus was on the rights of the citizen rather than the rights of man, and attention was directed towards a set of political rights, such as the right to vote. By the early twentieth century, as enfranchisement gradually became universal, citizens' calls for rights were increasingly social in nature. The establishment of welfare states in European nations went some way towards satisfying such demands, as housing, education and health care came to be seen as social rights (Marshall 1992).

Universal human rights, as opposed to the rights citizens demanded of states, returned to global political prominence after 1945. The reappearance of human rights has sometimes been explained as being a consequence of the exposure of Nazi wartime atrocities, or as a result of the heroic actions of key figures such as Eleanor Roosevelt (Glendon 2001). But, as Mark Mazower points out, attempts to establish a new doctrine of human rights succeeded only because nation-states were prepared to accept this as part of a broader conception of liberal political thought which maintained that the individual required protection from the state (Mazower 2004).

The post-war turn to human rights manifested itself in a number of ways. Perhaps the most iconic was the United Nations Universal Declaration of Human Rights (UDHR) of 1948. Comprised of 30 articles, the UDHR proclaimed the existence of a series of civil, political, economic, social and cultural rights, including 'the right to a standard of living adequate for health and well being of himself and his family, including food, clothing, housing and medical care' (United Nations 1948). In 1946 the right to 'the enjoyment of the highest attainable standard of physical and mental health' was enshrined within the charter establishing the World Health Organization (World Health Organization 1946). The International Covenant on Economic, Social and Cultural Rights (ICESCR), which was ratified in 1966 and came into effect for member countries 10 years later, provided legal bite to such declarations (United Nations, 1966).

During this period another set of health rights were established around the use of human beings in medical research. A series of international codes governing medical experimentation were created following the Nuremberg Trials of the Nazi doctors (Schmidt 2004; Weindling 2004; Annas and Grodin 1995). The Nuremberg Code (1947) stressed the importance of the voluntary participation of the research subject and the Helsinki Declaration (World Medical Association, 1964) asserted that researchers should 'seek the potential subject's freely-given informed consent, preferably in writing'. Although these codes were symbolically very important, they had less immediate impact at the national level than might be supposed. Patients were often used in medical trials in both the UK and the USA in the 1960s without either their knowledge or their consent (Hedgecoe 2009; Hazelgrove 2002; Rothman 1991). Patients' rights, whether these applied to the individual or to the wider population, were hard to define and even harder to impose (Mold 2012).

By the 1970s the language of human rights was being used by non-governmental organizations and other actors to make demands at the national and international level (Moyn 2010). In health, action coalesced initially around the concept of primary health care, which aimed to provide health services at the community level (Brown *et al.* 2006). Primary health care was the focus of the Alma-Ata conference in 1978 and the resulting declaration proclaimed that health 'is a fundamental human right' (Alma-Ata 1978). Human rights language was used throughout the 1970s and early 1980s to advance the development of primary health care (Cueto 2004) and also in attempts to address the social determinants of health (Irwin and Scali 2007), as well as in specific health campaigns, such as those against breast milk substitutes and the dumping of pharmaceutical drugs on markets in developing countries (Hilton 2009).

Health as a human rights issue was propelled further onto the global agenda in the late 1980s and early 1990s in the wake of HIV/AIDS. The work of the American physician, Jonathan Mann, has often been seen as being central to the conceptualization of HIV/AIDS within a human rights framework (Fee and Parry 2008). Mann's research on AIDS in Africa convinced him that the epidemic had social and economic causes as well as infectious ones. Mann developed the WHO's first Global Strategy on AIDS based on human rights principles, emphasizing non-discrimination against people with AIDS and equitable access to health care (Gruskin *et al.* 2007). Human rights principles were put forward as a tool for the analysis of AIDS and as means to address the many problems it posed (Tarantola 2008).

During the mid-1990s, a range of other health issues, such as reproductive health, mental illness and disability, were also conceptualized as human rights matters (Gruskin *et al.* 2007). Indeed, the health human rights agenda continued to expand into the first decades of the twenty-first century. Health rights outcomes became linked to international development, as seen within the Millennium Declaration and the resulting Millennium Development Goals (United Nations 2000a). In 2000 the United Nations Committee on Economic, Social and Cultural Rights issued a General Comment on the Right to Health, expanding at length on the right to health contained within the ICESCR (United Nations, 2000b). A special rapporteur on the right to health was appointed by the UN in 2002 to report on global efforts to ensure everyone has the right to the highest attainable standard of physical and mental health.

Yet, despite such developments, it is not possible to point to a clear narrative of progress around health rights. As will be discussed in greater detail later, complexities and anomalies remain. The United States, for example, refuses to ratify the ICESCR for fear of generating a legal right to access to health care for its citizens. As Anne-Emmanuelle Birn notes, even if the right to health care was guaranteed worldwide, 'the right to health – as opposed to the right to health care – will still be far from achieved' (Birn 2008: 37). In part, this is because the meaning of health rights and health as a human right continues to be contested. Demonstrating how and why such contestations remain is one of the central themes of this book.

The key to solving such a puzzle is developing an understanding of where health rights and the notion of health as a human right came from. The history of health rights is relatively underexplored. Although the history of rights, and human rights in particular, is an expanding area of historiographical enquiry (Cmiel 2004), few of these texts make reference to the history of health rights (Hoffmann 2010; Moyn 2010). There are useful overviews of the development of health as a human right (Birn 2008; Tarantola 2008; Gruskin *et al.* 2007; Marks 2002) and work on the WHO and the right to health (Meier, this volume; Meier 2010). To situate health rights, the exploration of the use of health rights language in a range of temporal and spatial locations is required. This book aims to provide such a fine-grained analysis.

Social theory, health and rights

There is a growing anthropological, sociological and political science literature on health rights assemblages – from the research on bioethics (e.g. Reubi 2012a; Mold 2011; Fox and Swazey 2008; Sunder Rajan 2007; Stevens 2000) to the work on human rights and AIDS (e.g. Zigon 2011; Robins 2008; Biehl 2007; Kavita 2006; Nguyen 2005; Epstein 1996) and access to medicines (e.g. Ferraz, 2009; Petryna, 2009; Abramovich and Pautassi, 2008; Gloppen, 2008; Oleson, 2006). In this section, we outline some of the questions, approaches and concepts articulated in this literature – many of which are addressed, used and further developed in the essays that make up this collection.

Assemblages of virtue and vitality

The related concepts of mentalities and apparatuses of government developed by Michel Foucault (2004) and others (Legg 2011; Dean 2010; Agamben 2009; Miller and Rose 2008; Li 2007; Valverde 2007; Rabinow and Rose 2003; Deleuze 1992) are powerful tools to help make sense of existing combinations of the moral and political language of rights with the knowledge and practices of biomedicine and health. Mentalities of government are forms of rationality made up of moral and philosophical propositions, institutions, forms of expertise, scientific statements, intellectual categories, laws and administrative measures, architectural environments, techniques and practices organized in complex assemblages or apparatuses. Concerned with the direction of human conduct, these mentalities and associated apparatuses make it possible to constitute something as an object of thought, identify it as a problem and devise strategies to intervene on it. We suggest that combinations of rights, medicine and health are best understood as such mentalities and apparatuses of government and, accordingly, term them assemblages of virtue and vitality. Before outlining some of the advantages of thinking with these twin concepts, we give two examples of such assemblages.

The first example is the assemblage of social rights and blood transfusion developed in post-war Britain and lauded by Richard Titmuss in *The Gift Relationship* (Titmuss 1970; cf. Reubi 2012a; Reubi 2010b; Fontaine 2002). At the heart of this apparatus were the concepts of social solidarity and the welfare state: citizens had a right to receive blood for transfusion from the welfare state when needed and, in return, had a duty to give their blood regularly to ensure that the national blood bank was adequately stocked. In addition to these social liberal concepts, this assemblage was further made of and characterized by: the National Blood Transfusion Service, a centralized, state-run agency part of the NHS and responsible for the collection, storage and redistribution of blood of the British territory; medical knowledge about ABO and Rhesus blood types; laboratory technicians and cold storage rooms; and propaganda specialists and educational films to ensure that the public was educated about blood transfusion and aware of the importance of becoming a blood donor.

The second example is the assemblage of human rights and HIV/AIDS that emerged at the end of the twentieth century (cf. Robins 2008; Biehl 2007; Nguyen 2005). This apparatus is constructed around the figure of the responsible patient – someone who seeks information about and manages his or her disease; someone who is an active member of patient support groups; and someone who advocates for more public awareness about the disease and increased funding for research. Other defining features of this assemblage comprise: public health prevention campaigns; provision of condoms and needle-exchange programmes; human rights notions of non-discrimination and non-stigmatisation of people living with HIV/AIDS (PLWAs) and of the right to health and access to antiretroviral treatments; and HIV/AIDS screening tests, counselling specialists and community health workers.

There are many advantages of thinking and narrating combinations of rights and health through the twin concepts of govern-mentalities and apparatuses. First, it enables researchers to avoid following lawyers in thinking that health rights are only norms and institutions and examine instead the rich assemblage of knowledge, socialities, spaces and practices that make them up (Kurasawa 2012; Reubi 2011). Second, it allows researchers to emphasize the different meanings of health rights across time and space and explain this by pointing at the changing arrangements and assemblages of which they are part (Douzinas, 2007). Third, it enables researchers to analyse how health rights are transposed and adapted to new cultural and geographical contexts by examining the ways in which their assemblage are transformed (Allen 2011; Collier and Ong 2005).

Making health rights

For anthropologists, sociologists, historians and political scientists working on health and rights, the assumption is, of course, that health rights assemblages are not pre-existing but have to be made – a protracted and difficult process that necessitates a lot of effort and perseverance. A key driving force in the production of health rights apparatuses are transnational networks of experts and advocates (Reubi 2012b; Merry 2006; Riles 2000; Keck and Sikkink 1998; Hass 1992). These networks are coalitions or communities of professionals with a recognized expertise in a specific area. One characteristic of these networks is that their members develop and share a same 'style of thinking' – a combination of knowledge, values and practices that allow the network's members to identify problems that need addressing and suggest particular explanations, analyses and solutions. Another distinctive trait of these networks is their transnational character. Their members are all part of a highly educated, cosmopolitan elite – they live in different countries, speak more than one language and work for international institutions such as the UN, the World Bank or the WHO, NGOs, thinktanks, universities and other civil society groups (Goodale 2009; Merry 2006; Guilhot 2005; Chatterjee 2004; Dezalay and Garth 1998). Furthermore, while members portray these networks as horizontal and non-hierarchical, they are frequently dominated by particularly charismatic leaders or political entrepreneurs (Robins 2008; Nguyen 2002; Keck and Sikkink 1998). Similarly, although members will come from a variety of disciplines, lawyers will tend to be a strongly represented disciplinary group in the networks (Dezalay and Garth 2012; Reubi 2012b).

The function of these expert and advocacy networks is twofold in relation to health rights assemblages. First, they help make them up (Reubi 2012b; Rushton 2010; Shiffman and Smith 2007; Merry 2006; Keck and Sikkink 1998; Hass 1992). This involves the articulation of new knowledge. A good illustration is the already mentioned work of Jonathan Mann and his colleagues at the WHO and, later, at the Harvard School of Public Health in devising human rights principles for public health, from AIDS to sexual and reproductive health (Fee and Parry 2008). Second, it also involves research into and the problematization of new issues. A good illustration has been recent attempts by both lawyers and anti-smoking advocates to reframe and present tobacco control as a human rights issue (Reubi, this volume). Finally, making a health right assemblage also involves attracting the attention of both the public and those in power. To do so, expert and advocacy networks will generally frame an issue to make it comprehensible and meaningful, run public campaigns, reach the media as well as lobby governments. The international campaign run by the Treatment Action Campaign (TAC), Médecins sans Frontières (MSF), Oxfam and others to draw attention to the plight of PLWAs in South Africa and the importance of access to cheap anti-retroviral drugs is a good example of such work (Oleson 2006).

Besides making health rights assemblages, expert and advocacy networks also help disseminate them (Goodale 2009; Robins 2008; Merry 2006; Keck and Sikkink 1998). This involves, of course, disseminating information about health rights to government officials, local business leaders, human rights advocates and community organizers. It also encompasses lobbying and pressurising governments, multinational corporations and others to adopt the new policies and monitoring compliance. This is often done through campaigns and embarrassing those in power by showing the distance between discourse and practice. Furthermore, disseminating health rights involves translating them and making them both comprehensible and attractive for local actors with their particular cultural sensitivities and interests. In that sense, expert and advocacy networks are 'mediators' (Robins 2008: 15) who translate or 'adjust the rhetoric and structure' of health rights assemblages 'to local circumstances' (Merry 2006: 135). As Merry explains:

> Appropriating global [health] rights frameworks and translating them to fit into particular situations ... often means transplanting institutions and programs such as [patient groups, treatment possibilities, human rights rules and so on]. This is at heart a process of translation across boundaries of class, ethnicity, mobility and education. Intermediaries [such as NGOs or social movement activists] who translate global ideas into local situations and retranslate local ideas into global frameworks play a critical role in the process. They foster the gradual emergence of local rights consciousness among grassroots people and greater awareness of national and local issues among global activists.
>
> (Merry, 2006: 134)

Of course, these dissemination and translation efforts are not always successful. As we see in some of the chapters in this volume, local actors with differing interests or worldviews often resist the rationales and practices associated with health rights assemblages successfully (cf. Lynteris, this volume; Zigon, this volume).

Problems

In contrast with lawyers and public health experts' enthusiasm for and cele-bration of rights (e.g. Schrecker *et al.* 2010; Birn 2008; Tarantola 2008; Hunt 2003; Mann *et al.* 1999), the aim of many sociologists, anthropologists and political scientists has been to uncover the problems and failures inherent to health rights assemblages. This is generally done in a critical humanitarian spirit with social scientists using their research to criticize existing injustices and improve society (e.g. Das 2007; Farmer 2004; Kleinman 1995; cf. also Wilkinson 2012). These scholars have identified a range of issues inherent to health rights assemblages, from the overly biomedical understanding of the right to health (Greco 2004) to the Western cultural bias inherent to human rights discourses (Goodale 2009; Fox and Swazey 2008). Here we examine the three issues that have been most discussed in the literature.

The first of these critiques is that health rights assemblages are just another form of power and domination (e.g. Zigon 2011; Goodale 2009; Sunder Rajan 2007; Guilhot 2005; Hardt and Negri 2000; Dezalay and Garth 1998; Fisher 1997). These authors question whether human rights lawyers and public health advocates really are a benevolent force purporting to protect those most vul-nerable from abuse. The critics are, as Goodale (2009: 93) has argued, 'sceptical about the well-intentioned activism of the cosmopolitan elite' that make and diffuse health rights. There are two main reasons for this scepticism. First, many of these authors argue that the new class of professional legal and moral experts who has come to dominate health rights assemblages both disempower victims by speaking for them and bureaucratize the language of rights through standardized moral principles, formal procedures and routinized practices (Reubi 2011; Holden and Demeritt 2008; Sunder Rajan 2007). Second, many of these authors also point out that this new class of professionals are in cahoots with the forces of empire (Guilhot 2005; Hardt and Negri 2000; Dezalay and Garth 1998). As Hardt and Negri (2000: 36) argue, 'humanitarian NGOs' such as 'Oxfam and Médecins sans Frontières' are 'some of the most powerful paci-fic weapons of the new world order;' they are 'the charitable campaigns and the mendicant orders of Empire'.

The second most debated problem inherent to health rights assemblages is their close relationship with neo-liberalism (e.g. Mold 2011; Wilson 2011; Zigon 2011; Goodale 2009; Sunder Rajan 2007; Merry 2006; Waldby and Mitchell 2006; Scheper-Hughes 2001). For many human rights lawyers and public health advocates, health rights are deemed to be a bulwark against the dangers of neo-liberalism, from privatisation to user fees (e.g. Schrecker *et al.* 2010; Forman 2008; Tarantola 2008; Hunt 2004). Social science research has shown this assertion to be problematic. First, it demonstrates that health rights and neo-liberalism presuppose and advance the same figure of the subject: individuals, who are both free and responsible in relation to their health, bodies and lives (Zigon 2011; Waldby and Mitchell 2006; Scheper-Hughes 2001; Cooter 2000). This, of course, limits the protection health rights can offer against neoliberal policies. Second, social science research also shows that health rights tend to be articulated around nation-states, which are the ultimate bearers of health rights obligations (Reubi 2011). In contrast, health rights are rather toothless in relation to transnational corporations – the neo-liberal actors par excellence.

The third and last problem is the judicialization of health rights (e.g. Reubi 2011; Biehl *et al.* 2009; Ferraz 2009; Petryna 2009; Abramovich and Pautassi 2008; Gloppen 2008). Litigation, especially in Latin America, has become an increasingly popular method for realising the right to health and, especially, the right to access to pharmaceuticals. At the start, these legal suits were focused on providing cheap access to anti-retroviral drugs and benefited the majority of the populations in the countries where the suits were successful. But, with time, an increasing number of claims have focused on new high-cost drugs for rare diseases. These are generally filled by patient organizations with the help of interested pharmaceutical companies. As a consequence, the costs associated with pharmaceutical assistance have skyrocketed and the focus on high-cost drugs for rare diseases has tended to favour a few middle-class claimants to the detriment of standard treatments for the wider population. In other words, the judicialization of the right to health has led to the widening of health inequalities.

Subjectivities

An important part of the anthropological and sociological literature on health rights assemblages explores how the latter have reconfigured the ways we understand ourselves and others as subjects and citizens (e.g. Reubi 2012a; Zigon 2011; Robins 2008; Kavita 2006; Nguyen 2005; Nguyen 2002). Building on the work of Michael Foucault and others (e.g. Dean 2010; Rose 2007; Foucault 2004; Hacking 2002; Isin 2002), this literature examines how the knowledge, experts, organizational forms and techniques that make up health rights assemblages transform our modes of being. For this literature, there is no universal, fixed subject in relation to which one can govern. Instead, it holds that notions of subjectivity and citizenship that exist at a given time and place are progressively constituted through a process of subjectification. This process sees human beings constitute themselves through the adoption and use of knowledge, practices and techniques derived from medico-political apparatuses such as health rights assemblages (Douzinas 2007).

Health rights assemblages have brought into being a range of new subjectivities and notions of citizenship over the last century. Two of these seem to have been particularly dominant in the West (Reubi 2012a; Reubi 2010b; Rose and Novas 2005; Novas and Rose 2000; Rabinow 1996). The first one, which prevailed until the late 1970s, is the citizen with social rights and social duties. As mentioned earlier, this figure of the citizen was the product of social-liberal theories of rule developed by thinkers such as Keynes and Beveridge and articulated around the notions of 'welfare', 'social solidarity' and 'society'. In the case of unemployment, illness, accident or old age, this social-liberal citizen was cared for by the welfare state. In return, he or she had an obligation to contribute to the working of the welfare state and both trust and submit to its experts. The notion of the blood donor is typical of the social-liberal subject: he or she is entitled to receive blood from the state when needed but is also expected to give his or her blood whenever deemed necessary by physicians. The second dominant figure of the subject in the last century is the active, autonomous and responsible individual. This subject, a product of neo-liberal theories of government based on notions such as 'markets' and 'entrepreneurship', has been predominant since the early 1980s. This individual is responsible for his or her health and expected to plan actively for the improvement, or at least maintenance of his or her health. Neo-liberal subjects do so by informing themselves on the internet, discussing their care with their doctors and buying private insurance schemes on the market.

Of course, these forms of health and biomedical subjectivity do not come into being in a vacuum, but develop alongside and mix with pre-existing notions of the subject. This is all the more so when subjectivities generated elsewhere are transplanted to new socio-cultural settings (Robins 2008; Merry 2006). These foreign forms of the subject will generally encounter resistance and go through a process of translation to adapt them to the new settings (Zigon 2011; Reubi 2010b; Robins 2008; Kavita 2006; Nguyen 2005; Nguyen 2002). For example, when transfusion medicine was introduced in Singapore after World War Two, the social-liberal figure of the blood donor was adapted to fit the local governing elite's project to develop and modernize the newly independent city-state: citizens were entitled to receive blood and in return were expected to give their blood as part of the local nation-building efforts (Reubi 2010b). Similarly, the neo-liberal figure of the responsible, active 'therapeutic citizenship' that was developed as part of the fight against HIV/AIDS in the West was partly transformed and associated with religious forms of subjectivity when transplanted to places as different as post-soviet Russia and post-apartheid South Africa (Zigon, this volume; Robins 2008; Nguyen 2005).

One cannot discuss the relationship between health rights and subjectivities without mentioning those that remain excluded from these rights (Fine 2012; Douzinas 2007; Rancière 2004; Asad 2003; Isin 2002; Agamben 1998; Arendt 1951). As Douzinas (2007: 96) has explained, 'the privilege[d] subject of rights ... has been a white, well-off, heterosexual male, who condenses in his person the abstract dignity of humanity.' In consequence, he argues, 'rights have been denied to [the] people' that do not fit this picture and are 'routinely portrayed as uneducated, uncivilized or simply unworthy of the privileges of the fully human' (Douzinas 2007: 97). Categories of people who have been denied health rights are many. Women in the past and present have often seen their reproductive and sexual rights curtailed in the name of morality, tradition or culture (Hulverscheidt, this volume). Similarly, the privilege of claiming health rights was, until the process of decolonisation in the 1950–70s, limited to particular racial groups (Hoffman 2010). More critical today, perhaps, is the persistent discrimination of health rights in relation to nationality and citizenship (Hoffman, this volume). Although the exclusion of many categories of people from health rights continues, it is important to note that, as Rancière (2004) has argued, these categories are subject to political contestation and change (cf. also Hoffman, this volume). Health rights, as this book will demonstrate, are not static entities with fixed boundaries and consequences.

Summary of chapters

The ebb and flow of health rights over both time and place is a critical theme of this book. We begin, in Part I, by exploring the discourses that surround health rights, citizenship and subjectivity. As discussed already, health rights did not begin with the UDHR or the establishment of the WHO, but were connected with much older discourses surrounding citizenship, social solidarity and the nation-state. In her chapter, Jane Seymour discusses the place of rights in relation to the provision of health care in Britain during the early twentieth century. She suggests that reciprocal responsibility, and not rights, were central to good citizenship and thus good health. Such an understanding points towards a social conceptualization of health rights and responsibilities conferred on the citizen, not universal rights available to all humans. Indeed, as Beatrix Hoffman demonstrates in her chapter, discourses of citizenship can be used to restrict health rights, and particularly access to health care. Focusing on the USA in the later twentieth and early twenty-first centuries, she explores the position of unauthorized immigrants in America with respect to health care. Health care for immigrants has long been a contentious issue, and, although unauthorized migrants have been able to use emergency care since the late 1980s, they do not have access to the programmes that provide health care for elderly or indigent American citizens. In the United States, health rights are thus linked to citizenship, with unauthorized immigrants deliberately excluded. In his contribution, Jarrett Zigon further explores the relationship between health, rights and citizenship. In the first part of his essay, Zigon unpacks the political subject imagined in the work of Western political philosophers and lawyers who are favourable to the universal language of human rights. In particular, Zigon outlines the universal figure of the subject that underlies Michel Ignatieff's theory of human rights: the individual that has a capacity to stand outside his or her own socio-cultural context and freely reflect, decide and act. In the second part of his contribution, Zigon explores the ways in which the Russian Orthodox Church (ROC) uses the language of human rights as part of its drug rehabilitation and HIV/AIDS prevention and treatment programmes. Interestingly, he shows how Ignatieff's political subject is lost in translation, as the ROC reconfigures human rights as a tool to transform drug addicts into good, neo-liberal Russian citizens.

The problematic making and remaking of health as a human right is explored in greater detail in Part II. In his chapter, Benjamin Meier charts the transformation of the right to health through the development of international health frameworks and institutions. Beginning in the late 1940s, with the UDHR and the establishment of the WHO, and concluding with the response to HIV/AIDS as a human rights issue in the 1980s, Meier plots the changing nature of health as a human right at the international level. As the tools and objects of global health governance evolved, so, too, did the notion of health as a human right. This was not, however, an uncontested process: the human right to health was a place where many political tensions, including those between Cold War adversaries and rich and poor nations, were voiced. The establishment of the notion of health as a human right at the global level opened up the possibility for specific issues to be conceived of as human rights problems. In her chapter, Marion Hulverscheidt considers how and why female genital mutilation (FGM) came to be seen as an abuse of human rights. She demonstrates that the framing of FGM as a human rights issue in the 1990s was only the most recent approach to the practice. In the late nineteenth century anthropologists 'discovered' FGM, but saw it as a custom to be described, not as an abuse to be condemned. During the 1960s, doctors emphasized the potential health dangers of FGM and, in the 1970s, feminist groups saw it as a violation of women's rights. The construction of FGM as a human rights issue has not, Hulverschedit suggests, completely taken over from these older discourses. Another example of the making of human rights is offered by David Reubi. In his contribution, he explores how a network of public health experts and human rights lawyers have sought to frame tobacco control as a human rights issue over the last 10 years. Reubi describes in detail the efforts made by this network to construct a right to tobacco control and have it accepted within both the tobacco control and the human rights fields. He also shows how, for this network of experts, human rights are a strictly legal concept interpreted by lawyers and a way to access to powerful, judicial monitoring and enforcement mechanisms. This, Reubi argues, is contributing to the current judicialization of the right to health.

Resistance to, contestation of and the translation of health rights are considered in greater detail in Part III of the book. In her contribution, Hannah Waterson examines the ways in which people living with HIV in Japan have engaged with human rights discourses to shape policy and practice. HIV was initially considered to be a disease of 'others', principally foreigners and gay men, helping to foster a restrictive approach. Echoing the response to HIV/AIDS at the global level, gay groups and other NGOs began to use human rights discourses to press for less discriminatory policies. Waterson's chapter also serves as a case study of the ways in which the local and the global interact to transform and transpose the human rights discourse, calling into question the very universality of human rights. Katerini Storeng and Dominque Béhague raise additional problems with the rights discourse in their essay which examines the utilisation of rights language by activists and others to frame a specific health issue, in this case safe motherhood. They explore the changing nature and relevance of rights talk, particularly as new discourses, such as that around evidence-based policy and practice, have come to the fore. Drawing on ethnographic research within the safe motherhood community, Storeng and Béhague argue that over the last 20 years, the rise of 'evidence-based' advocacy in global health has lead to a resistance and move away from the rhetoric of rights. They also show how, where the language of rights has remained important, its very meaning was changed, to bring it in to line with the evidence-based ethos. These reformulations notwithstanding, there are scenarios that appear to remain resistant to the language and practice of human rights. In his chapter, Christos Lynteris considers the response to the SARS epidemic in China in 2003. The rights of individuals suspected of carrying the virus were quickly restricted in order to prevent the disease from spreading, a practice commonly employed across time and space. Lynteris shows how, in China during the SARS outbreak, the language of rights was, despite numerous tentatives, unable to impose itself. Instead, a biopolitical rationale intended to restrict the movement of migrant workers was the dominant discourse and remained so throughout the outbreak. In this scenario, health was not a right, but, rather, a duty to the state.

There is a sense then, in which Lynteris' chapter returns us to our beginning, with responsibilities and the role of the state remaining relevant at the opening of the twenty-first century just as they were at the start of the twentieth. The essays in this collection show that languages of citizenship remain important both in understanding where health rights came from and how they operate in local and national contexts. Constructing health as a human rights issue was a contested and incomplete process and one that had often unintended effects. Moreover, the technical discourses surrounding the systemisation and implementation of health as a human right may themselves further transform the notion of health rights. The changes over time and space in the meaning and application of health rights pointed to by this book are unlikely to be the final formulations of this dynamic concept.

Bibliography

Abramovich, V. and L. Pautassi (2008) 'Judicial Activism in the Argentine Health System: Recent Trends', *Health and Human Rights* 10(2):53–65.

Agamben, G. (1998) *Homo Sacer: Sovereign Power and Bare Life*, Stanford, CT: Stanford University Press.

——(2009) *'What is an Apparatus?' and Other Essays*, Stanford, CT: Stanford University Press.

Allen, J. (2011) 'Powerful Assemblages?', *Area* 43(2):154–157.

Annas, G. and Grodin, M. (eds) (1995) *The Nazi Doctors and the Nuremberg Code: Human Rights in Human Experimentation*, New York: Oxford University Press.

Arendt, H. (1951) *The Origins of Totalitarianism*, New York: Harcourt Brace.

Asad, T. (2003) *Formations of the Secular: Christianity, Islam and Modernity*, Stanford: Stanford University Press.

Barbot, J. (2006) 'How to Build an "Active" Patient? The Work of AIDS Associations in France', *Social Science and Medicine* 62:538–51.

Biehl, J. (2007) *Will to Live: AIDS Therapies and the Politics of Survival*, Princeton, NJ: Princeton University Press.

Biehl, J., Petryna, A., Gertner, A., Amon, J. and P. Picon (2009) 'Judicialisation of the Right to Health in Brazil', *The Lancet* 373(9682):2182–84.

Birn, A. E. (2008) 'Health and Human Rights: Historical Perspectives and Political Challenges', *Journal of Public Health Policy* 29:32–41.

Bolton, T. (2008) 'Consent and the Construction of the Volunteer: Institutional Settings of Experimental Research on Human Beings in Britain during the Cold War.' PhD thesis, University of Kent.

Brown, T. M, Cueto, M. and Fee, E. (2006) 'The World Health Organization and the Transition from "International" to "Global" Public Health', *American Journal of Public Health* 96: 62–72.

Burchell, G., Gordon, C. and Miller, P. (eds) (1991) *The Foucault Effect: Studies in Governmentality*, Chicago: University of Chicago Press.

Chatterjee, P. (2004) *The Politics of the Governed: Reflections on Popular Politics in Most of the World*, Princeton, NJ: Princeton University Press.

Cmiel, K. (2004) 'The Recent History of Human Rights', *American Historical Review* 109: 117–35.

Collier, S. and Ong, A. (2005) 'Global Assemblages, Anthropological Problems', in A. Ong and S. Collier, *Global Assemblages: Technology, Politics and Ethics as Anthropological Problems*, Malden, MA: Blackwell, 124–44.

Collini, S. (1979). *Liberalism and Sociology: L.T. Hobhouse and Political Argument in England, 1880–1914*, Cambridge: Cambridge University Press.

Cooter, R. (2000) 'The Ethical Body', in R. Cooter and J. Pickstone, *Companion to Medicine in the Twentieth Century*, London: Routledge, 451–68.

Cueto, M. (2004) 'The Origins of Primary Health Care and Selective Primary Health Care', *American Journal of Public Health* 94:1864–74.

Das, V. (2007) *Life and Words: Violence and the Descent into the Ordinary*, Berkeley: University of California Press.

Dean, M. (2010) *Governmentality: Power and Rule in Modern Society*, London: Sage.

Deleuze, G. (1992) 'What is a Dispositive?', in T. J. Armstrong (ed.) *Michel Foucault Philosopher*, New York: Routledge, 159–68.

Dezalay, Y. and Garth, B. (1998) 'Droits de l'homme et philanthropie hégémonique', *Actes de la Recherche en Sciences Sociales* 121(1):23–41.

——(eds) (2012) *Lawyers and the Construction of Transnational Justice*, Oxford: Routledge.

Douzinas, C. (2007) *Human Rights and Empire: the Political Philosophy of Cosmopolitanism*, Abingdon: Routledge.

Epstein, S. (1996) *Impure Science: AIDS, Activism and the Politics of Knowledge*, Berkeley: University of California Press.

Farmer, P. (2004) *Pathologies of Power: Health, Human Rights and the New War on the Poor*, Berkeley: University of California Press.

Fee, E. and Parry, M. (2008) 'Jonathan Mann, HIV/AIDS and Human Rights', *Journal of Public Health Policy* 29:54–71.

Ferraz, O. (2009) 'The Right to Health in the Courts of Brazil: Worsening Health Inequities?', *Health and Human Rights* 11(2):33–45.

Fine, R. (2012) 'Cosmopolitanism and Human Rights', in T. Cushman, *Handbook of Human Rights*, New York: Routledge, 100–109.

Fisher, W. (1997) 'Doing Good? The Politics and Anti-politics of NGO Practices', *Annual Review of Anthropology* 26:439–64.

Fontaine, P. (2002) 'Blood, Politics and Social Science: Richard Titmuss and the Institute of Economic Affairs, 1957–1973', *Isis* 93:3, 401–34.

Forman, L. (2008) 'Rights and Wrongs: What Utility for the Right to Health in Reforming Trade Rules on Medicines', *Health and Human Rights* 10(2):37–52.

Fox, R. and Swazey, J. (2008) *Observing Bioethics*, New York: Oxford University Press.

Foucault, M. (2004) *Naissance de la biopolitique, cours au Collège de France, 1978–1979*, Paris: Seuil/Gallimard.

Glendon, M. A. (2001) *A World Made New: Eleanor Roosevelt and the Universal Declaration of Human Rights*, New York: Random House.

Gloppen, S. (2008) 'Litigation as a Strategy to hold Governments Accountable for Implementing the Right to Health', *Health and Human Rights* 10(2):21–36.

Goodale, M. (2009) *Surrendering to Utopia: An Anthropology of Human Rights*, Stanford, CT: Stanford University Press.

Greco, M. (2004) 'The Politics of Indeterminacy and the Right to Health', *Theory, Culture and Society* 21(6):1–22.

Gruskin, S., Mills, E. J. and Tarantola, D. (2007) 'History, Principles and Practice of Health and Human Rights', *The Lancet* 370:449–55.

Guilhot, N. (2005) *The Democracy Makers: Human Rights and International Order*, New York: Columbia University Press.

Hacking, I. (2002) *Historical Ontology*, Cambridge, MA: Harvard University Press.

Hardt, M. and Negri, A. (2000) *Empire*, Cambridge, MA: Harvard University Press.

Hass, P. (1992) 'Epistemic Communities and International Policy Coordination', *International Organization* 46(1):1–35.

Hazelgrove, J. (2002) 'The Old Faith and the New Science: the Nuremberg Code and Human Experimentation Ethics in Britain, 1946–73', *Social History of Medicine* 15:1 109–35.

Hedgecoe, A. (2009) '"A Form of Practical Machinery" : the Origins of Research Ethics Committees in the UK, 1967–72', *Medical History* 53, 331–50.

Hilton, M. (2009) *Prosperity For All: Consumer Activism in an Era of Globalization*, Ithaca and London: Cornell University Press.

Hoffman, S.-L. (2010) 'Introduction: Genealogies of Human Rights', in S.-L. Hoffmann (ed.) *Human Rights in the Twentieth Century*, Cambridge: Cambridge University Press, 1–26.

Holden, K. and Demeritt, D. (2008) 'Democratising Science? The Politics of Promoting Biomedicine in Singapore's Developmental State', *Environment and Planning D: Society and Space* 26:68–86.

Hunt, L. (2007) *Inventing Human Rights: A History*, New York: W.W. Norton & Co.

Hunt, P. (2003) *Report of the Special Rapporteur on the Right of Everyone to the Enjoyment of the Highest Attainable Standard of Physical and Mental Health*, Geneva: UN Economic and Social Council.

——(2004) *Report of the Special Rapporteur on the Right of Everyone to the Enjoyment of the Highest Attainable Standard of Physical and Mental Health, Addendum: Mission to the World Trade Organization*, Geneva: UN Economic and Social Council.

Irwin, A. and Scali, E. (2007) 'Action on the Social Determinants of Health: a Historical Perspective', *Global Public Health* 2:235–56.

Ishay, M. R. (2004) *The History of Human Rights: From Ancient Times to the Globalization Era*, Berkeley: University of California Press.

Isin, E. (2002) *Being Political: Genealogies of Citizenship*, Minneapolis: University of Minnesota Press.

Jasanoff, S. (2005) *Designs on Nature: Science and Democracy in Europe and the United States*, Princeton, NJ: Princeton University Press.

Kavita, M. (2006) 'Politico-moral Transactions in India AIDS Service: Confidentiality, Rights and New Modalities of Governance', *Anthropological Quarterly* 79(1):33–74.

Keck, M. E. and Sikkink, K. (1998) *Activists Beyond Borders: Advocacy Networks in International Politics*, Ithaca, NY: Cornell University Press.

Kleinman, A. (1995) *Writing at the Margin: Discourse between Anthropology and Medicine*, Berkeley: University of California Press.

Kurasawa, F. (2012) 'Human Rights as Cultural Practices', in T. Cushman, *Handbook of Human Rights*, New York: Routledge, 155–63.

Legg, S. (2011) 'Assemblage/Apparatus: Using Deleuze and Foucault', *Area* 43(2): 128–133.

Li, T. M. (2007) 'Practices of Assemblage and Community Forest Management', *Economy and Society* 36(2):263–293.

Mann, J., Gruskin, S., Grodin and Annas, G. (eds) (1999) *Health and Human Rights: a Reader*, New York: Routledge.

Marks, S. P. (2002) 'The Evolving Field of Health and Human Rights: Issues and Methods', *Journal of Law, Medicine and Ethics* 30:739–54.

Marshall, T. H. (1992) 'Citizenship and Social Class', in T. H. Marshall and T. Bottomore, *Citizenship and Social Class*, London: Pluto Press, 3–51.

Mazower, M. (2004) 'The Strange Triumph of Human Rights, 1933–50', *The Historical Journal* 47:379–98.

Meier, B. M. (2010) 'Global Health Governance and the Contentious Politics of Human Rights: Mainstreaming the Right to Health for Public Advancement', *Stanford Journal of International Law* 46: 1–50.

Merry, S. E. (2006) *Human Rights and Gender Violence: Translating International Law into Local Justice*, Chicago: University of Chicago Press.

Miller, P. and Rose, N. (2008) *Governing the Present: Administrating Economic, Social and Personal Life*, Oxford: The Polity Press.

Mold, A. (2011) 'Making the Patient Consumer in Margaret Thatcher's Britain', *The Historical Journal* 54(2):509–28.

——(2012) 'Patients' Rights and the National Health Service in Britain, 1960s–1980s', *American Journal of Public Health* 102(11):2030–28.

Moyn, S. (2010) *The Last Utopia: Human Rights in History*, Cambridge, MA: Harvard University Press.

Nguyen, V.-K. (2002) 'Sida, ONG et la politique du témoignage en Afrique de l'Ouest', *Anthropologies et Sociétés* 26(1):69–87.

——(2005) 'Antiretroviral Globalism, Biopolitics and Therapeutic Citizenship', in A. Ong and S. Collier, *Global Assemblages: Technology, Politics and Ethics as Anthropological Problems*, Malden, MA: Blackwell, 124–44.

——(2010) *The Republic of Therapy: Triage and Sovereignty in West Africa's Time of AIDS*, Durham, NC: Duke University Press.

Novas, C. and Rose, N. (2000) 'Genetic Risk and the Birth of the Somatic Individual', *Economy and Society* 29(4):485–513.

Oleson, T. (2006) '"In the Court of Public Opinion": Transnational Problem Construction in the HIV/AIDS Medicine Access Campaign, 1998–2001', *International Sociology* 21(1):5–30.

Petryna, A. (2009) *When Experiments Travel: Clinical Trials and the Global Search for Human Subjects*, Princeton, NJ: Princeton University Press.

Porter, D. (1999) *Health Civilisation and the State: A History of Public Health From Ancient to Modern Times*, London: Routledge.

Rabinow, P. (1996) *Essays on the Anthropology of Reason*, Princeton, NJ: Princeton University Press.

——(2003) *Anthropos Today: Reflections on Modern Equipment*, Princeton, NJ: Princeton University Press.

Rabinow, P. and Rose, N. (2003) 'Foucault Today', in P. Rabinow and N. Rose, *The Essential Foucault: Selections from the Essential Works from Foucault, 1954–1984*, New York: New Press, vii–xxxv.

Rancière, J. (2004) 'Who is the Subject of the Rights of Man?', *South Atlantic Quarterly* 103(2/3):297–310.

Reubi, D. (2010a) 'The Will to Modernize: a Genealogy of Biomedical Research Ethics in Singapore', *International Political Sociology* 4:142–58.

——(2010b) 'Blood Donors, Development and Modernisation: Configurations of Biological Sociality and Citizenship in Post-colonial Singapore', *Citizenship Studies* 14 (5):473–93.

——(2011) 'The Promise of Human Rights for Global Health: a Programmed Deception?', *Social Science and Medicine* 73:625–28.

——(2012a) 'The Human Capacity to Reflect and Decide: Bioethics and the Reconfiguration of the Research Subject in the British Biomedical Sciences', *Social Studies of Science* 42(3):348–68.

——(2012b) 'Making a Human Right to Tobacco Control: Expert and Advocacy Networks, Framing and the Right to Health', *Global Public Health* 7(Suppl. 2): S176–90.

Riles, A. (2000) *The Network Inside Out*, Ann Arbor: University of Michigan Press.

Robins, S. (2008) *From Revolution to Rights in South Africa: Social Movements, NGOs and Popular Politics after Apartheid*, Woodbridge: James Currey.

Rose, N. (2007) *The Politics of Life Itself: Biomedicine, Power and Subjectivity in the Twenty-First Century*, Princeton, NJ: Princeton University Press.

Rose, N. and Novas, C. (2005) 'Biological Citizenship', in A. Ong and S. Collier, *Global Assemblages: Technology, Politics and Ethics as Anthropological Problems*, Malden, MA: Blackwell, 439–63.

Rothman, D. (1991) *Strangers at the Bedside: A History of How Law and Bioethics Transformed Medical Decision Making*, New York: Basic Books.

Rushton, S. (2010) 'Framing AIDS: Securitization, Development-ization, Rights-ization', *Global Governance* IV(1):1–17.

Scheper-Hughes, N. (2001) 'Commodity Fetishism in Organs Trafficking', *Body and Society* 7(2–3):31–62.

Schmidt, U. (2004) *Justice at Nuremberg: Leo Alexander and the Nazi Doctors' Trial*, Basingstoke: Palgrave Macmillan.

Schrecker, T., Chapman, A., Labonte, R. and De Vogli, R. (2010) 'Advancing Equity on the Global Market Place: how Human Rights can Help', *Social Science and Medicine* 71:1520–26.

Sellars, K. (2002) *The Rise and Rise of Human Rights*, Stroud: Sutton Publishing.

Shiffman, J. and Smith, S. (2007) 'Generation of Political Priority for Global Health Initiatives: a Framework and Case Study of Maternal Mortality', *The Lancet* 370:1370–79.

Stevens, M. (2000) *Bioethics in America: Origins and Cultural Politics*, Baltimore, MD: Johns Hopkins University Press.

Sunder Rajan, K. (2007) 'Experimental Values: Indian Clinical Trials and Surplus Health,' *New Left Review* 45:67–88.

Tarantola, D. (2008) 'A Perspective on the History of Health and Human Rights: from the Cold War to the Gold War', *Journal of Public Health and Policy* 29:42–53.

Titmuss, R. (1970) *The Gift Relationship: From Human Blood to Social Policy*, London: Allen & Urwin.

Tutton, R. and Corrigan, O. (eds) (2004) *Genetic Databases: Socio-Ethical Issues in the Collection and Use of DNA*, London: Routledge.

United Nations (1948) 'The Universal Declaration of Human Rights'. Available online: www.un.org/en/documents/udhr/index.shtml.

——(1966) 'International Covenant on Economic, Social and Cultural Rights'. Available online: www2.ohchr.org/english/law/cescr.htm.

——(2000a) 'United Nations Millennium Declaration'. Available online: www.un.org/millennium/declaration/ares552e.pdf.

——(2000b) 'The Right to the Highest Attainable Standard of Health'. Available online: www.unhchr.ch/tbs/doc.nsf/(Symbol)/40d009901358b0e2c1256915005090be?Opendocument.

Valverde, M. (2007) 'Genealogies of European States: Foucauldian Reflections', *Economy and Society* 36(1):159——178.

Waldby, C. and Mitchell, R. (2006) *Tissue Economies: Blood, Organs and Cell Lines in Late Capitalism*, Duke, NC: Duke University Press.

Weindling, P. (2004) *Nazi Medicine and the Nuremberg Trials: From Medical War Crimes to Informed Consent*, Basingstoke: Palgrave Macmillan.

Wilkinson, I. (2012) 'Social Suffering and Human Rights', in T. Cushman, *Handbook of Human Rights*, New York: Routledge, 146–54.

Wilson, D. (2011) 'Creating the "Ethics Industry": Mary Warnock, *In Vitro* Fertilization and the History of Bieothics in Britain', *Biosocieties* 6(2):121–41.

World Health Organization (1946) 'Constitution of the World Health Organization'. Available online: www.who.int/governance/eb/who_constitution_en.pdf.

World Medical Association (1964) 'Declaration of Helsinki, Ethical Principles for Research Involving Human Subjects'. Available online: www.wma.net/en/30publications/10policies/b3/17c.pdf.

Zigon, J. (2011) *'HIV is God's Blessing': Rehabilitating Morality in Neoliberal Russia*, Berkeley: University of California Press.

Part I

Rights, citizenships and subjectivities

1 Not rights but reciprocal responsibility

The rhetoric of state health provision in early twentieth-century Britain

Jane K. Seymour

The Universal Declaration of Human Rights claims to be a universal prescription for a better world. Its preamble states that the peoples of the United Nations 'have determined to promote social progress and better standards of life in larger freedom'. The ideal of human nature on which this rests is set out in Article 1 of the Declaration, which asserts, 'All human beings are born free and equal in dignity and rights. They are endowed with reason and conscience and should act towards one another in a spirit of brotherhood.' (United Nations 1948) The word 'should' in this formulation indicates the normative character of rights discourse, which is concerned to establish universally applicable standards of right and wrong. More particularly, since they 'principally involve the relationship between the state and the individual' (Mann *et al.* 1994: 10), it is the rights and wrongs committed under the authority of government that human rights are most concerned with. When the United Nations (UN) was formed during the Second World War, it was pitted against the Axis powers and the abhorrent atrocities committed by Hitler's Nazi regime in particular. The history of the beginnings of the UN therefore illuminates this focus on the protection of the rights of individuals or groups from potential abuses by powerful institutions, including governments.

But a notable concern with the relationship of modern nation states with individual citizens preceded the Second World War by at least 40 years, in Britain at least. During the later decades of the nineteenth and early decades of the twentieth century, however, it was not rights that formed the central aspect of this anxiety, but responsibilities. Throughout this era, debate about the relative roles of the individual and the state in establishing a stable and harmonious society were framed in terms of 'citizenship'. For progressive liberal thinkers during this era, this term had a particular set of meanings and associations that were drawn from the social, political, economic and, especially, the ethical context of the time. The term 'citizenship' was understood to encapsulate, in a holistic sense, the relationship between the individual and the collective more broadly, as well as the narrower juxtaposition of citizen and state. The slippage between these two pairings, which is evident in contemporary writing on the subject, as many of the quotations that follow will illustrate, points to the identification of the nation state with the wider concept of society as a whole at this time. In fact, heavily influenced by the philosopher T.H. Green, progressive liberals in Britain saw the state as the 'society of societies' (Green 1997: 452), and social relations were regarded as crucial to the definition of both the individual citizen and the purposes and mechanisms of the state. It was duty to others, the expression of reciprocal social obligations, that formed the core of this understanding of citizenship. At this time, then, citizenship, tended to place emphasis on obligations and not entitlements, apparently a completely foreign discourse to that of human rights.

Yet, citizenship then, as human rights today, was a normative discourse that was conceived as a means of attaining a better quality of life for all. There are many similarities between the early twentieth-century discourse of responsibility and the contemporary one of human rights, including the ameliorative intention to improve the opportunities and well-being of both individuals and populations. Although one discourse emphasizes rights, and the other responsibilities, both agree that these are complementary objects, two sides of the same coin. Where the early twentieth-century ideal of citizenship implied communal progress built on a model of social and political participation, human rights, too, rely on popular engagement and social mobilization: '[W]ithout an active civil society, paper commitments to rights mean very little' (London 2008: 67). Both seek to tackle the question of how the state relates to individual citizens and both are tied to democratic forms of governance. Indeed, human rights share an intellectual and political heritage with citizenship, because the postwar concern with rights evolved from the pre-war preoccupation with responsibilities. Both human rights and citizenship were constructed in the pursuit of high ideals and for the general good of humanity.

However, there is also distance between the two discourses and it is my aim in this chapter to make intelligible the alternative regime of relations between citizen and state that flowered at the end of the nineteenth century and into the twentieth. The sociologist T. H. Marshall described a narrative of citizenship over the eighteenth, nineteenth and twentieth centuries that focused almost exclusively on citizens' rights – as he recounted the progressive establishment of first civil rights, then political rights and, finally, social rights by British citizens (Marshall and Bottomore 1992). Thus, the twentieth century has become subsequently, in keeping with Marshall's scheme, the era of 'social citizenship', when citizens gained access to social rights of welfare, healthcare, housing and so on. However, as I shall demonstrate, the distinctive feature of citizenship in the late nineteenth and early twentieth century was not the emphasis on rights to material social goods, but rather the ethical nature of the relation between the individual and society, and a eudaemonic programme that highlighted moral and spiritual well-being. This is illustrated in particular in the approach of George Newman, Chief Medical Officer (CMO) at the Ministry of Health between 1919 and 1935, to the provision of health services by the state. Access to healthcare is one of the welfare measures that Marshall counted as one of the features of social citizenship. However, Newman's concern was with more than material rights. The aim he held to be at the heart of his public health work was 'the betterment of man's estate' (Newman 1920: 36) and the ideal to which this appealed was that of citizenship. This chapter examines Newman's programme of preventive medicine and its relationship to the contemporary discourse of citizenship in order to illustrate how the rhetoric of state health provision during the interwar period was dominated not by the pursuit of rights for all but the fulfilment of responsibilities by both citizens and the state.

Liberalism and citizenship in the early twentieth century

During the nineteenth century, British politics was dominated, at least in theory, by the liberal doctrine of *laissez faire*, which advocated a small state offering minimal interference with individual freedoms (Keynes 1926). In the latter half of the century, however, this principle began to be challenged. During Gladstone's second period as Prime Minister in the early 1880s, the Liberals themselves began to depart in practice from their own orthodox principles. The introduction of legislation such as the Ground Game Act (1880), the Irish Land Act (1881) and the Agricultural Holdings Act (1883), for example, all protected the rights of tenants, thereby eroding the rights of landowners. Gladstone referred to these paternalistic interventions as 'constructionism' and, despite qualms, supported such measures for primarily pragmatic reasons. As the volume of legislation increased, the distance between theory and practice grew and created a philosophical crisis in liberal politics. This was arguably the crucial factor in the development towards the end of the century of a reformed liberalism, known as the 'new liberalism' (Vincent and Plant 1984: 39–41). By the early twentieth century, the growing number of interventions by the state into the welfare of the population cemented the need for a reformulation of expectations concerning the relative roles of citizen and state. The classical liberalism of the Victorian era had valued individual self-sufficiency and viewed the state's role as essentially a negative one of removing limits to individual action. But up to and around the turn of the century, it was gradually recognized by new liberals that the central aim of liberal policies, individual freedom, could be constrained by structural factors. Poverty, disease, unemployment, all began to be recognized as social and economic inequalities that were circumstances beyond the power of individuals alone to transform. For new liberals, then, government had a legitimate role in protecting the interests of disadvantaged citizens and promoting greater social equality.

If this intellectual shift followed in the train of the politics of pragmatism, this indicates the powerful effect of changing social and economic structure in the late Victorian era. Urbanisation and industrialization had brought problems of poverty and inequality to the fore. They also rendered older liberal ideals of independence and self-help increasingly out of touch with the reality of working people's lives. The system of organized industrial capitalism that had arisen over the course of the preceding century had turned individual workers from artisans or tenant labourers into wage-earning factory hands. When the working poor had clear ties to places and communities, the expectation had been that within the framework provided by the parish and the tenancy system, they should take responsibility for their own independence. But this ideal of self-sufficiency was incompatible with recognition of the dependence of industrial workers on the fortunes and fairness of their employers. In response to this, new liberals reformulated their ideal of independence by reconsidering their understanding of the individual and of society. Classical liberalism held the freedom of individuals, believed to be rational and autonomous, as paramount and saw society merely as an aggregate of the actions of individuals. This produced an emphasis on self-help and self-reliance. New liberals, by way of contrast, recognized that the individual could not exist in complete autonomy but was embedded within a social and environmental context (Collini 1979; Freeden 1978; Weiler 1982). Progressive liberals at the end of the nineteenth century did not lose sight of the individual but talked rather in terms of his self-development or self-realization within a community, emphasising interdependence instead of independence.

One clear indication of this emphasis on interdependence was the prevalence of organic imagery in late nineteenth- and early twentieth-century rhetoric about society, a trope that highlights the impact of developments in biology on social and political thought during the latter half of the nineteenth century (Freeden 1978: 10–11, 18–19). Society was often compared to an organism, in which each individual represented an aspect or an organ of this living whole. The economist and new liberal theorist J. A. Hobson (1858–1940), for example, was convinced that 'humanity in all its various aggregations is a social stuff' so that, 'whatever forms of coalescence it assumes … there will exist a genuine organic unity' (Hobson 1914: vi). Although more sceptical of the 'mysticism' of describing society 'as if it were a physical organism', L. T. Hobhouse (1865–1929), another prominent new liberal and a pioneering sociologist, was happy to embrace this idea as helpful metaphor:

> For an organism is a whole consisting of independent parts. Each part lives and functions and grows by subserving the life of the whole. It sustains the rest and is sustained by them, and through their mutual support comes a common development. And this is how we would conceive the life of man in society so far as it is harmonious.
>
> (Hobhouse 1911: 87)

This idea of society as an organic whole furthered arguments for its coherent existence and for the necessity of the co-operation of its different elements, emphasising a reciprocal relationship between the individual and the social body (Freeden 1978: 96). If 'the life of the body is not perfected by oppressing the life of the cells, but by maintaining it at its highest point of efficiency' then this was also the case for the life of society and the life of its members (Hobhouse 1911: 90). This gave the state a legitimate role in freeing individual citizens from the oppressive conditions of social disadvantage on the pragmatic grounds that doing so had benefits for all in improving the overall functioning of society, which could be understood either in terms of the nation state or the human race as a whole.

The transformation of liberal thinking that depended on this new vision of the social interdependence of human nature made liberalism a force for progressive politics in the early twentieth century (Seymour 2012: 87–101, 112–20). The strength of the nation was felt to be in the strength of the commonweal, which meant that the health, well-being and, crucially, productivity of every citizen was important. These concerns with public welfare as the basis of national success resonated with contemporary calls for national efficiency that emerged from across the political spectrum (Searle 1971). In *fin de siècle* Europe, many writers had already proposed that the European races were degenerating both physically and morally (Pick 1989). Against this general background, the Boer War (1899–1902) ushered in an era of great anxiety about national fitness in both Britain and her Empire. This protracted and bloody campaign dented Britain's military and imperial confidence because it defied the expectation that her professional army would quickly defeat the Boer farmers. It prompted a public fuss over the reportedly very poor physical state of army recruits and, in 1903, an Inter-Departmental Committee on Physical Deterioration was appointed to 'make a preliminary enquiry into the allegations concerning the deterioration of certain classes of the population' (Inter-Departmental Committee on Physical Deterioration 1904: v). The Committee's report in 1904 stated that no clear evidence could be established for notable decline in the fitness of the working classes, but there were several 'acknowledged evils' in living and nutritional conditions that were adversely affecting health (ibid.: 92). All of this raised public awareness of the squalor in which the poorer classes of the community were living, especially in urban areas. Concern for the health and living conditions of the poor, therefore, had in part a very pragmatic root in promoting the progress of the nation. Underpinning it was the perceived need to improve the efficiency not just of Britain's military and empire, but also of her economic machinery. Radical calls for the overthrow of capitalism were rejected but it was recognized that the wheels of the industrial mechanism might turn more smoothly if all citizens had a shared stake in the generation of wealth. Thus social justice was rendered identical with social interest (Freeden 1978: 223). It was this thinking that broadly underlay the Liberal Government's reforms of 1906–14, including the introduction of free school meals, old age pensions, national health insurance and other measures such as workers' compensation for injury.

The national interest was not understood solely in economic or military terms, however, but as being underpinned by an ethical or moral component. For new liberals, the plight of the poor was a moral issue, both because of concern about the effect of sordid living conditions on the moral growth of poor families and their members, and because of what it indicated about the morality of the nation. New liberalism was therefore concerned not only with the material transformation of society. Indeed, at the root of their reforming programme was an ethical agenda to renew the character of the nation, for only this would allow its entire people to reap the benefits of social change. As Hobhouse wrote:

The 'social organism' is a perfect organism only when its members feel that they depend on one another. Hence no deep or lasting improvement can come without a change in the spirit of our industrial system ... No mere change of machinery can undo the moral damage[.]

(Hobhouse 1893: 4)

Ethics had been central to the liberal tradition ever since Adam Smith, who was a moral philosopher as well as a pioneering political economist. As Liberal MP Herbert Samuel put it: 'The trunk of the tree of Liberalism is rooted in the soil of ethics' (Samuel 1902: 6). During this period, straddling the end of the nineteenth and the beginning of the twentieth centuries, the ethical basis of liberalism came under renewed scrutiny as concern grew over the basis of freedom within a modern industrialized society such as Britain. As new emphasis was placed on the interdependence of individuals and on the inevitable social context of the development of character, the moral growth of both citizens and society was brought into fresh focus. In a society of interdependent individuals, the character of each member formed the foundation of the national morality, which was, in turn, the ethical matrix for the development of every citizen. The moral character of individual and community were intertwined: '[S]ocial development is also in the end personal or individual development' (Hobhouse 1911: 85). For a society to reach its highest state of development, it needed to offer each of its members scope for his or her own personal growth, which meant offering them opportunities to escape the squalor and misery of poverty and disease in order to develop characters of probity and responsibility. Underlying all welfare efforts in this period was an all-pervasive and all-important interest in ethical or moral social reform. Indeed, it was the moral effects of poverty, as much if not more so than its material effects, that reformists such as the new liberals sought primarily to tackle (Harris 1992: 132–33).

This is evident especially in the persistence of the ideal of voluntary effort, both in terms of philanthropic activity and self-help (Lewis 1995, 1999). These had been the main themes of Victorian approaches to welfare and they did not vanish with the new acceptance of state intervention, but were integrated within it. While it was increasingly the case that progressives envisaged the state and voluntary organizations working together towards many welfare goals, the voluntary sector was by no means delegitimized by state involvement in welfare provision (Macadam 1934). Indeed, as evinced by bodies such as the British Institute for Social Service (founded in 1904) and the National Council for Social Service (founded in 1919), both of which gained strong support from public and political figures, there was an undiminished zeal for charitable efforts towards building a better society in the early twentieth century. Philanthropic efforts were widely valued for their moral significance. Traditional face-to-face modes of giving reinforced the relationship between the benefactor and beneficiary of charity, which was understood to have a positive moral effect on both, but especially on the recipient. The casework methods of the Charity Organization Society (COS) were built on this personal interaction, for example. In this sense, voluntary effort was thought to have an advantage over state activity because participating in charitable schemes brought the poor into direct contact with exemplars of the values of good citizenship in the persons of middle-class charity workers. It was also understood as a moral education for the citizen engaged in charitable works, teaching them about the plight of the poor and demonstrating the need for the more fortunate to contribute to the welfare of their poorer fellows. Thus, the reform of the circumstances of the poor had a moral significance for everyone.

Harris has highlighted the patronising nature of charitable welfare efforts at this time (Harris 1992). Social reformers such as the COS and the Fabians tended to share a high-minded conviction that charitable or state benefits for the poor were only acceptable within a mode that clearly implied a reciprocal duty to behave according to middle-class moral codes that promoted thrift, self-reliance and temperance and deplored fecklessness, dependence and indulgence. For many social workers and social scientists, the inculcation of 'citizenship [was] the ultimate goal of social welfare.' 'Their aim as social reformers was not to keep the poor in their place, but to force the poor into active and prudent participatory citizenship' (Harris 1992: 132–33). The intention of this rhetoric was, in other words, to justify the coercion of the poor in parallel with the reform of their circumstances. However, it has tended not to be recognized that citizenship was as key to promoting state-sponsored and voluntary intervention aimed at improving the circumstances of the poor as it was in improving the poor themselves. Although the normative purpose of citizenship is undeniable, there was genuine concern in many quarters about the plight of the poor. Those who saw the poor as prevented from reaching their innate human potential favoured social reforms because they wished to dismantle the material and mental barriers to complete self-realization and full participation in the social life. The emphasis on releasing the poor from the physical and psychological conditions of poverty was often greater than that on reforming the poor. It should be recognized that citizenship was a joint effort of society and the state, emphasising the obligations of individuals, yes, but also of the state and of society as a whole (Seymour 2012: 249–73, 280–98).

And so, citizenship had a dual aspect. On the one hand, citizenship was about what the state and the community more widely could do to foster 'the full development of the faculties and the due enjoyment of life' for all citizens (Hobhouse 1893: 3). On the other, it was about training citizens into virtuous and responsible participants in civil society, as upholders of bourgeois social values (Freeden 2003). The reciprocity at the heart of this formula has widely been considered unequal in the face of prevailing social inequalities and it is certainly true that in many quarters this might reinforce a domineering and judgmental approach to the poor. But in its most progressive and democratic incarnations, citizenship was understood as an endeavour that pulled the entire community together and had a role in improving the characters of the rich as well as the poor. Citizenship in its most idealist vein saw each citizen as offering a different but equally valuable contribution to the community, according to his or her own talents, abilities and inclinations. This meant that the community ought to foster the development and invite the participation of every citizen – and that every citizen, high or low, ought to strive to reach his or her potential for both individual and communal benefit.

The influence of evangelicalism

We have seen how one of the key themes of new liberal thought about society was morality or ethics. This preoccupation was itself derived from evangelical Christianity, which had been central to public, political and social life for the Victorians. It is hard to overestimate the centrality of evangelicalism to the normative spirituality and morality of British society throughout the nineteenth and into the early twentieth centuries, for it had a notable effect on all forms of Christianity in Britain, from Dissenters, to Anglicans and Catholics (Bebbington 1989: 106–7). It would be equally hard to overstate the importance of trends in evangelicalism for the development of new liberalism and consequently of citizenship (Seymour 2012).

The nineteenth century has been called the evangelical century (Bebbington 1989: 149) but, in response to a series of challenges, evangelical thought underwent something of a reorientation in the latter half of the century. The first threat to evangelical tenets came from higher criticism of the Bible. This scholarship aimed at uncovering the historical origins, aims and purposes of Biblical texts, emphasising a rational approach and thereby undermining the traditional evangelical view of the Bible as direct revelation from God. Then, the explosion in evolutionary thinking that occurred in the 1860s after Darwin's publication of *On the Origin of Species* cast further doubt on the Biblical account of the origins of humanity, when the book of Genesis had already been called into question by geological science. There were those who sought to resolve the tension between rationality and revelation, including the authors of *Essays and Reviews*, a volume published in 1860. Written by broad church Anglicans who disputed the literal authority of the Bible and the relevance for the modern world of the morality it contained, it was hugely controversial at the time of publication. However, in its emphasis on integrating reason and science into an understanding of God, it signalled the shifts already occurring in evangelicalism that would continue to reverberate for decades to come. Over time, although the Bible remained the central Christian text, its importance as the indisputable word of God was eroded.

Alongside this, the importance of Christ's atonement and the emphasis on human sin in general was also diminished. As a traditional evangelical theology preoccupied with sin, hellfire and salvation through conversion and Christ's sacrifice on the cross became less pervasive, it was succeeded by a less stern version of evangelicalism in which the emphasis was different (Bebbington 1989: 145). As humanity's failings took on a softer connotation, the traditional evangelical focus on service to God began to be transformed into service to humanity. Activism, associated with the desire to convert others, had always been at the centre of evangelical faith, classically expressed in missionary work and in voluntary organizations of all kinds. Activism remained a vital strand in late Victorian religious life but it was often directed more into social and charitable work, which became an end in itself. This was in large part stimulated by the growing recognition of the 'social problem', which led to efforts to save bodies and not just souls. Some saw such activism as working towards the achievement of the Kingdom of God on earth, rather than only in Heaven (Packer 2003: 241–42). For others, this humanitarian and social consciousness began to be expressed in non-religious terms but was inherited from the same source and had the same fervour: 'Earnestness remained when Christianity faded' (Bebbington 1989: 150). It is no mere coincidence that the reform of liberalism followed closely on this transformation.

The moral norms of the late nineteenth and early twentieth centuries were ultimately derived from the values of evangelical Christianity, even though the emphasis on Christian belief itself was beginning to fade. Undoubtedly, for many activists, philanthropists, charity workers, social workers and Liberal voters, their motivation remained intimately connected with faith. But even those new liberals who counted themselves agnostic or atheist could not escape the fact that the humanitarian consciousness and moral assumptions underlying their worldview were bestowed on society by the evangelical tradition. Religious conversion may have faded into the background, but the middle classes had inherited a conviction that theirs was the right way of life and in the later nineteenth and early twentieth centuries they invested much effort into 'converting' the working classes to the merits of temperance and sabbatarianism and the evils of gambling and sexual licence (Packer 2003: 239). These were essentially middle-class values, which had supported a capitalist economy and existing social structures and yet which were transformed into the basis of a progressive political consciousness.

The true significance of citizenship lay in its encapsulation of a moral philosophy grounded in the essentially social nature of the individual. It implied a symmetry of rights and duties. Rights and duties existed on both sides, naturally, because, 'rights imply duties ... Rights and duties are the same facts looked at from opposite points of view' (Jones 1919: 109). The state's right to levy taxes, for example, was the individual's duty to contribute to the commonwealth looked at in reverse. The individual's right to claim relief in cases of poverty was, contrariwise, the flipside of the state's duty to provide for those of its citizens unable to support themselves. Because the state and the citizen were bound by social relations, they were linked by reciprocal and concordant ethical imperatives. This placed responsibility to others at the core of citizenship. The philosopher Sir Henry Jones (1852–1922) believed that this had inspired a new spirit of the age: 'We are reinterpreting the idea of freedom,' he wrote, 'and setting out to prove that "perfect freedom" expresses itself only in mutual service' (ibid.: 26–27).

Although the Liberal Party went into decline after the First World War, the new liberal ideas underlying mainstream progressive politics remained important (Freeden 1986) and citizenship retained its relevance to discussions about the role of the state in individual welfare. Political figures such as Christopher (later Viscount) Addison (1869–1951) continued to work towards the ideals of new liberalism, although not necessarily from within the Liberal fold. Having served as Minister for Reconstruction under Lloyd George during the war, he afterwards became Minister of Health in 1919. He was removed from this post in 1921, becoming Minister without Portfolio until his resignation in the same year, over the halting of the housing programme he had worked for while at the Ministry of Health. After he lost his seat in the 1922 general election, Addison moved to join the Labour Party, from within which he continued his political career, first as an MP and government minister and later as a Labour peer. Liberal MP Percy Alden (1865–1944) similarly decamped to Labour, as, somewhat earlier, had the future Chancellor of the Exchequer, Philip Snowden (1864–1937). The Labour Party was heir not only to personnel but also to the progressive programme of the Liberals. James Ramsay MacDonald (1866–1937), leader of the Labour party in the interwar years and Britain's first Labour prime minister, was closer to liberalism than to socialism in his political ideology and continued to espouse citizenship. He repudiated Marx and shared the ethical ideals of the new liberals, supporting 'ideals of moral citizenship', embodied in such phrases as 'each for all and all for each' (Barker 1972: 90). MacDonald, like the new liberals, was concerned with the relation of the individual and his development to the social context: 'Socialism,' he wrote, 'is a theory of social organization, which reconciles the individual to society' and 'has discovered how the individual in society can attain to a state of complete development' (ibid.: 100). And it was not only political figures in the interwar period who represented the continuing relevance of new liberal thinking. George Newman, who was a friend of both Addison and MacDonald, embodied the presence of new liberal ideals within Whitehall up to 1935 and his programme of preventive medicine was built on the ideal of citizenship.

Citizenship and health: the ideas of George Newman

Newman was born in 1870 into a Quaker family. His whole family was involved in missionary and charitable work, for the Religious Society of Friends had been heavily influenced by mainstream evangelicalism early in the nineteenth century. During Newman's childhood and youth, the Quaker response to evangelical thought began to alter in reaction to the same factors that were gradually transforming the evangelical tradition across the Christian spectrum. Indeed, the Quakers came to the forefront of the new emphasis on social work as God's work. This trend was already underway in the last decades of the nineteenth century, but by the beginning of the twentieth century Quakers viewed themselves as having a special role to play in the spiritual and moral renewal not just of their own community, but also wider society (Packer 2002, 2003).

Particularly important in this was the figure of John Wilhelm Rowntree (1868–1905), a young man who captured the imagination of his own generation of Quakers in his belief that young Friends had a particularly valuable contribution to make in the creation of a harmonious society because of their distinct theological heritage, which emphasized the presence of God within every human being: '[W]ith our clearer perception of the indwelling nature of the Spirit [we] ought to strike more easily below class distinction and form to the recognition of the true brotherhood of man' (Rowntree 1905: xvi). John Wilhelm stated his intention to 'devote [his] life to making the Society of Friends ... a real and living force in the world' (ibid.: xxiv). But the major focus of this was 'the work of bringing spiritual life and vigour back to our England' (ibid.: xvi). Thus, for John Wilhelm, spiritual reform was primary to social change. In this, he was representative of the influence of religion on political and social thought at this time. Despite his underlying spiritual aims, however, there was a definite practical inflection towards social work: 'Friends should be drawn out into more public service, and accustom themselves to a wider and more hopeful view of their responsibilities' (ibid.: xxxvii). His early death, after a career in which he was dogged by health problems and yet remained very active within the Society of Friends, only increased the aura surrounding John Wilhelm. The general esteem in which he was held was shared by Newman, who declared on John Wilhelm's death in 1905:

> O yes, we Quakers have been given something of a vision; if only, if only we w[oul]d proclaim it. We might make the world just a bit nearer to a larger & truer thought of God. Now John Wilhelm has left us, some of us must buck up & do ... something.
>
> (cited in Kennedy 2001: 288)

Newman's career in public health was his own contribution to this Quaker mission for spiritual and social improvement. As a child he had harboured ambitions of following in the footsteps of his father and becoming a missionary, perhaps in India. But while at medical school in Edinburgh, Newman's eyes were opened to the squalor of the city's slums: '[N]o words can possibly describe the *beastly* filth & misery of underground Edinbro', he wrote to his aunt. He began to realize the need in the home field: 'Social problems! Indeed – they want the light & cleanliness of Christ – they want some few lives to be given up & sacrificed for their good' (Newman [1889]). He held religious meetings in the tenements of Edinburgh while he was at university there and when he subsequently moved to London, he also worked with the poor in the slums of Covent Garden. His career in public health began with part-time appointments as a medical officer in London and Bedfordshire, before he gained his first full-time appointment as the local Medical Officer of Health for Finsbury, another deprived area of London. After making a name for himself here, he was appointed as CMO to the Board of Education in 1907 and subsequently to the post at the Ministry of Health when it was formed in 1919. Although his

medical training and interests led him into public health, this was never separate for Newman from his sense of mission (Hammer 1995: 24–26). The philosophy underpinning his views on preventive medicine originated in his youthful
missionary fervour but as he matured, and throughout his adult career, it was
aimed firmly at social service.

As well as remaining all his life an active and committed Friend, Newman
was also confirmed in his liberal politics. This political engagement was first
developed during his days at Bootham, a Quaker school in York. The Liberal
Party had, in the course of the nineteenth century, espoused the cause of religious equality and thus become the party of nonconformists, including Quakers
(Isichei 1970: 200–202), and so the political education at Bootham was steeped
in the liberal tradition. Newman shared a keen interest in the Liberal Party with
his fellow pupil and friend Arnold S. Rowntree (1872–1951), a cousin of the
brothers John Wilhelm and Benjamin Seebohm Rowntree, both sons of Joseph
Rowntree, the confectionary magnate and philanthropist (Smith 2000: 55). This
friendship endured for life and both boys retained their liberal leanings when
they became adults. Arnold Rowntree became Liberal MP for York from 1910
to 1918, during which time he worked towards social reforms such as national
insurance, fighting for the rights of low-paid workers in particular (Packer
2003: 249–51). Newman's own engagement with social issues was evident from
his teens. During his time at Bootham, he contributed seven essays covering
political and social concerns to the school's *Bootham Observer*, a prolific number
given that most other contributors wrote only two or three pieces (Smith 2000: 57–
58). In his adulthood, Newman could best be described as a new liberal. In this, he
was once more aligned with the Rowntree family, who not only through political activities but also newspaper ownership were promoters and pioneers of
new liberal policies (Packer 2003). For both Newman and the Rowntrees, their
faith and the sense of 'social witness' that derived from it converged on new
liberal ideals for both the moral and material renewal of society.

When it came to public health work, then, Newman's philosophy was per-
meated with the new liberal ideal of citizenship. Newman's preferred term for
public health work was 'preventive medicine', a terminology that was broadly
accepted by the turn of the century and, by the 1920s, widely understood and
uncontroversial. Preventive medicine had evolved from an older environmental
understanding of public health, through the re-orientation from sanitation and
engineering to state medicine and into greater alignment with curative medicine
(Fee and Porter 1992). While still inclusive of sanitary work, vaccination programmes and epidemiological investigations, it was now also concerned with
personal hygiene and disease prevention. As with citizenship, preventive medicine was an object of two balanced and related aspects, the role of the state and
the role of the individual. Indeed, the term 'preventive medicine' was surely
preferred by Newman and many of his contemporaries to its alternative of
'state medicine' because the former term included non-statutory activities, had
no specific locus and therefore implicated every and all bodies in its successful
prosecution. One crucial pillar of preventive medicine was hygienic living,

meaning simply the adaptation of one's way of life to promote health, in regard to factors such as diet, sleep, exercise, alcohol consumption and dental cleanliness. This required a fully participatory involvement from each and every member of the community for its full benefits to be realized in terms of the national health. It was a quintessential example of a reciprocal responsibility.

It has become almost a truism that the 1930s was the decade in which the shift away from a sanitarian, environmental conception of public health found its culmination in a preoccupation with personal health. In particular, historians frequently note that this re-orientation resulted in a new onus on the individual to look after his or her own health, which is interpreted as removing the burden of responsibility from the state's health authorities. 'Increasingly, public health authorities focused on what the individual should do to ensure personal hygiene.' (Lewis 1986: 5). Newman's writings illustrate the trend towards individual hygiene, encouraging citizens to take care of their own well-being through healthy living. In his annual reports, from the early 1920s onwards, he emphasized the importance of 'an educated people willing and able to practise the way of health' (Newman 1920: 6). Anne Karpf has dubbed this a 'punitive individualism, where each citizen has a moral duty to make themselves fit' (Karpf 1988: 35). There is no doubt that Newman did perceive personal hygiene as a moral duty, in the sense derived from the contemporary moral philosophy underlying the emphasis on social obligation. The understanding of human nature as essentially social saw the individual as having a responsibility to others as much as to him- or herself. In fact, Newman considered each person 'under obligation to cultivate his own health and capacity, and so to conduct himself as not to conduce to the hurt or risk of his neighbours' (Newman 1922: 169). But to characterize this as 'punitive' misses the essentially relational content of morality in the interwar years, the understanding that individuals were not divisible from their place within the community, as well as the emphasis on the counterpart to individual efforts – the activities of state and society to promote the well-being of all citizens.

Newman saw the public's health, like any other aspect of the nation's progress, as dependent on 'a partnership … between those who govern, and those who are governed' (Newman 1929: 207). He framed the emphasis on individual responsibility for personal and communal health in very positive terms, as part of the reciprocal duty that existed between citizen and state. The individual's power to effect a positive impact on his or her own health was viewed as an opportunity for citizens: it meant the involvement of every citizen in the project of national well-being, representing simultaneously an expansion of the public health project and of the responsible autonomy of citizens. The practice of personal hygiene offered scope for each citizen to improve his or her life at the same time as advancing the progress of the nation, because the fitness, productivity and well-being of everyone was valuable to the community as a whole. Thus, preventive medicine was a key ground for the operation of an ethic of citizenship. Indeed, Newman felt it was a special case in the relationship of citizens and state:

> All wise government no doubt depends on the assent of the governed, but in public and private medicine an even fuller assent is needful, if the individual is to reap his full advantage and at the same time act loyally as a member of the community.
>
> (Newman 1922: 169)

Personal health was a crucial aspect of civic responsibility. 'For the people to regulate their homes and the conditions under which they work with reason and good sense,' observed Newman, was not an 'infringement of individual liberty'. Rather, 'it has proved repeatedly to lead to an increase in both individual liberty and responsibility'. Responsibility and liberty, far from being mutually exclusive or mitigating categories, were rendered identical by the philosophy that viewed man's social obligations as his ultimate matrix for self-development. This was not applicable, in Newman's vision, only to the working classes but to both 'capitalist and workman' (Newman 1931: 109). It is clear that, for Newman, hygienic practices promised to increase the moral freedom of *all* citizens. True to his Quaker principles, he was essentially an egalitarian and saw every human being as equally worthy. Preventive medicine in Newman's understanding was not about a paternalist disciplining of the lower classes but about drawing all citizens, of every part of society, together in a united effort.

In Newman's vision of preventive medicine, the conditions that would bring about true citizenship could not be forced or bought because any coercion or bribes would prevent true self-determination. Thus, the state could train citizens in the ways of civic duty, and offer them opportunities to gain true freedom through the development and fulfilment of their responsibilities, but only individuals themselves could pursue this process for themselves:

> Unlike other social movements of emancipation, that of personal and communal health demands and requires the assent and daily co-operation of those it would benefit. Health is not something which can be imposed by authority, it begins and flourishes only as it is practised. There is nothing under the sun more democratic[,] individualistic and co-operative.
>
> (Newman 1931: 108–9)

Newman opined that 'the best State is that which does most for the individual citizen and enables him to do most for himself' (ibid.: 235). This was the conception at the heart of the new liberal view of the state and of the ideal of citizenship: that state and citizen were bound to work together if they pursued the highest form and quality of life for all within society.

For Newman, there was never any question of full citizenship being entirely the individual's endeavour. Indeed, his perception of the importance of the individual to society as a whole presented a powerful motive for the group to foster individual growth. Newman talked of:

[T]he paramount concern of the State in the lives and upbringing of its citizens. It is the direct interest of the State to recognize that the common-wealth is a vital and growing organism, and not a machine, preserving its very existence by stimulating and developing the aggregate of individual *capacity* and *responsibility*, by which alone the strength and reproductive power of the State itself is sustained, and by which alone the growing obligations of the individual can be fulfilled and opportunity offered for their fulfilment.

(Newman 1931: 109–10)

For individuals to thrive in the living of rich and morally responsible lives, the community needed to offer the conditions to make this possible for every citizen:

We must encourage and assist him to live up to the top of his capacity, physically, mentally and morally – to be creative and productive, to do, and enjoy doing, worthy things, to co-operate harmoniously with human society, and to extend by his endeavour and ideals the frontiers of life.

(ibid.: 193)

If the individual had a responsibility to himself and to his community, it was incumbent on the state to foster its citizens and enlarge their lives.

In common with other new liberals, Newman saw the state as having a cru-cial role to play in freeing citizens to live full and healthy lives – this was a formal expression of the communal obligation to the individual's well-being. And therefore the state had an important contribution to make to preventive medicine. The state in this period did, in fact, carry out or support numerous endeavours in the field of public health, as the official annual reports of the Ministry of Health attest, from the provision of sanitary measures, including water supply, sewerage and refuse removal, to treatment facilities for fevers, tuberculosis and venereal disease, and ante- and post-natal care for mothers and infants, as well as the administration of medical services in connection with the Poor Law – the list is long. There were also several activities, such as housing and town planning, provision of public recreation grounds and public baths, that were neither traditional sanitary nor medical concerns but were considered of relevance to the health of the community. A neat and tangible summary of the medical services provided to the individual only (that is excluding work, such as sanitation or intelligence gathering, that would be seen to benefit the community rather than the individual immediately or directly) was given in the Ministry's annual report for 1934:

The contacts of the public medical services may be briefly summarized:

(a) Before birth – ante-natal advice and treatment under the maternity and child welfare service.

(b) At birth – maternity and midwifery provision under the maternity and child welfare service and maternity benefit under the National Health Insurance scheme.

(c) Between birth and school age – under the maternity and child welfare service.

(d) During school age – under the school medical service.

(e) During his working life if an insured person – domiciliary medical advice and treatment through Local Insurance Committees constituted under the National Health Insurance scheme.

(f) At any time when destitute – domiciliary and institutional medical advice and treatment under the Poor Law.

(g) For Infectious Diseases, Tuberculosis, Venereal Disease at any stage of his career – under the provision made by Local Authorities.

(Ministry of Health 1933–34: 88)

The provision detailed here clearly represented a commitment by the state to promote the health of its citizens, especially its working population, its mothers and its children. For Newman, the gradual proliferation of such activities over the later nineteenth and early twentieth centuries represented the growing commitment of the state, for combined philosophic, social, political, economic, scientific and humanitarian reasons, to the good of the individual. Newman understood the state as representative of the community and as having an overriding obligation to the individual that was the reciprocal of the citizen's duty to the commonweal. Citizenship was the summary of this mutual bond of obligation and contribution.

For Newman, preventive medicine was one key aspect of citizenship and his version of citizenship was both the means and the end of a democratic society of equals, each with his or her own contribution to make to the overall life of the social body. He was an idealist, and there is much to admire in his ideals. Nevertheless, Newman's style of thinking, although it was characteristic of the progressive milieu during the first half of the twentieth century, was eclipsed by the different sensibilities of the post-war era. From the perspective of our own era, Newman and the new liberals look at best naive in their ambitions for social reform. At worst, their ideology can be viewed as propping up the system of industrialized capitalism that was then and is now potentially so damaging to the interests of workers. It was certainly an incremental and gradualist template for amelioration and not a radical or revolutionary one. But it is important not to lose sight of the genuine concern with social reform shared by progressive liberals over the first half of the century, although it is unfamiliar to us in its emphasis on moral reform prior to material change. Despite its tendency to propagate the norms of the middle classes that were inherited from evangelical Christianity, citizenship in the early twentieth century was ultimately aimed at making life better, fuller, richer for all.

Conclusion: universal human rights?

The discourse of human rights is presented as a universally applicable template, as discussed at the beginning of this piece, for 'social progress and better standards of life in larger freedom' (United Nations 1948). It therefore appears to express a series of universal ethical norms, which are based on man's innate nature as a rational, moral and rights-bearing being. However, the mainstream progressive politics of the early twentieth century did not view human individuals and citizens in the same light. Rather, they were conceived as interdependent and responsibility bearing, with human development and fulfilment dependent on the recognition of obligations imposed by the essentially social nature of human beings.

The lesson from a study of citizenship in the first half of the twentieth century, then, is that views of the 'essential' nature of man and the moral discourses tied to these are not universal. They are specific to the particular social, cultural, religious, intellectual and political conformations from and within which they arise. The ethical ideal of citizenship espoused by Newman and his contemporaries was born within the context of liberal and evangelical traditions, developed in the face of the new social problems created by the industrial revolution. It offered a template of how individuals, citizens, communities and states should interact in order to achieve harmony and happiness, in a manner that avoided radical challenge to the political order of the day. Human rights, as heirs to the tradition of citizenship, also form a normative discourse that has been constructed within a liberal-capitalist context and that supports the economic and political structures of such a system. Responsible citizens and rights-bearing subjects alike are not born, they are made within the social and cultural context that disciplines them to recognize the truths of prevailing discourse. In the case of both human rights and citizenship, this context is derived from the Christian tradition, its moral norms, and its interaction with rationalism (another European construct, this time of the Enlightenment). The differences between the two regimes developed as these factors evolved and were reconfigured in tandem with social and intellectual change over the twentieth century.

The ethics of health and healthcare will always be normative, although the prescription will vary depending on the perspectives, contexts and preoccupations of the prevailing discourse on the subject. We should, therefore, be cautious of assertions that a 'human rights approach to health is critical to address growing global health inequalities' (London 2008), if only because they contain claims that the best, if not the sole, way to make progress in improving lives and health is to channel resources into human rights programmes that create rights-bearing citizens. We ought to recognize that if we choose such a path, we are potentially excluding other definitions of human well-being and other ideals of human nature that are formed within alternative paradigms of society, community and spirituality. We should also understand that the currently championed discourse of human rights is likely, in time, to be eclipsed, or at least modified, by another, as yet unformed and unknown, version of the ethics of health and welfare.

Bibliography

Barker, B. (ed.) (1972) *Ramsay MacDonald's Political Writings*, London: Allen Lane.

Bebbington, D.W. (1989) *Evangelicalism in Modern Britain: A History from the 1730s to the 1980s*, London: Unwin Hyman.

Collini, S. (1979) *Liberalism and Sociology: L.T. Hobhouse and Political Argument in England 1880–1914*, Cambridge: Cambridge University Press.

Fee, E. and D. Porter (1992) 'Public Health, Preventive Medicine and Professionalisation: England and America in the nineteenth century', in *Medicine in Society*, ed. A. Wear, Cambridge: Cambridge University Press.

Freeden, M. (1978) *The New Liberalism: An Ideology of Social Reform*, Oxford: Clarendon Press.

——(1986) *Liberalism Divided: A Study in British Political Thought 1914–1939*, Oxford: Oxford University Press.

——(2003) 'Civil Society and the Good Citizen: Competing conceptions of citizenship in twentieth-century Britain', in *Civil Society in British History*, ed. J. Harris, Oxford: Oxford University Press.

Green, T.H. (1997) *Collected Works*, ed. P. Nicholson, 5 vols, vol. 2, Bristol: Thoemmes Press.

Hammer, M. (1995) '"The Building of a Nation's Health": The life and work of George Newman to 1921', unpublished thesis, University of Cambridge.

Harris, J. (1992) 'Political Thought and the Welfare State 1870–1940: An intellectual framework for British social policy', *Past and Present*, 135: 116–41.

Hobhouse, L.T. (1893) *The Labour Movement*, London: T. Fisher Unwin.

——(1911) *Social Evolution and Political Theory*, New York: Columbia University Press.

Hobson, J. A. (1914) *Work and Wealth: A Human Valuation*, London: Macmillan.

Inter-Departmental Committee on Physical Deterioration (1904) *Report of the Inter-Departmental Committee on Physical Deterioration. Vol. I: Report and Appendix* [Cd. 2175], London: HMSO.

Isichei, E. (1970) *Victorian Quakers*, Oxford: Oxford University Press.

Jones, H. (1919) *The Principles of Citizenship*, London: Macmillan.

Karpf, A. (1988) *Doctoring the Media: The Reporting of Health and Medicine*, London: Routledge.

Kennedy, T.C. (2001) *British Quakerism, 1860–1920: The Transformation of a Religious Community*, Oxford: Oxford University Press.

Keynes, J.M. (1926) *The End of Laissez-Faire*, London: Hogarth Press.

Lewis, J. (1986) *What Price Community Medicine? The Philosophy, Practice and Politics of Public Health Since 1919*, Brighton: Wheatsheaf Books.

——(1995) 'Presidential Address: Family provision of health and welfare in the mixed economy of care in the late nineteenth and twentieth centuries', *Social History of Medicine*, 8: 1–16.

——(1999) 'The Voluntary Sector in the Mixed Economy of Welfare,' in *Before Beveridge: Welfare Before the Welfare State*, ed. D. Gladstone, London: IEA Health and Welfare Unit.

London, L. (2008) 'What is a Human-Rights Based Approach to Health and Does it Matter?', *Health and Human Rights*, 10: 65–80.

Macadam, E. (1934) *The New Philanthropy: A Study of the Relations between the Statutory and Voluntary Services*, London: George Allen & Unwin.

Mann, J.M. (1996) 'Health and Human Rights', *British Medical Journal*, 312: 924–25.

Mann, J.M., L. Gostin, S. Gruskin, T. Brennan, Z. Lazzarini and H.V. Fineberg (1994) 'Health and Human Rights', *Health and Human Rights*, 1: 6–23.

Marshall, T.H. and T. Bottomore (1992) *Citizenship and Social Class*, London: Pluto Press.

Ministry of Health (1933–34) *Annual Report of the Ministry of Health*, London: HMSO.

Newman, G. [1889] Letter from George Newman to Caroline Westcombe Pumphrey, Newman Correspondence, Wellcome Library, MSS 6206/154.

——(1920) *On the State of the Public Health: Annual report of the Chief Medical Officer of the Ministry of Health*, London: HMSO.

——(1922) *On the State of the Public Health: Annual report of the Chief Medical Officer of the Ministry of Health*, London: HMSO.

——(1929) *On the State of the Public Health: Annual report of the Chief Medical Officer of the Ministry of Health*, London: HMSO.

——(1931) *Health and Social Evolution*, London: George Allen & Unwin.

Packer, I. (ed.) (2002) *The Letters of Arnold Stephenson Rowntree to Mary Katherine Rowntree, 1910–1918*, Cambridge: Cambridge University Press.

——(2003) 'Religion and the New Liberalism: The Rowntree family, Quakerism, and social reform', *Journal of British Studies*, 42: 236–57.

Pick, D. (1989) *Faces of Degeneration: A European Disorder, 1848–c. 1918*, Cambridge: University of Cambridge Press.

Rowntree, J. (ed.) (1905) *John Wilhelm Rowntree: Essays and Addresses*, London: Headley Bros.

Samuel, H. (1902) *Liberalism: An Attempt to State the Principles and Proposals of Contemporary Liberalism in England*, London: Grant Richards.

Searle, G.R. (1971) *The Quest for National Efficiency: A Study in British Social and Political Thought 1899–1914*, Oxford: Blackwell.

Seymour, J.K. (2012) 'Citizenship, the State, and the Chief Medical Officer: Sir George Newman and interwar health policy', unpublished PhD thesis, University of London.

Smith, H. (2000) 'A Quaker Inheritance: An analysis of family values, religion and the childhood and youth of George Newman (1870–1948)', *Quaker Studies*, 5: 49–67.

United Nations (1948) *Universal Declaration of Human Rights*. Available online: www.un.org/en/documents/udhr/index.shtml (accessed 10th January 2012).

Vincent, A. and R. Plant (1984) *Philosophy, Politics and Citizenship: The Life and Thought of the British Idealists*, Oxford: Blackwell.

Weiler, P. (1982) *The New Liberalism: Liberal Social Theory in Great Britain, 1889–1914*, New York: Garland Publishing.

2 Unauthorized immigrants and the denial of the right to health care in the United States

Beatrix Hoffman

On 9 September 2009 President Barack Obama addressed the United States Congress to announce the sweeping reform proposal that would become the Patient Protection and Affordable Care Act of 2010. After explaining how his plan would expand health insurance coverage and control health costs, the President began to refute charges that had been levied by his opponents. Claims that the revamped health system would 'insure illegal immigrants,' he assured the audience, were 'false.' Suddenly, Republican Congressman Joe Wilson shouted out, for all the world to hear, 'You lie!' But Obama did not lie when he insisted that 'illegal' (unauthorized or undocumented) immigrants would be excluded from the health care law, known as the PPACA or Affordable Care Act, which passed in 2010. Such immigrants will not be allowed to purchase coverage in the new private health insurance 'exchanges' run by the states, neither will they be eligible for any of the expanded public insurance coverage provided under the Act. Although exclusion of unauthorized immigrants from health care and coverage was nothing new, the Obama–Wilson exchange made the issue more public than ever before, broadcasting a bipartisan consensus that health care rights for the undocumented would be unpalatable to the American voter.

Between 1990 and 2007 the number of unauthorized immigrants in the US increased from an estimated 8.5 million to 11.8 million (an increase that has since ground to a halt, mostly due to the economic crisis) (Passel *et al.* 2012). More than half of these immigrants do not have any form of health insurance. Unauthorized immigrants to the US are not eligible for Medicare, the federal health insurance programme for the elderly and severely disabled, or for Medicaid, the federal/state programme for the poor, even if they pay the taxes that support these programmes. Instead, immigrants seek care in hospital emergency rooms or at community clinics that are not required to check immigration status, or they do not seek necessary care at all. Overall, unauthorized immigrants have the highest rates of un-insurance of any population in the US, and the greatest difficulty accessing health care (Camarota 2009; Chavez 1983; Chavez *et al.* 1992; Ku 2001).

This chapter discusses the case of unauthorized immigrants in the twentieth- and early twenty-first century United States as an example of exclusion from the right to health care. Human rights, by definition, belong to all people regardless of citizenship or location (Hunt 2000, 3–4). However, international covenants acknowledge that individual states have the right to establish controls over who enters their borders, and the idea of conferring rights on unauthorized immigrants remains politically unpopular. As a result, the rights of migrants and unauthorized immigrants are little recognized and rarely enforced. A few countries in the European Union (EU) and Latin America do offer comprehensive health services to all residents, including immigrants and migrants, but many such programmes are being curtailed or cancelled due to financial pressures (Govan 2012a, 2012b).

Given that so few countries enforce rights to health care access for the unauthorized despite human rights agreements, it comes as no surprise that the United States does not either. But the US is unique among developed nations in denying economic and social rights not just to immigrants, but also to its own citizens. The United States refused to ratify the International Covenant on Economic, Social and Cultural Rights, and remains the only prosperous nation without universal health coverage for its own citizens. Attempts to create a universal social insurance system in the US failed repeatedly during the twentieth century (Hoffman 2012, Starr 2011). Obama's 2010 Affordable Care Act greatly expands access, but will still leave over 20 million people without health insurance. Americans have no official legal right to medical care, except to emergency care and, as discussed later, that right has only been in force since 1986.

Despite its crucial role in the drafting of international human rights agreements after World War Two, the US has refused a commitment to enforcing economic and social rights within its own borders (Alston 1990). The rejection of these rights, including the right to health care, is deeply rooted in the US political culture of individualism and rhetorical anti-statism. Even the nation's most expansive social programmes confer 'entitlements' but do not embody 'rights.' Medicare and Medicaid, passed in 1965, did not create a right to health care coverage; these programmes 'could be repealed at any time … there is no federal constitutional right to this sort of government assistance or to its continuation once it has been undertaken' (Wing 1993, 177). The 2010 Affordable Care Act is not a sweeping social entitlement but rather a system of insurance regulation and subsidy. It mandates that individuals purchase health insurance, and requires insurance companies to sell policies without regard to the purchaser's health condition. The Act provides subsidies to help individuals obtain coverage, but does not confer a formal right to health care (Hoffman 2012). In the case of undocumented immigrants, it explicitly denies such a right.

Since the 1970s, the US has increasingly restricted immigrants from social insurance and welfare benefits, ostensibly to discourage newcomers from entering the country. While excluding immigrants has served to draw the limits of the welfare state, health and welfare policies have also served as a kind of immigration policy (Fox 2012). The exclusion of undocumented immigrants from the Affordable Care Act continues this trajectory of using health care policy to advance an anti-immigrant agenda. The denial of access to undocumented immigrants must be understood in the context of both the US history of rejecting social and economic rights, and its history of wildly ambivalent policies toward immigration.

Unauthorized immigration in the United States[1]

The United States is a 'nation of immigrants' and celebrates its immigrant heritage. At times, immigration and migration have been encouraged to alleviate labour shortages in industry and agriculture. But nativism has also been a common thread throughout US history, and in various eras the government has attempted to restrict immigration and deport unauthorized residents (Daniels 2004). Immigration restriction, while often linked to economic conditions and labour competition, has also been inextricably connected with notions of race. Immigrant groups have been welcomed or excoriated depending on the extent of their perceived racial difference and their potential to assimilate with the dominant culture. Notions of Asian racial difference, as well as the threat of competition from Chinese labourers, led to the Chinese Exclusion Act of 1882, which ended the era of open immigration. Following the great wave of immigrants from Southern and Eastern Europe, many of whom were Catholic or Jewish, the Immigration Act of 1924 created nationality quotas on entry into the US, favouring immigrants from Northern Europe and the British Isles and virtually halting immigration from Southern and Eastern Europe, Asia and Africa. As historian Mae Ngai writes, 'the national origins quota system proceeded from the conviction that the American nation was, and should remain, a white nation' (Ngai 2004, 27).[2]

However, due in part to the demand for migrant farm labour, the 1924 Act did not impose quotas on immigration from Mexico or Latin America. The treatment of Mexican immigrants and migrants as legal or illegal depended on conditions in the agricultural economy. Mexican workers flowed across the border in large numbers during the 1920s when their labour was welcomed. During the Great Depression, Mexican immigrants and even US-born individuals with Mexican ancestry became the target of campaigns for deportation and 'repatriation.' An estimated 400,000 people of Mexican origin were forced to leave the country. Then, during World War Two, labour demand soared again, and the US created the *bracero* program to bring Mexican migrants to Southwestern farms as 'guest workers' (Daniels 2004; Ngai 2004).

The 'schizoid' nature of US immigration policy, as historian Roger Daniels puts it, continued in the post-war era (Daniels 2004). The 1952 McCarran-Walter Act increased controls on the US–Mexico border. The 1965 Hart-Celler Immigration Act abolished the 1924 national origins quotas and provided new paths to legal immigration, mostly through family status, but also paradoxically (by imposing a total numerical limit of 120,000 on all legal immigration from Western Hemisphere countries) led to the greatest wave of 'illegal' immigration in US history. In 1976, Congress created new national quotas of 20,000 for each

Western Hemisphere country, forcing the vast majority of Mexican migrants and immigrants into illegal status (Ngai 2004, 261). The 1986 Immigration Reform and Control Act again embodied basic contradictions, imposing new penalties on employers of undocumented workers but also creating an 'amnesty' programme for immigrants who had been in the country a certain number of years (Daniels 2004).

Immigration restriction and control has been frequently tied to health and welfare policy. Migrants who were welcomed for their labour could be expelled for seeking services from local health and welfare providers. Like immigration policy, government programmes often sent a mixed message. The Social Security pension system, created in 1935, did not officially discriminate by race or national origin, but in practice initially excluded the majority of Mexican residents and black Americans because it did not cover agricultural or domestic workers. Starting in the 1970s, the federal government began restricting programmes based on citizenship status. Immigrants were first officially barred from Medicaid, the federal health insurance programme for the poor, in 1973 (Fox 2012, 294). The most severe restrictions on immigrant eligibility for social services were imposed by the Clinton-era welfare reform law of 1996 (the Personal Responsibility and Work Opportunity Act) which not only barred the undocumented from all federal social benefits including Medicare and Medicaid (with certain emergency exceptions), but also excluded legal immigrants from eligibility for their first five years in the country. Although evidence has always shown that immigrants overwhelmingly come to the US to work, not to receive government benefits, the association of immigrants with 'welfare dependency' has continued in the public mind (Chavez 2008; Fox 2012).

The common, but incorrect, assertion that immigrants come to the US to take advantage of social welfare programmes helped drive the debate on the Affordable Care Act (ACA). Even after the President's announcement that the new program would not include the undocumented, opponents circulated mass emails urging citizens to oppose the ACA because it would provide 'free health care for illegal immigrants' (Politifact 2009). The notion that unauthorized immigrants would reap benefits embodied everything conservatives loathed about the Obama proposal. But, as noted, the Democrats had already decided on exclusion for political reasons.

Access and exclusion

Despite this history of official exclusion from government health insurance programmes, there are some ways that unauthorized immigrants have been able to obtain medical care in the US Private health care providers might accept patients regardless of citizenship or national origin, so long as they could pay for their care. Given the poverty of most undocumented immigrants and migrants, this option has rarely been a realistic one. Local (state, county and municipal) services for the poor often did not impose citizenship requirements, although many did discriminate by race and national origin. Even some federal government health programmes have been available to the undocumented: the Migrant Health Centres and community health centres established in the 1960s mostly offer their services regardless of immigration status. Some undocumented immigrants – perhaps around a third, although no reliable statistics are available – are able to obtain private health insurance through their employment (Ludden 2009). Finally, the 1986 law creating a right to emergency care (EMTALA) allows non-citizens to access care via hospital emergency rooms. This haphazard and mostly unplanned patchwork of accessible services, coupled with official exclusion from most public insurance programmes, reflects the nation's continuing ambivalence toward both immigration and universal rights to health care.

In general, legal status did not determine eligibility for most social services until after the 1960s (Fox 2012). Restrictions were imposed based on race or national origin, not citizenship. Although less formal and institutionalized than the official discrimination against African-Americans in the US South, an extensive system of Jim Crow (racial separation) targeted Mexicans in border areas, regardless of whether they were new immigrants or their families had been in the country for centuries (Gutierrez 1995). While some county and private hospitals in the Southwest and California treated both Mexican and Anglo (white) patients, other health facilities were for whites only or were strictly segregated by national origin, which was also a marker for race. In Los Angeles in the 1920s, for example, separate public health clinics were established for 'Americans' and 'Mexicans' (Abel 2004; Molina 2006). Although public hospitals, clinics and asylums did not bar immigrants from using their services, newcomers could be deported for becoming a 'public charge,' and health and welfare facilities in some states were required to report any 'aliens' who threatened to become a burden on taxpayers (Fox 2012: 131–32). During the Depression, Los Angeles relief authorities argued that people of Mexican origin suffering from tuberculosis were becoming public charges, and forced thousands of families, including US citizens of Mexican ancestry, to repatriate to Mexico (Abel 2007).

Migrant farm workers, unauthorized or not (currently, about 25 per cent are US citizens), have historically suffered the poorest health status and the least access to health care of all socioeconomic groups in the US (NCFH 2012). However, because of their importance to the agricultural economy and the fact that, by definition, they crossed state boundaries, their health has received the attention of the federal government. The US Constitution stipulates that Congress may regulate only interstate commerce, or activity that crosses state lines. The Migrant Health Act of 1962 originated in concerns about migrants' supposed propensity to contagious disease. Mexican workers entering the US to work in the *bracero* and other contract labour programmes were required to pass through Public Health Service stations at the border, where they were 'dusted with an insecticide, vaccinated, examined for evidence of venereal disease, given a … chest X-ray, and examined for any other condition which would make the laborer inadmissible or unfit for agricultural work.' Once workers had passed through the stations, the government turned over responsibility for their health to employers (Robinson 1958). Reliance on employer voluntarism predictably proved ineffective, and by the early 1960s poor health conditions among migrant labourers had become a national scandal. In 1962 Congress passed the Migrant Health Act, which provided federal grants to local health providers willing to care for migrant workers. The Act's sponsors argued that the legislation was intended to protect American citizens from contagious disease, and, even more important, to sustain the agricultural labour force. '[Q] uite apart from humanitarian considerations,' the Migrant Health Act would 'help assure in the national interest the continued availability of an essential labor supply' (Health Clinics 1962: 13).

The United Farm Workers, the most influential farmworker rights organization in US history, also opened clinics and health centres in the 1960s and 1970s as part of its push to improve the terrible health conditions of migrant agricultural labourers. Today over 100 migrant health centres receive federal funding, but advocates estimate that only between 10 and 15 per cent of migrants have access to the services. Unauthorized workers fearing deportation are reluctant to attend these clinics, and due to low literacy levels many are not even aware of the clinics' existence, which are advertized primarily through pamphlet literature (Castañares 2002; Rudd 1975).

Federally funded community-based health centres are an important source of care for undocumented immigrants, who are banned from Medicaid, the federal-state health insurance programme for the poor. These centres, which were originally created as part of President Lyndon Johnson's War on Poverty in the 1960s, offer free or sliding-scale services (fees based on ability to pay) and are not required to ask patients about their citizenship status. At Alivio Medical Center in Chicago, for example, which provides $1 million a year in uncompensated care to the indigent poor, more than half of the patients in 2001 were undocumented (Mendieta 2001). Clinics located in public schools are an important source of care for children of unauthorized immigrant parents (all children, including immigrants, have a right to public education in the US). The state of Texas provides funding for four school-based health centres that 'make no distinction between citizen and non-citizen students' (Texas Comptroller 2006). The 2010 Affordable Care Act provides $11 billion in federal funding to expand community health centres, with the goal of doubling their capacity to 40 million patients by 2015. (NACHC 2010) Although this provision of the Act is not explicitly intended to improve access for immigrants, it may do so in practice.

The most recent anti-immigrant backlash, however, has made unauthorized people more reluctant than ever to utilize community health services, and made it more difficult for providers to offer them. For example, in Vallejo, California, in 2009, a local taxpayers' group demanded that the town's clinic stop providing care to undocumented immigrants (Jordan 2009). New anti-immigration legislation at the state level has threatened immigrants' access to health care even further. Arizona's 2010 law allows police to demand immigration documents and makes failure to produce them a crime. The Alabama immigration law, passed in 2011, requires public schools and employers to check immigration status of students and potential workers. Following its passage, fearful parents removed their children from schools. Families became afraid to leave their homes, and some immigrants fled the state altogether (Gomez 2012). Deportation raids sometimes target health facilities. According to one 2012 report, in several states 'Local, state and federal law enforcement authorities have staked out some migrant clinics, detained staff taking patients to medical appointments and set up roadblocks near their facilities and health fairs as part of immigration crackdowns' (Galewitz 2012). Although court challenges are curtailing some of the more draconian aspects of the new state laws, they are undoubtedly having a chilling effect on immigrants' freedom of movement and ability to access health services.

The most common way for uninsured Americans and immigrants alike to seek medical care is via hospital emergency rooms. EMTALA, the Emergency Medical Treatment and Active Labor Act of 1986, established a universal right to emergency care in the US. Democratic Congressman Pete Stark of California proposed EMTALA in response to a rash of 'patient dumping' cases in his district, in which private hospitals transferred very sick and injured patients to public hospitals because the patients did not have insurance coverage. Patient dumping had become a national scandal in the 1980s, with an estimated 250,000 patients transferred in an unstable condition each year (Hoffman 2006b). EMTALA requires hospital emergency rooms to screen and stabilize all patients who come to their doors, no matter their health insurance status. The law was intended to end the dumping crisis, but it also unintentionally made hospital emergency rooms the 'safety net' provider for those who could not obtain care anywhere else, including undocumented immigrants.

Following EMTALA, and in the absence of a right to comprehensive health services, emergency rooms came to serve as primary and emergency health care centres for many immigrants (and others). However, undocumented immigrants still account for only a small percentage of non-urgent visits to emergency rooms, and they continue to use all types of health services at far lower rates than US citizens or legal immigrants. Even so, undocumented immigrants are often blamed for overburdening hospital emergency rooms, especially in the Southwest. According to the American Hospital Association, in 2000 'the 24 southernmost counties from Texas to California accrued \$832 million in unpaid medical care, a quarter of which was directly attributable to illegal immigrants' (Janofsky 2003). Despite statistics showing that a majority of patients utilizing emergency rooms for primary care are US citizens, problems of emergency room overcrowding and high costs in border areas have become defined by immigration opponents as an illegal immigration problem (Cunningham 2011; Hoffman 2006a).

Exclusion from the Affordable Care Act

The official exclusion of unauthorized immigrants from government health pro-grammes is nothing new, as this chapter has shown, but the treatment of the undo-cumented in the 2010 health reform law represents a troubling development. For the first time, undocumented immigrants will be banned from purchasing certain types of private health coverage. The Affordable Care Act requires states by 2014 to create 'health insurance exchanges,' a set of competing, regulated insurance plans (mostly private, although some may be non-profit) among which uninsured individuals and families may 'shop' for coverage. Government oversight of the exchanges is supposed to improve quality and keep down the costs of coverage (Starr 2011). The controversial 'individual mandate', requiring all individuals to buy insurance if an employer or public plan does not cover them, does not apply to undocumented immigrants, and the law goes one step further by forbidding unauthorized immigrants from purchasing coverage at all in the exchanges. Although a huge legal controversy swirled around the constitutionality of the individual mandate (the US Supreme Court did declare the mandate constitutional in June 2012), virtually nothing has been said about the constitutional implications of banning a class of people from purchasing a private product.

Latino rights organizations strongly opposed the exclusion of undocumented immigrants during the framing of the initial health reform proposals in 2009, but also made the political choice to support the Affordable Care Act in the end. The National Council of La Raza, a major civil rights organization, notes that the Obama health care reform does contain provisions that are helpful to legal immigrants, who will have full access to the health insurance exchanges and will be equally eligible for subsidies to make coverage more affordable. Medicaid's five-year waiting period for legal immigrants, however, will continue. La Raza are hopeful that the law's increased funding for community health centres and more emphasis on primary care may lead to better access for the undocumented who continue to remain uninsured. 'While the health care reforms laws are imperfect,' argues a 2011 La Raza statement, 'they take steps to fix our broken health care system' (National Council of La Raza 2011).

However, the new law will increase burdens on certain parts of the health care system and even threaten their viability. The Congressional Budget Office estimates that 23 million people in the United States will still be without health insurance five years after the major provisions of the Affordable Care Act come into effect, and this number is likely to be much higher if some states refuse to implement the Medicaid expansion. One-third of those who remain uninsured will be unauthorized immigrants (McGreal 2010). The uninsured will still have the right under EMTALA to seek care in emergency rooms; yet, the Affordable Care Act will drastically reduce government subsidies for safety-net hospitals that serve large numbers of indigent and undocumented patients (Schechter 2012). Such hospitals, already in financially precarious condition, could be forced into bankruptcy. The chief executive of a Brooklyn safety-net hospital stated in the *New York Times*, 'I was told in Washington that they understand that this is a problem, but immigration is just too hot to touch' (Bernstein 2012). Some critics point out that excluding millions from health coverage and forcing them into emergency rooms could defeat the Affordable Care Act's central purpose of reducing medical costs, and that 'the politics of immigration might be preventing us from saving money on health care' (Bernier 2012).

Immigrant and migrant health rights as human rights

Some US organizations have protested the law's exclusion of immigrants on religious, moral, and ethical grounds, including arguments that health care is a human right. The US Council of Catholic Bishops asserted that 'health care is a basic human right and not a privilege' of all people that should not depend on 'where they live or where they were born' (Galarneau 2011). The American College of Obstetricians and Gynecologists argues that 'Immigrant women living within our borders should have the same access to basic preventive health care as US citizens without regard to their country of origin and documentation of their status,' and that immigrant access to health care is a crucial component in any strategy to reduce racial and income health disparities in the US (ACOG 2009).

But a campaign to expand health care access to immigrants on human rights grounds will be extremely difficult to carry out in the United States, which has refused to implement any of the numerous international covenants declaring health care to be a right. Although the US played a major role in drafting the 1948 United Nations Universal Declaration of Human Rights, it has not ratified the International Covenant on Economic, Social, and Cultural Rights (ICESCR). President Jimmy Carter brought the ICESCR to Congress for ratification in 1978, but progress stalled due to opposition from conservatives, and the subsequent Reagan administration opposed the Covenant aggressively. Republican officials sought successfully to affirm a clear distinction between individual rights and social rights, and to argue that the latter threatened the former. Conservative activist Phyllis Schlafly summarized the Republican stance on social rights when she declared that ratification of the ICESCR would lead to 'a legally binding commitment to legislate unlimited taxes' and 'would constitute a giant step toward a socialist state' (Alston, 1990, 378). The covenant for social and economic rights has since dropped out of US political discourse, and few Americans – including political leaders – seem to be aware of its existence.

Official rejection of economic and social rights is reflected in the US health care system, which has allowed up to 45 million Americans to go without any kind of health coverage. The US system is built on job-based insurance, which is offered at the discretion of the employer and can be taken away any time. Health coverage is sold and administered by myriad private insurance companies, most of which are for-profit entities that view themselves as offering a commercial product rather than a public service (Hoffman 2012; Starr 2011). As mentioned earlier, even the public insurance programmes, Medicare (for the elderly) and Medicaid (for the poor), do not establish fundamental rights to health care. Indeed, they are currently undergoing political attack from the Right, including proposals to replace Medicare coverage with a system of vouchers for purchasing private insurance policies (Medicare Plan 2012).

The 2010 Affordable Care Act intends to expand health insurance but does not establish a right to health care. Even if fully implemented, it will not reach the goal of universal coverage. In addition to the undocumented immigrants who will remain uninsured, individuals can opt out of the required coverage through paying a relatively modest fine. Over 20 million will still not have health insurance after full implementation of the law in 2014, and if some states decline to expand Medicaid coverage of the poor (as allowed by the recent Supreme Court ruling), additional millions will be left out.

Apart from failing to create universal coverage, the Affordable Care Act leaves the employer health insurance system intact, and requires those not insured by their employer or a public programme to purchase (with subsidies if necessary) private coverage in the new health insurance exchanges. The ACA does ban traditional practices of private insurance companies that allowed them to exclude customers with pre-existing health conditions and to cancel the policies of individuals who got sick. Insurers are also required to offer certain preventive health services free of charge. Supporters of the Act argue that these stipulations confer significant new rights on health insurance consumers, and the Obama administration portrays them as a 'New Patients' Bill of Rights' (Patients' Bill of Rights 2010). But, while the law will create new obligations to purchase health insurance (except for undocumented immigrants), there is still no official right to access to health care in the US, apart from emergency room care (for which patients still receive a bill).

The practical lack of rights in the US system contrasts with a broad (albeit vague) public belief that medical care is not like other commodities and that human beings should have a right to basic care (Hoffman 2012). For example, 90 per cent of respondents in one recent Massachusetts survey agreed that access to health care should be a right regardless of ability to pay (Jacoby 2009). During the 2008 presidential election campaign, Barack Obama declared his support for the notion that health care is a right, not just an individual responsibility (Obama 2010). Americans defend the one existing right to care – emergency care – by stating that 'we don't leave people to die in the streets.'

The contradiction between the right to health care impulse and the actual workings of the new health law will come to a head around the issue of undocumented immigrants. Even those immigrants who wish to and who could afford to purchase insurance in the new exchanges will be banned from doing so. Curtailing an individual's right to purchase a product appears to be a new type of discrimination against immigrants. Immigrant rights and human rights groups might adopt a strategy focusing on the denial of health rights as a type of discrimination based on race and national origin (Hernandez-Truyol 1997). Such arguments, based on civil rights, will currently carry greater rhetorical weight than emphasizing economic and social rights, which are not recognized in the US.

In the longer term, however, health rights activists must draw attention to the United States's outlier status in the international human rights community. Few Americans realize that virtually all other high-income nations (and many low- and middle-income ones too) have affirmed and seek to implement economic and social rights, including the right to health care access. Greater understanding of the international human rights context could lead to more direct challenges of the US refusal to apply a human right to health care not just to immigrants, but also to its own citizens.

Notes

1 59 per cent of the estimated 11.8 million undocumented immigrants to the US in 2007 were Mexican. This chapter focuses on Mexican immigrants to the United States, on whom the author's research has centered to date. In US political rhetoric, 'undocumented' is often used as a synonym for 'Mexican,' underscoring the racialization of the immigration debate.
2 As many scholars (e.g., Roediger 1999) have shown, Irish and Southern and Eastern European immigrants were initially characterized as 'non-white.'

Bibliography

Abel, Emily K., 2004. '"Only the Best Class of Immigration:" Public Health Policy toward Mexicans and Filipinos in Los Angeles, 1910–40.' *American Journal of Public Health* 94 (6), June: 932–39.

——, 2007. *Tuberculosis and the Politics of Exclusion: A History of Public Health and Migration to Los Angeles*. New Brunswick, NJ: Rutgers University Press.

ACOG (American College of Obstetricians and Gynecologists) Committee for Underserved Women, 2009. 'Health Care for Undocumented Immigrants,' ACOG Committee Opinion No. 425, January.

Alston, Philip, 1990. 'US Ratification of the Covenant on Economic, Social and Cultural Rights: The Need for an Entirely New Strategy.' American Journal of International Law 84 (2), April: 365–93.

Bernier, Nathan, 2012. 'How will the affordable care act affect illegal immigrants,' July 5, 2012, kuhf.fm.news. http://app1.kuhf.org/articles/1341526931-How-Will-the-Affordable-Care-Act-Affect-Illegal-Immigrants.html.

Bernstein, Nina, 2012. 'Hospitals Fear Cuts in Aid for Care to Illegal Immigrants.' *New York Times*, July 26.

Buettgens, M. and Mark A. Hall, 2011. 'Who Will be Uninsured after Health Insurance Reform?,' Urban Institute Real Time Policy Analysis, March 10, www.rwjf.org/coverage/product.jsp?id=71998.

Camarota, Steven, 2009. 'Illegal Immigrants and HR 3200: Estimate of Potential Costs to Taxpayers,' Memorandum, Center for Immigration Studies, September, www.cis.org/IllegalsAndHealthCareHR3200.

Castañares, Tina, 2002. 'Outreach Services,' *Migrant Health Issues Monograph Series*, No. 5, National Center for Farmworker Health, Inc.

Chavez, Leo R., 1983. 'Undocumented Immigrants and Access to Health Services: A Game of Pass the Buck.' *Migration Today* XI (1): 15–19.

——, 2008. *The Latino Threat: Constructing Immigrants, Citizens, and the Nation*. Palo Alto, CA: Stanford University Press.

Chavez, Leo. R., Estevan T. Flores, and Marta Lopez-Garza, 1992. 'Undocumented Latin American Immigrants and US Health Services: An Approach to a Political Economy of Utilization.' *Medical Anthropology Quarterly* 6 (1), March: 6–26.

Cunningham, Peter, 2011. 'Nonurgent Use of Hospital Emergency Departments,' Statement before the US Senate Health, Education, Labor and Pensions Committee,

Subcommittee on Primary Health and Aging, May 11, http://hschange.org/CONTENT/1204/1204.pdf.

Daniels, Roger, 2004. *Guarding the* Golden Door: *American Immigration Policy and Immigrants Since 1882*. New York: Hill & Wang.

Departments of Health and Human Services (HHS), Labor, and Treasury, 2010. 'Patients' Bill of Rights' July 1, www.healthcare.gov.

Fox, Cybelle, 2012. *Three Worlds of Relief: Race, Immigration, and the American Welfare State, from the Progressive Era to the New Deal*. Princeton, NJ: Princeton University Press.

Galarneau, Charlene 2011. 'Still Missing: Undocumented Immigrants in Health Care Reform.' *Journal of Health Care for the Poor and Underserved* 22 (2): 422–28.

Galewitz, Phil, 2012. 'Fear Keeps Migrant Workers from Getting Health Care.' *Kaiser Health News*, June 6.

Gomez, Alan, 2012. 'In Wake of Immigration Law, Some Migrants Return to Alabama.' *USA Today*, February 21.

Govan, Fiona, 2012a. 'Spanish Illegal Immigrants no Longer Given Free Health Care.' *The Telegraph*, May 10.

——, 2012b. 'Spanish Doctors and Nurses Protest over Health Care Law for Immigrants.' *The Telegraph*, August 6.

Gutierrez, David, 1995. *Walls and Mirrors: Mexican Americans, Mexican Immigrants, and the Politics of Ethnicity*. Berkeley: University of California Press.

Health Clinics, 1962. 'Health Clinics for Migratory Farmworkers: Hearing before a Subcommittee of the Committee on Interstate and Foreign Commerce, House of Representatives,' February 13, 1962. US Government Printing Office.

Hernandez-Truyol, Berta Esperanza, 1997. 'Reconciling Rights in Collision: An International Human Rights Strategy' in Juan F. Perea, *Immigrants Out!: The New Nativism and the Anti-Immigrant Impulse in the United States*. New York: New York University Press.

Hoffman, Beatrix, 2006a. 'Sympathy and Exclusion: Access to Health Care for Undocumented Immigrants in the United States' in Keith Wailoo, Julie Livingston, and Peter Garbaccia (eds), *A Death Retold: Jesica Santillan, the Bungled Transplant, and Paradoxes of Medical Citizenship in the United States*. Chapel Hill: University of North Carolina Press.

——, 2006b. 'Emergency Rooms: The Reluctant Safety Net' in Rosemary Stevens, Charles Rosenberg, and Lawton R. Burns (eds), *Bringing the Past Back In: History and Health Policy in the United States*. New Brunswick, NJ: Rutgers University Press.

——, 2012. *Health Care for Some: Rights and Rationing in the United States since 1930*. Chicago: University of Chicago Press.

Hunt, Lynn, 2000. 'The Paradoxical Origins of Human Rights' in Jeffrey N. Wasserstrom, Lynn Hunt, and Marilyn B. Young (eds), *Human Rights and Revolutions*. Lanham, MD: Rowman & Littlefield, 2000.

Jacoby, Jeff, 2009. 'What "right" to health care?.' *Boston Globe*, September 13, www.boston.com.

Janofsky, Michael, 2003. 'Burden Grows for Southwest Hospitals.' *New York Times*, April 14.

Jordan, Miriam, 2009. 'Illegal Immigration Enters the Health-Care Debate.' *Wall Street Journal*, August 15.

Ku, Leighton and Sheetal Matani, 2001. 'Left Out: Immigrants' Access to Health Care and Insurance.' Health Affairs 20 (1), January: 247–56.

Kullgren, Jeffrey T., 2003. 'Restrictions on Unauthorized Immigrants' Access to Health Services: The Public Health Implications of Welfare Reform.' *American Journal of Public Health* 93 (10), October: 1630–33.

Ludden, Jennifer, 2009. 'Health Care Overhaul Ignores Illegal Immigrants.' NPR.com, July 8.

McGreal, Chris, 2010. 'US Healthcare Bill Leaves Illegal Immigrants Excluded.' *Guardian*, March 22.

Medicare Plan, 2012. 'Majority oppose Paul Ryan's Medicare plan.' *Boston Globe*, August 22.

Mendieta, Ana, 2001. 'Hospitals pay medical costs of undocumented,' *Chicago Sun-Times*, December 11.

Molina, Natalia, 2006. *Fit to be Citizens? Public Health and Race in Los Angeles, 1879–1939*. Berkeley: University of California Press.

NACHC, 2010. National Association of Community Health Centers, Expanding Health Centers under Health Reform, June 2010. www.nachc.com.

National Council of La Raza, 2011. 'Dear Representative,' January 18. www.nclr.org.

NCFH, 2012. National Center for Farmworker Health, 'Facts about Farmworkers.'

Ngai, Mae M, 2004. *Impossible Subjects: Illegal Aliens and the Making of Modern America*. Princeton, NJ: Princeton University Press.

Obama, Barak, 2010. 'Obama: Health Care Should Be a Right.' *Huffington Post*, July 7. www.huffingtonpost.com/2008/10/07/obama-health-care-should_n_132831.html.

Passel, Jeffrey, D'Vera Cohen, and Ana Gonzales-Barrera, 2012. 'Net Migration from Mexico Falls to Zero, and Perhaps Less.' Pew Research Center Report, April 23. Pew Research Center. www.pewhispanic.org.

Politifact, 2009. 'The Democrats' Health Care Bills would Provide "Free Health Care for Illegal Immigrants."'August 28. www.politifact.com.

Robinson, Norma J., 1958. 'The Public Health Program for Mexican Migrant Workers,' *Public Health Reports* 73 (9), September): 851–60.

Roediger, David, 1999. *The Wages of Whiteness: Race and the Making of the American Working Class*. New York: Verso.

Rudd, Peter, 1975. 'The United Farm Workers Clinic in Delano, California: A Study of the Rural Poor.' *Public Health Reports* 90 (4), July – August: 331–39.

Schechter, David, 2012. 'Health Care for Undocumented Immigrants Unresolved by Uupheld Law.' www.WFAA.com, June 29.

Starr, Paul, 2011. *Remedy and Reaction: The Peculiar American Struggle Over Health Care Reform*. New Haven, NJ: Yale University Press.

Texas Comptroller, 2006. 'Undocumented Immigrants in Texas: A Financial Analysis of the Impact to the State Budget and Economy,' www.window.state.tx.us/specialrpt/undocumented/.

Wing, Kenneth, 1993. 'The Right to Health Care in the United States.' *Annals of Health Law* 2, February: 161–93.

3   Rights, responsibility and health services

Human rights as an idiomatic language of power

Jarrett Zigon

In discussing various problematizations available for contemporary anthropological reflection, Paul Rabinow briefly addresses with wonder Michael Ignatieff's claim that human rights has emerged 'as the language of human good' (quoted in Rabinow 2003: 21). Rabinow's response is short and probing – he is attempting to raise questions rather than answer or analyse them in full. But in addressing the writings of this scholar-activist-politician, Rabinow suggests that not only are human rights in practice an important anthropological focus of research, but so too is human rights as an idiomatic language and the way in which this language is framed, articulated and reproduced by activists at all points of manifestation in its transnational flow. In this chapter, I respond to Rabinow's anthropological imperative to explore critically human rights discursive and non-discursive practices in order to disclose how these become embedded within local institutional relationships and therefore affect local possibilities and potentialities of moral and political subjectivity.

In his reading of Ignatieff, Rabinow appears most concerned with apparent, if not ambiguous, claims of the hegemony of human rights as a moral discourse in the world today. It is this that he addresses, for example, when Ignatieff writes: 'The legitimacy of human rights is not its authoritative universalism, so much as its capacity to become a moral vernacular for the demand for freedom within local cultures' (quoted in Rabinow 2003: 23). Although Rabinow is somewhat sceptical of this claim to vernacularization, it has become somewhat of a truism among some anthropologists that this is, in fact, the case. Thus, for instance, Sally Engle Merry argues that due to the process of translation between the worlds of transnational human rights and local cultural practices, human rights often only appear in the world in the vernacular (Merry 2006a, 2006b). It must be recognized, however, that because transnational human rights discourse is the 'strong language' in contrast to the 'weak language' (Asad 1986) of the vast majority of local cultural practices with which it interacts, power inequality preserves the discursive foundations of transnational human rights over and against any significant challenges of vernacularization.[1]

This general preservation of transnational human rights discourse, however, should not be considered the result of more attractive or compelling, meaningful and practical possibilities made available through this language – the view it seems Ignatieff and other activists would take. Rather, in many cases, it results from the related and inseparable power inequality from the flow of international funding, media support and international and governmental rhetoric and policy all aimed at disseminating the transnational moral discourse of human rights. As Pheng Cheah has put it, this 'contamination' of human rights discourse and the local organizations attempting to put it into practice significantly calls into question the claim that this discourse and its practice is a 'pure totality' free of capital and power interests (Cheah 1997: 249–54). Because of this very real institutional, and therefore semiotic, inequality between transnational human rights and local cultural practices, as well as the changes of subjectivities that often results from interacting with local human rights organizations and institutions, it is not entirely clear that human rights become vernacularized in any way similar to how Ignatieff and Merry suggest.

Rather than speaking of the vernacularization of human rights, it is perhaps more appropriate to speak of human rights as a floating signifier or an empty signifier whose meaning, because ultimately disconnected from any signified, is always open to contestation, ambiguity and rearticulation by diverse and often contradictory parties (see Brown 1995). That is to say, the essential ground-lessness of the concepts of human rights renders this language potentially meaningful for any number of unrelated and possibly opposed projects. One reason this is so is because human rights does not constitute a new and singular discourse. Alain Badiou writes that a new discourse becomes necessary when what he calls a truth event is inadmissible and unnameable within existing dis-courses, and therefore, only a new discursive language is able to articulate the new truth (Badiou 2003: 46). Clearly, this is not the case with human rights. Rather, the language of human rights as established in the 1948 UN Universal Declaration of Human Rights fits perfectly into a number of already well-established discursive traditions such as natural law, liberalism, socialism, independence and liberation movements, and Catholicism to name only a few. Because of this, in many cases, human rights language does not need to be vernacularized because it already fits very well into diverse and well-known local discourses of power. What occurs in many cases, then, is not vernacular-ization, but rather a performative shift of the floating signifier of human rights such that this fragmentary, fuzzy and transferrable idiom can be pragmatically utilized by diverse and oftentimes opposed projects.

In this chapter, I will address this aspect of human rights language and argue that it has allowed human rights to become a language of power. In order to make this argument, I will begin by considering the way in which Michael Ignatieff, one of the human rights industry's most clear and well-known advocates, articulates one of the dominant views of human rights. It will become clear that, although this view necessitates a faithful belief that human rights con-stitutes a coherent discourse, Ignatieff's defence of this discourse belies the floating signifier aspect of this language. I will then turn to the example of the Russian Orthodox Church and its recent adoption of human rights language in support of its health and social services. What this example reveals is that this adoption can only be understood within a complex configuration of post-Soviet politics that has come to be dominated by the discourse of neoliberalism and the way in which the floating signifier of human rights has provided a link between the conservative politics of the Church, post-Soviet nation building, and neoliberal global political-economics. Finally, I will conclude by suggesting that the Russian Orthodox case is not unique to this conservative institution, but rather is indicative of the way in which the floating signifier of human rights has, for the most part, become a language of power that is idiomatically articulated through diverse local organizations and practices such as those of health and social services.

Human rights, agency and floating signification

In *Human Rights as Politics and Idolatry*, Ignatieff (2001) gives an impassioned argument for the universality of human rights and the capacity of rights to enable agency. Central to his argument is that human rights provide individuals with a transcendent and universal normative appeal against the abuses that may be rendered against them by particular state action or cultural practices. This normative appeal of rights, so argues Ignatieff, provides individuals with a form of agency unavailable by other means to resist repressive state and cultural regimes of power. As he puts it in describing the global spread of human rights as moral progress:

> We know from historical experience that when human beings have defensible rights – when their agency as individuals is protected and enhanced – they are less likely to be abused and oppressed ... The Universal Declaration of Human Rights represented a return by the European tradition to its natural law heritage, a return intended to restore *agency*, to give individuals the civic courage to stand up when the state ordered them to do wrong.
>
> (Ignatieff 2001: 4–5; emphasis in original)

The moral progress brought about by the post-war human rights revolution, according to Ignatieff, is marked by a return to a natural law tradition, which is intended to 'restore *agency*'. Thus, although Ignatieff may not claim that human rights is a new discourse in the sense that Badiou would define this, at the least he seems to be making the strong claim that human rights is a central component of an already well-established discourse he names natural law. Nevertheless, his subsequent discussion of human rights throughout the rest of the text tends to belie this claim. For example, although in the section of the text directly following this quote, Ignatieff briefly makes reference to the post-war international juridical revolution that was part of 'a wider reordering of the normative order' (Ignatieff 2001: 5), throughout the text he more often and ambiguously refers to such phenomena as human rights 'norms', 'language', 'values' and 'culture'. Thus, his own struggle to articulate any coherent and consistent discursive framework for referencing human rights suggests that Ignatieff is perhaps a bit too quick to equate, or even to associate, human rights with the discursive tradition of natural law.

On my reading of the text, then, I suggest that the moral progress Ignatieff claims human rights brings about is best understood in terms of 'the *language* that systematically embodies the moral intuition that ... our species is one, and each of the individuals who compose it is entitled to equal moral consideration' (Ignatieff 2001: 3–4; emphasis added). Whether this idiomatic language takes the form of law or everyday moral normative standards for being with others does not seem to be Ignatieff's concern in this text, rather what is important is 'the degree that this *intuition* gains influence over the conduct of individuals and states' (Ignatieff 2001: 4; emphasis added). Far from a coherent and consistent discourse, then, the language of human rights as Ignatieff tends to articulate it in this text is better conceived as a floating idiomatic[2] signifier available to be utilized for diverse ends.

Nevertheless, by identifying human rights as a return to the natural law discursive tradition, and therefore enabling a restoration of agency, or as he puts it elsewhere, 'the very purpose of rights language is to protect and enhance individual agency' (Ignatieff 2001: 18), Ignatieff seems to be identifying *agency* as a key human capacity for realizing the rational nature of human beings. Indeed, this is exactly how Ignatieff defines agency when he writes:

> By agency, I mean more or less what Isaiah Berlin meant by 'negative liberty,' the *capacity* of each individual to achieve rational intentions without let or hindrance. By rational, I do not necessarily mean sensible or estimable, merely those intentions that do not involve obvious harm to other human beings. Human rights is a language of individual empowerment, and empowerment for individuals is desirable because when individuals have agency, they can protect themselves against injustice. Equally, when individuals have agency, they can define for themselves what they wish to live and die for.
>
> (Ignatieff 2001: 57; emphasis added)

Moral progress, then, is measured by the extent to which agency as a key human capacity can flourish, which, it would seem, more or less depends on a particular political, cultural, or legal configuration of rights. Thus, rights in this perspective provide a normative appeal through which non-rights respecting political and cultural configurations can be overcome and allow the possibility of a human being to freely choose the form of life he or she so wishes (Ignatieff 2001: 68–77). I will return to this questionable line of argument later.

First, I would like to turn to Ignatieff's claim that his perspective of rights and agency is not founded on a theory of human nature, but is rather self-evident from the social and historical evidence of the practice of human rights (Ignatieff 2001: 54–6). This position stems from Ignatieff's attempt to defend the notion of human rights from critical attacks on several flanks, such as those from a religious perspective, an 'Asian' perspective and the postmodern relativistic view. Rather than defending human rights on what he calls 'metaphysical' grounds, Ignatieff argues that a close empirical and historical analysis shows human flourishing is most possible when rights provide the conditions for agentive resistance against repression and excessive power. Thus, whether it is the lack of rights that partially defined the contexts of the Holocaust, the Gulag, or the Great Leap Forward and the tens of millions of deaths that resulted from them, or the place of rights and thus agency in securing the apparent fact of Sen's claim that no famine has ever occurred in a democracy, Ignatieff argues the primacy of rights and agency is not a matter of endorsing a particular theory of human nature, whether this theory be solely Western or not, but rather a simple matter of right-minded socio-historic analysis (Ignatieff 2001: 54–5, 90–91).

But, as we have already seen, Ignatieff claims that the rise of the modern human rights regime is a return to the natural law discursive tradition, which is indeed based on a particular theory of the integral relationship between objective moral norms, law, and human nature. In addition to the rational nature of human beings that most natural lawyers assume, Ignatieff's explicit connection between rights and agency also relies on a view that, in Ignatieff's own words, respects the autonomy of agents (Ignatieff 2001: 18). This Kantian perspective of the human person is not only based on a particular theory of human nature, it is also perhaps the central theoretical foundation of modern secularism and liberalism (Asad 2003a; Mahmood 2005). Indeed, that this view is central to secular-liberalism is not something Ignatieff would deny. In fact, he argues human rights can only be successful if a secular-liberal notion of 'moral individualism' is at the basis of the human rights agenda (Ignatieff 2001: 67).

Although certainly recognizing that all humans are born into particular socio-historic-cultural configurations, moral individualism assumes that human beings have the *capacity* to reflectively stand outside of (or be free of) these relations and autonomously decide (or decide for oneself, that is, give the law to oneself) the kind of relation one wants to have with any particular form of life. Ignatieff, of course, understands that all humans are born initially into a particular form of life with its particular set of power relations, but maintains that under the proper conditions established through human rights, individuals can realize their true autonomous nature and 'choose the life they see fit to lead' and 'freely shape [its] content' (Ignatieff 2001: 57, 73). Apparently, in Ignatieff's view, such a capacity is not recognized as resting on a particular assumption and theory of human nature but simply *the fact* of human nature; an assumed fact on which his and many others' view of human rights rests.

Almost imperceptibly we have shifted or floated from one discursive tradition to another – from natural law to liberalism – by means of the signifier human rights. It could, of course, be argued that natural law and liberalism are not two distinct discourses, but even the most cursory glance at these two traditions reveals that although the two may overlap at particular historical and conceptual moments, for the most part they are quite divergent and ultimately do not depend on each other for their respective discursive coherence. Thus, what began as a claim of the return to a natural law tradition has somehow slipped into a defence of human rights in terms of the discursive tradition of liberalism. From the perspective that I am arguing for in this chapter, this is not a matter of poor argumentation on the part of Ignatieff, but rather the result of the very slipperiness of the floating signifier of human rights that allows it to so easily shift between, and become embedded within, diverse discursive traditions and political and moral projects.

My concern in this section has not been to defend a particular view of social life or culture against the moral individualism of human rights. I am not particularly interested in 'culturalist' or 'relativist' critiques of human rights. Rather, my task has been to disclose the theoretical assumptions of this particular, but dominant, view of human rights. Ignatieff assumes that the modern human rights language is a return to the natural law discursive tradition, and thus constitutes the former if not as a new discourse, then certainly a return to an already well-established and meaningful discourse. As such, the assumption seems to be that human rights is able to be utilized universally for resisting repressive power, and therefore, to allow for the realization of human freedom. But, as I will show in the rest of this chapter, this assumption does not always hold. For as a floating signifier human rights is a fragmented, fuzzy and ultimately groundless language that is able to be co-opted into a number of diverse and oftentimes contradictory political and moral projects, many of which Ignatieff would likely not endorse.

I suspect, nevertheless, that Ignatieff might reply to my argument so far with something like the following: perhaps it can be conceded that the 'goodness' of human rights cannot be argued theoretically or even coherently, but this fact does not entail that when human rights are put into practice they are not successful, even if imperfectly so.[3] In fact, this is precisely the line he takes in avoiding what he calls 'metaphysical' debates over the foundations of human rights when he writes: 'Far better, I would argue, to forgo these kinds of foundational arguments altogether and seek to build support for human rights on the basis of what such rights actually *do* for human beings' (Ignatieff 2001: 54; emphasis in original). Ignatieff is confident that even if 'metaphysical' and theoretical arguments for human rights fail, his endorsement of human rights as protecting and enhancing human agency is fully grounded in sociohistorical pragmatic evidence. In the rest of this chapter, then, I will consider some ethnographic and historic evidence in order to see just what 'rights actually *do*' when put into practice, and in so doing show that the politico-moral consequences of human rights in practice has pragmatic effects that, on the one hand, contradict Ignatieff's claims concerning the relation between rights and agency and, on the other, may in some cases be far from what Ignatieff would likely endorse. As will become clear, this is so because of the very slipperiness of human rights language and the way that this slipperiness allows human rights to become co-opted and embedded within diverse projects.

The Russian Orthodox Church and human rights[4]

In 2006 I started ethnographic research with a Russian Orthodox Church drug rehabilitation centre located outside St Petersburg. The Church considers this centre an integral part of its HIV/AIDS prevention and treatment programme. In a city and country that since the late 1990s has suffered the dual epidemics of heroin use and HIV/AIDS, the Russian Orthodox Church (ROC) provides one of the few services, and the only non-fee service, for drug users in St Petersburg. This Church-run programme is important for our purposes because just as I started my research in 2006, the Russian Orthodox Church began to develop and eventually adopted its own official document on human rights, in which it names injecting drug use (IDU) as one of the social issues towards which its notion of rights can be addressed (ROC 2008). What is particularly interesting about the ROC's 'Basic Teaching on Human Dignity, Freedom and Rights' (hereafter referred to as 'Basic Teaching') is that it claims explicitly that human rights should exist in order to support what it calls God-given morality and the Russian nation. Thus, Russian Orthodox human rights are conceived as that which provides the normative standards by which individuals can more easily be disciplined into morally good citizen-subjects (Zigon 2011).

To be effective, Russian Orthodox human rights need to be implemented in specific social spaces, and the Church-run rehabilitation centre can be seen as just such a location. At this centre, approximately 25 rehabilitants at any one time go through a three-month programme that is aimed at spiritual-moral education and the development of what staff and rehabilitants call normal persons capable of living a normal life (*normal'naya zhizn'*). These goals are brought about through a disciplinary-therapeutic regime that consists of religious education, prayer and confession, daily work to maintain and support the farm on which the rehabilitation centre is located or what is called labour therapy, and nightly group therapeutic sessions such as art or talk therapy. According to staff, as well as many rehabilitants, all of this therapeutic work is meant to cultivate a sense of responsibility, which is considered the most important moral virtue needed not only to overcome heroin addiction, but also to live a normal life in contemporary Russia.

The importance of responsibility in terms of living a normal life is echoed in the ROC's human rights document, which makes an integral link between the inherent dignity that is the foundation of human rights and the responsibility that this dignity entails. This link between dignity and responsibility necessitates that individuals work actively on themselves to become more moral persons, thus the document states that dignity should lead one to 'understand his responsibility for the direction and way of his life. Clearly, the idea of responsibility is integral to the very notion of dignity' (ROC 2008: 2). It is precisely this sense of responsibility that the Church-run programme attempts to instil within rehabilitants by means of its disciplinary-therapeutic practices.

In fact, in the Church's view, responsibility is considered necessary for the moral defence of individuals' inherent dignity, the concept on which, like the

UN version of human rights, the Church's version of human rights is founded. From the Church's perspective, if human rights are meant to secure a moral nation by means of securing moral persons, then this is done through the defence of the God-given inherent dignity of each individual, which can only be secured through the enactment of moral responsibility. Thus, for example, Patriarch Kirill[5] has argued in a speech on human rights and moral responsibility that there are two aspects of dignity. The first aspect is that dignity reveals the fact that a person has an inherent worth and, thus, second, 'that the life of a subject corresponds to this worth' (Kirill 2006a). This link between responsibility and dignity is necessary because, from the Orthodox perspective, dignity is something with which all persons are naturally endowed from God, but without the enactment of moral responsibility this dignity can become darkened by not living an appropriately moral life. Yet, because this dignity is always there as the basis of the essential worth of a human being no matter how much it may have become darkened through sin, it remains to be purified and grown. The 'Basic Teaching' makes this clear: repentance provides 'a powerful stimulus for seeking spiritual work on the self (*dukhovnoi raboty nad soboi*), making a creative change in [a person's] life, preserving the purity of the God-given dignity and growing in it' (ROC 2008).

Human rights for the Church, then, is that which can help defend against the darkening of inherent dignity, on the one hand, and support the 'spiritual work on the self' necessary to preserve and grow in this dignity, on the other. Human rights do this in two ways. First, human rights provide the normative standards and context in which a person can more easily choose to do the morally appropriate thing. This is possible because the Church does not separate rights from moral responsibilities, and therefore a social context based on these rights will necessarily entail the enactment of such responsibilities. Second, and similar to the way in which human rights help reveal the God-given worth of individuals, by providing a context in which persons are more likely to enact responsibility for oneself and toward others, human rights help bring about a personal state of freedom from evil. Again, the Church-run rehabilitation programme can be considered as such a context in which this work on the self can be done.

But, human rights as allowing the possibility for a personal state of freedom from evil is only the first step toward the main goal of the ROC's human rights doctrine; for ultimately human rights are meant to bring about a society free from evil. Here again, this is only possible with the linking of rights and responsibilities, which are meant to always be related to 'the neighbour, family, community, nation and all humanity' (ROC 2006). Arguing that this link is necessary for the moral stability of society, Kirill claims that freedom and human rights 'ought to be harmonized with morality and faith, and this harmonization, in turn, ought to be reflected in the structure of contemporary society' (Kirill 2006b). Ultimately, then, when human rights provide the normative structure within which moral responsibilities can be enacted, social life, the nation and the international order find moral and political stability. Thus, the 'Basic Teaching' concludes: 'Unity and inter-connection between civil and political, economic and social, individual and collective human rights can promote a harmonious order of societal life both on the national and international level' (ROC 2008). Human rights from the ROC perspective, therefore, structure a society in which both individual persons, society as a whole, and ultimately the nation can more easily harmonize and move toward what the Orthodox Church calls moral perfection.

A certain family resemblance can perhaps be seen here between these claims of the Russian Orthodox Church and the role of human rights in society, and Ignatieff's claim that human rights as a return to a natural law discursive tradition restores individual agency. For Ignatieff,[6] an international and national framework of human rights allows individuals to enable their natural capacity of agency to resist cultural, social and political wrongs against the dignity of their person, ultimately leading to, it would seem, a society, nation and world in which such dignity is always respected. As I have been arguing, this is more or less how the ROC envisions a human rights regime. The difference, however, is that the ROC takes this view of what human rights can do for bringing about a moral society to its logical conclusion – that is, for the ROC human rights are explicitly claimed to provide the moral structure by which individuals can become more responsibilized citizen-subjects of the Russian nation.

This is so because from the Church's perspective human rights provide a structure within which moral behaviour becomes more easily enacted and therefore helps make society and the persons living in it more moral. In this sense, the ROC's notion of human rights is about providing the means by which a moral society can be cultivated and secured. This is clearly seen in the 'Basic Teaching', where it is written that the:

> [S]ocial value and effectiveness of the entire human rights system depend on the extent to which it helps to create conditions for personal growth in the God-given dignity and relates to the responsibility of a person for his actions before God and his neighbours.
>
> (ROC 2008)

This approach to human rights as that which provides the moral structures and standards of society raises the question of the contemporary relationship between the ROC and the Russian state. How to reorganize Church–state relations in the post-Soviet period was a central question throughout much of the 1990s and was settled with the 1997 Federal Law on Freedom of Conscience and Religious Associations. This law gave the ROC a legal footing for its claimed priority status within the contemporary plurality of religions in Russia. No doubt due to the Church's 'special contribution' to the 'development of Russia's spirituality and culture' recognized by the 1997 law, the ROC receives public, political, and financial support from the state that other religions do not. In fact, the 1997 law was the result of a political project strongly supported by the ROC for controlling the religious pluralism that came to characterize the post-Soviet religious field, the result of which is that there is now at least a tacit expectation on the part of the Russian government that it will receive both public and private support from the ROC. This political situation reflects the position of the ruling faction of the Church, to which both the late Patriarch Aleksii II and the current Patriarch Kirill clearly belong – that Church–state relations should be defined according to the ancient Orthodox Byzantium notion of *simfoniia*, which is 'a model of governance in which the Church and state are engaged in an active partnership aimed at achieving the best possible material and spiritual conditions for human development' (Papkova 2008: 69). It is my contention that this political concept of *simfoniia* underlines the political vision of the ROC's human rights I described earlier.

The concept of *simfoniia* also privileges the ROC for defining, shaping and propagating the moral values that define the Russian nation and her people. Helping Russian society endure the struggles and difficulties of the post-Soviet transformation, and especially those viewed as the result of globalization and neoliberalism, are considered essential to the Church's part in this partnership. In fact, the main post-Soviet era social and moral documents of the ROC, which have been either authored or co-authored by the now Patriarch Kirill and include the 'Basic Teachings' on human rights, are best understood as establishing a theological position that is both anti-globalization and anti-neoliberalism (Agadjanian and Rousselet 2005: 32). This position of the ROC appears to mirror, support, and work in tandem with the current political rhetoric of the Putin–Medvedev regime, which claims to seek to re-establish Russia's political stability and power in opposition to the universalizing nature of the ideology of globalization and neoliberalism.

The Church-run drug rehabilitation and HIV prevention and care programme can be seen as a local space structured according to Orthodox human rights to provide the spiritual and moral support considered necessary to overcome the moral 'diseases' of globalization and neoliberalism. In a country that has one of the highest number of heroin users and fastest growing HIV epidemics in the world, and yet has very few services available for the people suffering from this dual epidemic, the Church-run programme is one of the only such available services in St Petersburg, one of the hardest hit cities of this health crisis. Thus, in this social context, which is made even more difficult by the neoliberal political environment that, despite political rhetoric, remains prevalent in Russia today, and which is partially defined by the radical decentralization of services, it is not surprising that the government supports the Church's taking the lead in the struggle against this health crisis. Similarly, the Church has recently made strong efforts to organize and offer a whole range of increasingly necessary social services that are not available otherwise. In this sense, the Church can be seen as filling the gap left by the radical decentralization of neoliberalism; or, put another way, the Church can be seen as providing the kind of services necessary for the successful realization of a neoliberal service sector economy.

According to those who run the drug rehabilitation and HIV prevention and care programme, the aim of the programme is to remake the moral subjectivity of rehabilitants into good, Orthodox people. Nevertheless, it is well recognized that, in most cases, this will not occur and, therefore, the secondary goal is to help make them into good responsibilized people capable of living normal lives in contemporary Russia. Despite the fact that the Church considers drug users to have significantly darkened their inherent dignity through their drug use and other activities such as stealing or prostitution that they may have engaged in because of their addiction, the Orthodox moral theology on which ROC human rights and the rehabilitation centre is based claims that within each person, including drug users, there is the ability to change and overcome their embodied immorality, purify their dignity and move towards God. This is the path of ethical work on the self on which the Church-run programme hopes to put rehabilitants by providing them a localized social service structured by Church-based human rights. While the Church-run programme recognizes that most of the rehabilitants will never fully convert to Russian Orthodoxy, it is expected that all of them can ethically work on themselves so as to become moral persons who are able to be responsibilized citizen-subjects and live normal lives in contemporary Russia. Short of full conversion, then, Orthodox human rights and the social services they help structure ultimately play their role in the great *simfoniia* of governance in contemporary Russia by providing the moral standards by which individuals can become responsibilized citizen-subjects, and in so doing, participate in the remaking and restabilization of the Russian nation.

But, the Church's use of human rights language and its practice in this programme has an unintended and ironic effect about which the Church seems to be unaware; for although the Church-run programme self-identifies and promotes itself as defined by, organized according to, and propagating Orthodox discourse and practices, much of what is actually said and done in this programme is very similar to alternative regimes of living such as those of neoliberalism. In other words, the Church-run programme and Russian Orthodoxy in general do not recognize that some of the fundamental moral dispositions and ethical skills it considers essential to Orthodox moral theology, and which are emphasized in the Church's human rights vision, are transferable and allow for successful living within competing discursive formations such as neoliberalism (cf. Comaroff and Comaroff 1986). It is for this reason that I have argued elsewhere that an unintended consequence of the Church-run rehabilitation centre is that it disciplines individuals into citizen-subjects who are better prepared to live in the Western-oriented and neoliberal world that, despite political rhetoric, is prevalent in Russia today and which the Church blames for the HIV and drug-using epidemic (Zigon 2011).

There need not be a direct equality in terms of the particular value concepts or discursive foundational assumptions between these competing discursive formations of Russian Orthodoxy and neoliberalism in order for subjects who have embodied the dispositional capacities of one of them to live sanely (Asad 2003b: 79) within the other competing formation. Thus, for example, the moral virtue and ethical disciplining of responsibility is central to both neoliberal and

Orthodox discursive regimes. But, if the particular disciplinary practices enacted in the Church-run programme and the underlying theological-discursive foundation for valuing responsibility as a virtue are not exactly that of neoliberal regimes, the disciplined and responsiblized subject cultivated within the Church-run programme supported by the language of human rights is still *better prepared* to live within the dominant neoliberal world of Russia than before entering rehabilitation. In this sense, Orthodox discourse does not need to share the neoliberal assumption of moral individualism to share the moral virtue of responsibility. Therefore, the Church-run programme unwittingly supports neoliberal regimes of living *not* because they share the same foundational moral assumptions and standards, but rather because of the very fact of the different foundational discursive assumptions. Thus, despite this difference, Orthodox and neoliberal discursive practices produce very similar disciplined subjects with very similar embodied dispositions such as responsibility. With such a result, it should come as no surprise that the more powerful and dominant discursive regime of neoliberalism benefits from the production of this new subjectivity. Human rights language serves as the idiomatic link that at one and the same time covers over and enables this ironic connection between the Russian Orthodox Church and neoliberal regimes of living.

What this example makes clear is that far from enabling a capacity of individual agency to resist repressive power, the ROC's notion of human rights is meant to provide the normative structure within which individuals can become good responsibilized citizen-subjects. The language of human rights, in this case, is used not so much to enable agentive freedom, or at least not in the sense Ignatieff envisions it, but to bind individuals closer to a particular state, and in so doing, to a particular dominant discourse of late and post-Cold War liberalism. It is possible for the ROC to adapt the language of human rights so easily to its post-Soviet political project because of the floating signifier character of this language. The language of international human rights and its key concepts – dignity, inherent respect, universality and responsibility – matches very well with many of the foundational moral concepts of the Orthodox Christian discursive tradition. In a world in which the idiomatic language of human rights carries with it increasing power and appeal, the ROC would no doubt be attracted to it for its potential political and rhetorical authority; even more so since much of the basic human rights language could easily be adapted, adjusted and safely embedded within the Church's already well-established discourse.

Some closing words

Human rights have become a dominant global moral language and yet, as the example of the Russian Orthodox Church's use of human rights shows, it still takes various forms and is utilized for different ends in different politico-social contexts. This is possible because human rights was never constituted as, neither could it become, a new discourse because its language so easily fits into any number of already existing discourses. As such, human rights language has survived essentially by becoming embedded within the already established articulations of diverse discursive traditions such as liberalism, neoliberalism and Russian Orthodoxy. Human rights, then, is akin to an idiom since as a floating signifier human rights language is easily fragmented, transferred and pragmatically performed for all kinds of diverse and contradictory purposes.

Since the late 1970s, and particularly since the end of the Cold War, human rights as an idiom has increasingly been utilized, either wittingly or unwittingly, as a moral foundation for the politics of neoliberalism. In this chapter, I have shown how this is the case with the Russian Orthodox Church and the way in which it frames the health and social services it offers in terms of human rights. It would be a mistake, however, to conclude that the Church's use of human rights ultimately results in the disciplining of individuals into good citizen-subjects simply because it is a conservative institution, for very similar consequences can be seen in the use of human rights in secular and supposedly apolitical institutions. This is particularly clear in the sphere of health services, where since the mid-1990s, human rights have been heralded as a foundation for the provision of such services and the right to health is increasingly claimed by the innumerable local NGOs providing such services and the handful of international organizations that support them.

Whether or not such rights-based services adequately provide for the well-being and health of the local populations they claim to serve is much debated. What is clear, however, is that such services tend to emphasize the necessity of rights being enacted within the context of increased personal responsibility and such emphasis, in turn, increasingly supports disciplinary regimes of responsibilization in the age of neoliberal governance (e.g., Biehl 2007; Robins 2006).[7] Despite neoliberal discursive emphasis on empowerment, which could be seen as a rhetorical strategy for cultivating self-responsibility and self-discipline within individuals (Lupton 1995: 59–61), these human rights regimes ultimately work directly on the fragile bodies of the sick and ill in order to *limit* individuals' acts, thoughts, emotions and relations in such a way that they adhere to a particularly defined politico-moral possibility (cf. Asad 2003a). In other words, since human rights are only entitled to those who are good citizens, the attempt to provide human rights to individuals is also the attempt to transform them into people of good citizenship. Thus to respond to Ignatieff's pragmatism of looking at what human rights do, it seems that the practice of human rights has, to a great extent, led to the cultivation and enactment of limits rather than enabling the expansion of politico-moral possibilities.

Through the disciplinary spaces made available by local non-governmental organizations claiming to provide services founded on the moral imperative of human rights, individuals simply seeking help or support for a particular health, social or political problem find themselves increasingly constituted (in language and in practice) as rights-bearing individuals made responsible for themselves and ultimately for the stability of the state, even if this takes the form of protesting that state's current configuration. For in the politico-moral limitations demarcated by the language of human rights, one's responsibility is to call for, struggle for, and eventually support a rights-respecting, democratic-capitalist regime with a human face. Within today's human rights language all other politico-moral possibilities are off the table.

I do not want to be misunderstood. Not all persons working for, or seeking help from, rights-based organizations are necessarily and fully transformed into such citizen-subjects. There is no doubt that individuals in contact with such organizations often adopt, utilize and experiment with rights talk and practice to the extent that it is useful for the ends they seek to accomplish only to leave it behind when it is no longer socially pragmatic (Merry 2006b: 44). Once again, we see the potential uses of the floating signifier. Nevertheless, because human rights is an iterable idiomatic language increasingly linked to disciplinary contexts and strategies of responsibilization, I suggest that even such short-term pragmatic usage leaves dispositional traces that have lasting effects on local socio-politico-moral ways of being. In this way, the idiom of human rights has become implicated in the service of power.

Notes

1 See Pitarch 2008 for a description of the complex and ambiguous nature of translating the UDHR into an indigenous language (the Mayan language Tzeltal). Although Pitarch does not make this point very strongly, it is clear that the translation distorts the UDHR to such a degree that the two texts are left as 'two distinct logics also operating in two distinct spheres' (118) and that when the language of human rights is used for strategic reasons against the Mexican state, it is used as a 'foreign language ... [the] external character [of which] makes it a valuable tool' (117).

2 I am grateful to Elinor Ochs for pointing out the idiomatic nature of human rights language.

3 I would like to thank Oskar Verkaaik for pointing this out.

4 This section has been adapted from Zigon 2011.

5 Kirill is the former Chairman of the Department for External Church Relations of the Moscow Patriarchate and widely considered the moral voice of the Church. He is the main author of several of the ROC's official documents on moral and social issues, including the 'Basic Teachings' and in conversations and interviews with priests and other Church members Kirill is often referenced as the Church's moral authority. Since the death of Aleksii II Kirill has become Patriarch of Moscow and All Russia. All references in this chapter to Kirill's writings and speeches are to those from when he was still a Metropolitan.

6 It should be noted that although Ignatieff was raised Russian Orthodox I am not trying to make any culturalist claims about the source of this family resemblance. The argument Ignatieff makes is not unique to him; he stands in this chapter simply as a representative of a dominant perspective within the transnational human rights industry.

7 Miriam Ticktin (2006) makes a similar argument concerning the disciplinary effects of humanitarian organizations and logic. I would argue, however, that Ticktin makes too strong a distinction between humanitarian and human rights regimes, as many humanitarian organizations tend to ground their services in terms of human rights to,

for example, health and medical services and utilize rights concepts such as dignity and respect as grounds for doing so.

Bibliography

Agadjanian, A. and K. Rousselet (2005) 'Globalization and Identity Discourse in Russian Orthodoxy', in V. Roudometof, A. Agadjanian and J. Pankhurst (eds), *Eastern Orthodoxy in a Global Age: Tradition Faces the Twenty-first Century*, Walnut Creek, CA: Altamira Press.

Asad, T. (1986) 'The Concept of Cultural Translation in British Social Anthropology', in J. Clifford and G.E. Marcus (eds), *Writing Culture: The Poetics and Politics of Ethnography*, Berkeley: University of California Press.

——(2003a) 'Redeeming the "Human" Through Human Rights', in *Formations of the Secular: Christianity, Islam, Modernity*, Stanford, CA: Stanford University Press.

——(2003b) 'Thinking about Agency and Pain', in *Formations of the Secular: Christianity, Islam, Modernity*, Stanford, CA: Stanford University Press.

Badiou, A. (2003) *Saint Paul: The Foundation of Universalism*, Stanford, CA: Stanford University Press.

Biehl, J. (2007) 'Pharmaceuticalization: AIDS Treatment and Global Health Politics', *Anthropological Quarterly*, 80(5): 1083–1126.

Brown, W. (1995) *States of Injury: Power and Freedom in Late Modernity*, Princeton, NJ: Princeton University Press.

Cheah, P. (1997) 'Posit(ion)ing Human Rights in the Current Global Conjuncture', *Public Culture*, 9: 233–66.

Comaroff, J. and J. Comaroff (1986) 'Christianity and Colonialism in South Africa', *American Ethnologist*, 13(1): 1–22.

Ignatieff, M. (2001) *Human Rights as Politics and Idolatry*, Princeton, NJ: Princeton University Press.

Kirill, M. (2006a) 'Human Rights and Moral Responsibility', www.mospat.ru (accessed 3 February 2007).

——(2006b) 'The Experience of Viewing the Problems of Human Rights and their Moral Foundations in European Religious Communities', www.mospat.ru (accessed 3 February 2007).

Lupton, D. (1995) *The Imperative of Health: Public Health and the Regulated Body*, London: Sage Publications.

Mahmood, S. (2005) *Politics of Piety: The Islamic Revival and the Feminist Subject*, Princeton, NJ: Princeton University Press.

Merry, S.E. (2006a) *Human Rights and Gender Violence: Translating International Law into Local Justice*, Chicago: University of Chicago Press.

——(2006b) 'Transnational Human Rights and Local Activism: Mapping the Middle', *American Anthropologist*, 108(1): 38–51.

Papkova, I. (2008) 'The Freezing of Historical Memory? The Post-Soviet Russian Orthodox Church and the Council of 1917', in M.D. Steinberg and C. Wanner (eds), *Religion, Morality, and Community in Post-Soviet Societies*, Washington, DC: Woodrow Wilson Center Press.

Pitarch, P. (2008) 'The Labyrinth of Translation: A Tzeltal Version of the Universal Declaration of Human Rights', in P. Pitarch, S. Speed and X.L. Solano (eds), *Human Rights in the Maya Region: Global Politics, Cultural Contentions, and Moral Engagements*, Durham, NC: Duke University Press.

Rabinow, P. (2003) *Anthropos Today: Reflections on Modern Equipment*, Princeton, NJ: Princeton University Press.

Robins, S. (2006) 'From "Rights" to "Ritual": AIDS Activism in South Africa', *American Anthropologist*, 108(2): 312–23.

ROC (Russian Orthodox Church) (2006) *Deklaratsiya o pravakh i dostoinstve cheloveka X Vsemirnovo Russkovo Narodnovo Sobora*, www.mospat.ru (accessed 1 December 2006).

——(2008) *Osnovy ucheniya Russkoi Pravoslavnoi Tserkvi o dostoinstve, svobode i pravakh cheloveka*, www.mospat.ru (accessed 10 July 2009).

Ticktin, M. (2006) 'Where Ethics and Politics Meet: The Violence of Humanitarianism in France', *American Ethnologist*, 33(1): 33–49.

Zigon, J. (2011) *HIV is God's Blessing: Rehabilitating Morality in Neoliberal Russia*, Berkeley: University of California Press.

Part II
Making health rights

4 The political evolution of health as a human right

Conceptualizing public health under international law, 1940s–1990s

Benjamin Mason Meier

Cited by health advocates throughout the world, human rights have become a cornerstone of global health governance, foundational to contemporary policy discourses and programmatic interventions (Reubi 2011). Yet human rights are not static concepts. Focused on the politically contingent transformation of human rights, this chapter traces the evolution of health norms as they were developed in human rights under international law and implemented through rights-based global health governance. Contemporary accounts presuppose that public health and human rights always 'evolved along parallel but distinctly separate tracks' (Gruskin, Mills and Tarantola 2007: 449), joined for the first time since the advent of the HIV/AIDS pandemic. As this chapter shows, such narratives present an incomplete history of the changing political conceptualizations of human rights for public health. This chapter analyses the contested politics underlying changing conceptions of a human right to health – from the establishment of the World Health Organization through the first decade of the HIV/AIDS pandemic. It assesses the political bases on which health rights have evolved in international law, through the policy documents outlined in Table 4.1, examining how international institutions, national governments and non-governmental organizations have conceptualized human rights law to achieve international health policy.

The foundations of human rights in public health

The international codification of universal human rights for health began in the context of World War Two. With growing calls among the Allied Powers for the creation of a post-War system to protect the individual from state tyranny, US President Franklin Delano Roosevelt announced that the post-war era would be founded on four 'essential human freedoms' – freedom of speech, freedom of religion, freedom from fear and freedom from want – with the final of these 'Four Freedoms,' freedom from want, heralding a state obligation to provide for the health of its peoples (Roosevelt 1941). Rising out of the war and drawing on the working- class struggles of the late nineteenth and early twentieth centuries, this freedom from want became enshrined in the lexicon of social and economic rights, with the Allied Powers bound together in seeking

Table 4.1 Evolving conceptualization of human rights for public health

Constitution of the World Health Organization (1946)	Universal Declaration of Human Rights (1948)	International Covenant on Economic, Social and Cultural Rights (1966)	Declaration of Alma-Ata (1978)	Global Strategy for the Prevention and Control of AIDS (1987)
Preamble Health is a state of complete physical, mental and social wellbeing and not merely the absence of disease or infirmity The enjoyment of the highest attainable standard of health is one of the fundamental rights of every human being without distinction of race, religion, political belief or economic or social condition Governments have a responsibility for the health of their peoples that can be fulfilled only by the provision of adequate health and social measures	**Article 25** (1) Everyone has the right to a standard of living adequate for the health and wellbeing of himself and of his family, including food, clothing, housing and medical care and necessary social services, and the right to security in the event of unemployment, sickness, disability, widowhood, old age or other lack of livelihood in circumstances beyond his control	**Article 12** 1. The States Parties to the present Covenant recognize the right of everyone to the enjoyment of the highest attainable standard of physical and mental health 2. The steps to be taken by the States Parties to the present Covenant to achieve the full realization of this right shall include those necessary for: (a) the provision for the reduction of the stillbirth rate and of infant mortality and for the healthy development of the child (b) the improvement of all aspects of environmental and industrial hygiene (c) the prevention, treatment and control of epidemic, endemic, occupational and other diseases (d) the creation of conditions that would assure to all medical service and medical attention in the event of sickness	1. The Conference strongly reaffirms that health, which is a state of complete physical, mental and social wellbeing, and not merely the absence of disease or infirmity, is a fundamental human right and that the attainment of the highest possible level of health is a most important worldwide social goal whose realization requires the action of many other social and economic sectors in addition to the health sector V. Governments have a responsibility for the health of their people that can be fulfilled only by the provision of adequate health and social measures. A main social target of governments, international organizations and the whole world community in the coming decades should be the attainment by all peoples of the world by the year 2000 of a level of health that will permit them to lead a socially and economically productive life. Primary health care is the key to attaining this target as part of development in the spirit of social justice	Non-discrimination is not only a human rights imperative but also a technically sound strategy for ensuring that infected persons are not driven underground, where they are inaccessible to education programmes and unavailable as credible bearers of AIDS prevention messages for their peers

state obligations that would prevent the deprivation witnessed during the Depression and World War Two (UN Conference on Food and Agriculture 1943).

Developing international human rights law for health through the United Nations (UN), the 1945 UN Charter elevated human rights as one of the principal purposes of the post-war international system, operating through the UN's Economic and Social Council (ECOSOC) to 'make recommendations for the purpose of promoting respect for, and observance of, human rights and fundamental freedoms for all' (UN 1945: Preamble). Concurrently elevating health within the UN, state representatives established the World Health Organization (WHO) as the UN's first specialized agency, with the Constitution of the World Health Organization (WHO Constitution) serving as the first international treaty to conceptualize a unique human right to health (Parran 1946).

Advancing human rights to support WHO's authority to coordinate health efforts across nations (International Health Conference 1946), states sought to facilitate international health cooperation, overcoming the political coordination challenges that had limited international health authority under the League of Nations (Borowy 2009). Seen in the preamble of the 1946 WHO Constitution, states framed their post-war health cooperation under the unprecedented declaration, 'the enjoyment of the highest attainable standard of health is one of the fundamental rights of every human being,' defining health positively to include 'a state of complete physical, mental, and social well-being and not merely the absence of disease or infirmity' (WHO 1946). Establishing WHO's authority far beyond that of its institutional predecessors (Masters 1947), WHO's mission was 'extended from the negative aspects of public health – vaccination and other specific means of combating infection – to positive aspects, i.e. the improvement of public health by better food, physical education, medical care, health insurance, etc.' (Stampar 1949). Through a rights-based focus on these underlying determinants of health, states declared in the WHO Constitution that 'governments have a responsibility for the health of their peoples which can be fulfilled only by the provision of adequate health and social measures' (WHO Constitution 1946).

Forming the political backdrop for the continuing evolution of these health obligations, states developed the 1948 Universal Declaration of Human Rights (UDHR) to proclaim the rights that were intended to bind the post-war world under a set of shared norms (Verdoodt 1964). With the UN advancing this 'common standard of achievement for all peoples and all nations' (UDHR 1948), the UDHR sought to define a comprehensive set of interrelated rights to underlie public health (Jenks 1946). With ECOSOC's Commission on Human Rights requesting that the UN's Division of Human Rights assemble a first draft of the UDHR to be put before the Commission (Alfredsson and Eide 1999), the initial draft for the First Session of the Commission on Human Rights Drafting Committee (the Drafting Committee) contained a wide range of provisions relevant to medical care, public safety, social security, and underlying determinants of health (Morsink 1999). Derived from proposals developed by US legal scholars (Committee of Advisers on Essential Human Rights 1946), many state delegates on the Drafting Committee were determined to recognize the importance of both 'medical care' and 'public health,' with preliminary emphasis on draft articles declaring that 'the state shall promote public health and safety' (UN ESCOR 1947). Reflecting the states represented in the Commission on Human Rights, this expansive rights-based vision of public health systems (at the national and community level) was presented in language similar to the WHO Constitution and in accordance with (1) the expansion of post-war European welfare policy, founded on the notion that 'social security cannot be fully developed unless health is cared for along comprehensive lines' (Beveridge 1942); (2) the early development of health rights in Latin America, encompassing 'the right to the preservation of his health through sanitary and social measures relating to food, clothing, housing and medical care' (Organization of American States 1948); and (3) the recent amendments to the Soviet Constitution, which established guarantees of medical care and 'maintenance in old age and also in case of sickness or disability' (Konstitutsiia SSSR 1936: Art. 120). Taken together, the First Session of the Drafting Committee framed a rights-based vision that reflected the experience of national health systems and recognized the importance of international solidarity in addressing determinants of the public's health.

However, over the three substantive sessions outlined in Table 4.2, the process of revising the UDHR exposed early divisions that would come to define international health policy during the Cold War.

At the opening of the Second Session of the Drafting Committee, the US representative introduced a completely revised text that focused on social security without any direct mention of health, viewing health as a benefit of work (rather than an independent right) and limiting state obligations only to those unable to secure their own 'livelihood' (rather than to all individuals). The representative of the Soviet Union objected vigorously to these US proposals, arguing that they were too vague and insisting on detailed delineations of universal obligations, with the US representative responding that 'no more detailed wording was practicable as different provisions for the protection of health were established in different countries' (Alfredsson and Eide 1999). While discussions continued to focus on the importance of underlying determinants of health, the Second Session framed this evolving consensus under the broad umbrella of 'social security,' with the adoption of specific protections related to mothers and children.

To delineate the aspects of social security crucial to the realization of human rights, the Third Session of the Drafting Committee reintroduced public health and medicine to the draft UDHR, even as these rights came to be framed under a state obligation to secure the conditions for individual work. With China and the Soviet Union seeking to enumerate the specific rights underlying health through obligations for a comprehensive system of 'social insurance,' the Chinese representative argued 'for the inclusion of a set of rights that had been considered being included in this article from the beginning – namely food,

Table 4.2 Final text from each of the UDHR drafting sessions

Session 1	Session 2	Session 3
Everyone, without distinction of economic and social conditions, has the right to the highest standard of health attainable. The responsibility of the State and community for the health and safety for its people can be fulfilled only by the provision of adequate and social measures.	1. Everyone has the right to social security. The State has a duty to maintain or ensure the maintenance of comprehensive measures for the security of the individual against the consequences of unemployment, disability, old age and all other loss of livelihood for reasons beyond his control. 2. Motherhood shall be granted special care and assistance. Children are similarly entitled to special care and assistance.	1. Everyone has the right to a standard of living, including food, clothing, housing and medical care, and to social services, adequate for the health and wellbeing of himself and his family and to security in the event of unemployment, sickness, disability, old age or other lack of livelihood in circumstances beyond his control. 2. Mother and child have the right to special care and assistance.

housing, clothing, and medical care' (UN 1950). Although the United States argued that 'only the right to housing and medical care should be explicitly stated,' the US representative came to support the full inclusion of determinants of health, albeit under a state obligation to realize a 'standard of living,' with this US agreement obviating the need for any discussion about health rights when the debate moved to the full UN General Assembly (UN 1950).

On 10 December 1948, the General Assembly unanimously (40–0, 2 abstentions) adopted the following text of article 25 of the UDHR:

(1) Everyone has the right to *a standard of living adequate for the health and well-being* of himself and of his family, including food, clothing, housing and *medical care* and necessary social services, and the right to security in the event of unemployment, sickness, disability, widowhood, old age or other lack of livelihood in circumstances beyond his control.
(2) Motherhood and childhood are entitled to special care and assistance. All children, whether born in or out of wedlock, shall enjoy the same social protection.

(UDHR 1948: Art. 25(1); emphasis added)

With agreement that human rights for health comprised both the fulfilment of necessary medical care and the realization of underlying determinants of health – explicitly including food, clothing, housing and social services as part of this holistic encapsulation of health determinants – states sought in the ensuing years to translate this declaratory language into binding obligations under international law.

The development of international law for a right to health

As the UN Commission on Human Rights moved to translate the hortatory rights of the UDHR into binding treaties under international law, health rights were transformed through the development of international legal obligations under the International Covenant on Economic, Social and Cultural Rights (ICESCR) (Green 1956). However, these processes to codify a human right to health faced conceptual limitations through the political constraints of the Cold War, hobbling efforts to advance public health discourses in human rights law (Tobin 2012).

With the WHO Secretariat initially asserting leadership for developing human rights standards on health, WHO suggested wide-ranging legal language to support the efforts of the Commission on Human Rights in developing an International Covenant on Human Rights. Drawn from the WHO Constitution and language abandoned in the drafting of the UDHR, WHO's expansive pro-posal for a right to health emphasized: (1) a positive definition of health; (2) the importance of social measures in realizing underlying determinants of health; (3) governmental responsibility for health provision; and (4) the role of public health systems in creating a wide range of measures for what would become 'primary health care' (WHO 1951a). Despite support from European and Latin American states, this WHO proposal was challenged in the Commission on Human Rights, with duelling US and Soviet amendments seeking to eliminate the expansive WHO proposal in its entirety, replacing it with each nation's respective view of health rights (see Table 4.3).

Rather than adopting either of these conflicting amendments – the United States' vague pronouncement of a right without corresponding obligations or the Soviet Union's limited obligations for medical care – states reached a com-promise, by which the US proposal was added to the first paragraph of the WHO proposal and the Soviet proposal on medical care was added as an additional obligation on state governments.

By a final vote of 10–0 (8 abstentions) – the abstentions from western states arising in objection to the obligation concerning medical care – the Commission on Human Rights concluded in 1951 with the following draft article for the International Covenant on Human Rights:

> The States parties to this Covenant recognize the right of everyone to the enjoyment of the highest standard of health obtainable. With a view to

Table 4.3 US and Soviet proposals for the right to health

US proposal	USSR proposal
The States Parties to the Covenant recognize the right of everyone to the enjoyment of the highest standard of health obtainable.	Each State Party hereto undertakes to combat disease and provide conditions that would assure the right of all its nationals to a medical service and medical attention in the event of sickness.

implementing and safeguarding this right, each State party hereto under-
takes to provide legislative measures to promote and protect health and in
particular:

1 to reduce infant mortality and to provide for healthy development of the
   child;
2 to improve nutrition, housing, sanitation, recreation, economic and working
   conditions and other aspects of environmental hygiene;
3 to control epidemic, endemic and other diseases;
4 to provide conditions which would assure the right of all its nationals to a
   medical service and medical attention in the event of sickness.

(Commission on Human Rights 1951)

Providing simultaneously for the general recognition of a right to health in an
opening paragraph with an enumeration of state obligations in subsequent
paragraphs, the revised draft of the right to health was the most detailed draft
among the economic, social and cultural rights, reflecting state obligations to
progressively realize a wide range of health determinants (Toebes 1999). While
a right to health continued to lack the support of western medical associations,
which were lobbying against government 'socialist' control of medical practice
(World Medical Association 1951), the WHO Secretariat received support from
its Executive Board (over the objections of the US Representative) to take a
continuing leadership role in the UN's efforts to develop the legal language of
the right to health (WHO 1951b).

With the Cold War superpowers continuing to be divided on the conceptualization of rights in the International Covenant, states were pressed to
replace the unified International Covenant on Human Rights with two separate
human rights covenants – one on civil and political rights and the other on
economic, social and cultural rights (UN General Assembly 1952). Indicative of
the political debates of the Cold War, the comprehensive vision of rights laid
out by states in the UDHR had unravelled along ideological and economic lines,
with the superpowers (and their respective spheres of influence) split on both a
belief in the universality of economic and social rights and the feasibility of
realizing these rights (Alston 1979). With the United States advocating the
advancement of international legal obligations only for civil and political rights
(those classic civil liberties already protected by western states' national con-
stitutions), US representatives dismissed 'aspirational' social and economic
rights (including a right to health) as a basis for a just world (UN 1952). This
unbending international disagreement on the nature of rights and divided UN
framework of two covenants notwithstanding, states continued to meet together in the Commission on Human Rights, finalizing the drafting of health
obligations for inclusion in what would become the ICESCR.

Although WHO initially sought an expanding role for human rights in
addressing underlying determinants of health – working with states to define
health comprehensively, in line with the WHO Constitution's proclamation of

health as 'a state of complete physical, mental and social well-being, and not merely the absence of disease or infirmity' (Commission on Human Rights 1952) – states came to reverse this early expansion of the right to health (Farley 2008). As the Soviet states withdrew temporarily from WHO in the late 1940s and early 1950s, denying socialized medicine a voice in World Health Assembly debates (Manela 2010), an unchallenged American influence (driven by US funding restrictions on the WHO Secretariat and a unified voting bloc of North, Central and South American states) succeeded in constraining WHO's efforts to advance a human right to health under international law (Goodman 1952). Reflecting a 1953 transition to WHO leadership more conducive to US influence, the WHO Secretariat abandoned its early efforts to develop expansive international legal language for public health – projecting itself as a 'technical organization' (Candau 1954), neglecting 'social questions' (WHO 1956), and finding legal rights 'beyond the competence of WHO' (WHO 1959). This WHO abdication of human rights authority enabled state efforts to weaken human rights norms for health (Meier 2010). Without WHO leadership, UN preparations for finalizing the right to health resurrected political debates on the inclusion of: (1) a definition of health; (2) the idea of 'social well-being'; and (3) the 'steps to be taken' by states (UNGA 1955). Following the six-year effort of the Commission on Human Rights to transform the UDHR into legally binding obligations, the debate then moved to the UN General Assembly to adopt the ICESCR's conceptualization of a right to health.

Through the 1957 debates of the General Assembly, state challenges to the ICESCR article on the right to health prevailed in eliminating from paragraph one both the definition of health and any reference to 'social well-being,' under the contradictory rationales that the definition was either unnecessarily verbose or irreconcilably incomplete. Narrowing state obligations in paragraph two, state challenges also succeeded in substituting 'the improvement of nutrition, housing, sanitation, recreation, economic and working conditions and other aspects of environmental hygiene' with the less specific 'improvement of all aspects of environmental and industrial hygiene' (with this later addition coming through the advocacy of the International Labour Organization) (UNGA 1957). On 30 January 1957, the General Assembly voted in favour of an amended right to health (54–0, with 7 abstentions), with the right to health retaining the following legal language in the years leading up to the 1966 adoption of the ICESCR:

1 The States Parties to the present Covenant recognize the right of everyone to the enjoyment of the highest attainable standard of physical and mental health.
2 The steps to be taken by the States Parties to the present Covenant to achieve the full realization of this right shall include those necessary for:

   (a) The provision for the reduction of the stillbirth rate and of infant mortality and for the healthy development of the child;

(b) The improvement of all aspects of environmental and industrial hygiene;

(c) The prevention, treatment and control of epidemic, endemic, occupational and other diseases;

(d) The creation of conditions which would assure to all medical service and medical attention in the event of sickness.

(UN General Assembly 1966)

With WHO continuing to avoid a rights-based approach to health, as human rights had become a basis for Soviet criticism of capitalist inequalities in health (Evang 1967), the UN's comprehensive 1968 review of human rights efforts included only perfunctory generalities on WHO's role in advancing the right to health – that:

> Through its programme of technical assistance, WHO is helping countries achieve the objectives set forth in the preamble to its constitution, and thus the full range of its activities are relevant to human rights by assisting countries to make a reality of their people's right to health.

(UN 1968)

Yet with WHO noting as early as 1968 that 'people are beginning to ask for health, and to regard it as a right,' this calculated neglect of human rights would soon turn to active engagement, returning to the political promise of international human rights as a means to realize international health cooperation (WHO 1968).

The implementation of human rights through primary health care

Concurrent with an expansion of human rights in UN governance in the 1970s (Morgan 2010), the WHO Secretariat came to see human rights principles as a normative foundation on which to frame public health policy, leading to international efforts to implement human rights through 'primary health care' – addressing health care in addition to the underlying social, political, and economic determinants of health (Litsios 1969). Recognizing the limitations of medical care in preventing disease and promoting health (WHO 1973), WHO turned to political efforts to structure national health systems for primary health care (Evang 1973). As developing nations entered the UN system and banded together under the Non-Aligned Movement, this new political force sought to influence the World Health Assembly, bring health policy in line with a New International Economic Order, and shift WHO efforts to support a rights-based approach to equity through primary health care (Chorev 2012). While primary health care had long garnered technical backing within the WHO Secretariat, the ideological support of human rights brought these technical health discourses to the fore of international health debates. With political support from developing states, WHO employed international negotiations, articles, and conferences to conceptualize human rights as a means to realize equity through underlying determinants of health (Mahler 1973).

With a 1973 change in the leadership of the WHO Secretariat, which paralleled developing country pressures to address international health inequities through national health systems, the Secretariat sought to revitalize human rights as a basis for WHO authority, extolling human rights obligations as a clarion call for the advancement of primary health care (Cueto 2004). Reflected in inter-agency studies and international debates, WHO sought to apply human rights frameworks and advocacy to realize underlying determinants of health, looking to a wide range of human rights standards to govern the public health implications of, among other things: human experimentation (WHO 1974); torture (Howard-Jones 1976); gender inequity (Sipilä 1979); and medical education (Torelli 1980).

An expansive concern for the wide range of human rights that underlay health notwithstanding, the WHO Secretariat gave preeminent focus to the human right to health, arguing that 'this provision is of primary importance from WHO's point of view, and the whole body of WHO activities is based on the right and principles contained therein' (WHO 1975). As international consensus developed around the primary health care policies necessary to implement the right to health, such human rights implementation framed a multisectoral approach to 'health in all policies' (Vigne 1979). To establish such rights-based policies, there was growing agreement that WHO had the political authority to coordinate these multisectoral actors in elaborating international legal obligations for underlying determinants of health (Roscam Abbing 1979).

Seeking a human rights framework to address inequities in economic determinants of health, meeting the political expectations of developing member states and placing greater emphasis on international development policies (Pannenborg 1979), scholars and practitioners began to focus on international economic arrangements that would assure 'health for all' (Commission on Human Rights 1973). Advancing economic growth as a means to realize the right to health, WHO focused on social and economic development as integral to public health (Eze 1979). Grounded in the WHO Constitution, subsequent international treaties, and the UN's debate on a human right to development, this socioeconomic approach to health aligned with public health scholarship on underlying determinants of health, provided a basis for incorporating human rights in international health policy, and formed the basis of what WHO officials referred to as 'the onset of the health revolution' (Lambo 1979).

WHO's 'Health for All' strategy provided a framework for its efforts to influence human rights implementation through socioeconomic development, structuring primary health care as a means to address underlying determinants of health. Officially defined by the World Health Assembly in 1977, and widely regarded as WHO's 'main thrust' in implementing human rights for public health (Taylor 1991), the Health for All strategy sought 'the attainment by all citizens of the world by the year 2000 of a level of health that would permit them to lead socially and economically productive lives' (World Health Assembly 1977). With developing states in the World Health Assembly viewing the inequitable distribution of resources for health to be a violation of human rights, this WHO strategy examined health within the broader social and economic context of development, finding that '[h]ealth is not a separate entity but an integral part of national development' – a view that led the WHO Secretariat to seek the national and international redistributions that would advance public health (Mahler 1978).

Elevating a rights-based approach to international health policy that had been wanting since the right to health was first proclaimed in the WHO Constitution, WHO and UNICEF convened the International Conference on Primary Health Care in September 1978. Held in Alma-Ata, USSR (now Almaty, Kazakhstan), this Conference brought together public health and development actors to address the policies necessary to realize the health determinants outside the control of the health sector (Mower 1985). Returning to the UDHR's promise of interconnected human rights for public health, WHO conceptualized a multisectoral model for primary health care, seeking social justice in the distribution of health resources. With representatives from 134 state governments, the Conference adopted the Declaration on Primary Health Care (a document that has come to be known as the Declaration of Alma-Ata), through which political representatives detailed the international rights-based consensus that primary health care was the key to advancing public health throughout the world (WHO 1978).

Reaffirming the human rights principles of the WHO Constitution, Article I of the Declaration of Alma-Ata outlined that:

> [H]ealth, which is a state of complete physical, mental and social well-being, and not merely the absence of disease or infirmity, is a fundamental human right and that the attainment of the highest level of health is a most important world-wide social goal whose realization requires the action of many other social and economic sectors in addition to the health sector.
>
> (Ibid)

Delineating the national policies necessary to implement human rights through primary health care, the Declaration of Alma-Ata outlined government obligations to reorient national social and economic development strategies to promote equity in health, laying out specific multisectoral obligations for:

(1) education concerning prevailing health problems
(2) promotion of food supply and proper nutrition
(3) an adequate supply of safe water and basic sanitation
(4) maternal and child health care, including family planning
(5) immunization against the major infectious diseases
(6) prevention and control of locally endemic diseases
(7) appropriate treatment of common diseases and injuries
(8) the provision of essential medicines.

(Ibid, § VII)

Intended to guide states in progressively realizing the right to health, the WHO Secretariat supported these national efforts to address underlying determinants of health through technical assistance, analysis, and monitoring, with the World Health Assembly developing formal guidelines for national policy under its 1981 Global Strategy for Health for All by the Year 2000 (WHO 1981).

Through the political advancement of such rights-based obligations, the Declaration of Alma-Ata conceptualized a programmatic vision for implementing human rights in primary health care; however, such obligations to realize distributive justice never took hold in national health policy (Taylor 1992). While this international health policy initially found support from the developed states (Bourne 1978), the rise of neoliberal economics – and with it, reflexive government opposition to health spending – closed any opportunity for WHO to advance primary health care (Chorev 2012). Developed states came to resist WHO's focus on primary health care, opposing the economic redistribution demands of developing states and scaling back international support for health policy under the mantle of 'Selective Primary Health Care' (through a narrower focus on growth-monitoring, oral rehydration, breastfeeding, and immunization) (Cueto 2004). Yet even as states stepped back from implementing human rights through expansive obligations for primary health care (WHO 1983), such rights-based standards endured in the politics of health policy, reconceptualized through a rights-based approach to public health in the international response to HIV/AIDS.

The operationalization of human rights in the public health response to HIV/AIDS

Despite a lack of political support for primary health care, human rights remained applicable to the advancement of public health, even as this implementation shifted from national health systems to individual health needs. WHO programme staff continued to refer to the normative standards of human rights throughout the early 1980s (Gunn 1983), and as a result, the Secretariat was politically poised to operationalize a rights-based approach to health with the advent of the HIV/AIDS pandemic. As developed states reduced their budgetary support for WHO primary health care programmes (Dietrich 1988), these same states increased their 'extrabudgetary' support for WHO's efforts to prevent and control the spread of the pandemic in the decade following the first reported case of AIDS (Vaughan *et al.* 1996). With these prevention efforts grounded in individual autonomy for health, WHO's rights-based approach to AIDS found support among transnational networks of non-governmental advocates, working closely with the WHO Secretariat to understand the risks for transmission, educate the public on prevention, and slow the spread of HIV.

The HIV/AIDS pandemic transformed human rights for global health as non-governmental advocates looked explicitly to these rights in framing health policy. With governments responding to the emergent threat of AIDS through traditional public health policies – including compulsory testing, named reporting, travel restrictions, and coercive isolation or quarantine – human rights were seen as a reaction to intrusive public health infringements on individual liberty and a bond among HIV-positive activists (Bayer 1991). Facilitated by academic discourse in Europe and the United States, advocates in the gay community and among people living with AIDS conceptualized human rights claims in opposition to restrictive public health measures (Mann and Carballo 1989). Where national legislation restricted the freedoms of these vocal minorities, human rights advocacy served to protect the vulnerable (Gruskin and Tarantola 2005). With improved understanding of heterosexual transmission and developing country prevalence, the rapid identification of a generalized pandemic created a pressing imperative for disease prevention and control through rights-based policy (WHO 1985). Supporting community-based advocacy in responding to this new threat, individual rights-based freedoms buttressed international health rights, framing social approaches to addressing underlying determinants of health.

In this period of burgeoning fear and advocacy, the establishment of WHO's Global Programme on AIDS (GPA) marked a turning point in the operationalization of individual human rights in public health policy – viewing discrimination as counterproductive to public health goals, abandoning coercive tools of public health, and applying human rights to focus on the individual behaviours leading to HIV transmission (Fee and Parry 2008). By focusing on underlying social determinants of HIV risk, human rights could play a supportive role in the public health response, as human rights violations were understood to be a key driver in the spread of the disease (Mann 1987a). The 1985 creation of WHO's Special Programme on AIDS – renamed and expanded in 1986 into the GPA – operationalized human rights in WHO programming through strategies to combat HIV discrimination, promote social equity, and encourage individual responsibility (Meier, Brugh and Halima 2012). Without medical treatment or biomedical prevention, the GPA sought to address social behaviours, with the promotion of human rights linked to the protection of public health (Mann and Kay 1991). Although human rights scholarship had long recognized the infringement of individual rights as permissible – even necessary – to protect the public's health, the GPA saw the respect of individual rights as a precondition for the public's health in the context of HIV prevention and control (Fee and Parry 2008). Quickly expanding within the WHO Secretariat, GPA staff, made up of the first epidemiologists to study HIV, recognized that discrimination had limited the public health response. They sought to develop a rights-based approach, providing the health education and supportive environment for individuals to take responsibility for changing their behaviours and thereby reduce their risk of infection (Mann 1987b). Memorializing this public health consensus to prevent HIV-related discrimination, the 1987 publication of 'Social Aspects of AIDS Prevention and Control' proclaimed that the HIV positive 'should remain integrated within society to the maximum possible extent and be helped to assume responsibility for preventing HIV transmission to others' (WHO 1987a). Emblematic of a tightening political relationship between WHO and non-governmental organizations to advance human rights, the GPA sought repeatedly to 'bring together the various organizations, particularly those organizations of the UN system and related organizations involved in human rights to discuss the relationship between AIDS, discrimination, and human rights' (WHO 1987b). With the GPA linking human rights organizations with HIV/AIDS advocates, this non-governmental interaction led to a deepening of human rights assessments of HIV prevention and control efforts – within the UN and across national governments (Mann and Kay 1991).

Tying together the efforts of international institutions, national governments, and non-governmental organizations under a universal framework for action, WHO's 1987 Global Strategy for the Prevention and Control of AIDS (Global Strategy) conceptualized universal human rights principles to prevent HIV transmission and reduce the impact of the pandemic (WHO 1987c). The Global Strategy focused on principles of non-discrimination and equitable access to care, stressing the need for public health programmes to respect and protect human rights as a means to achieve the individual behaviour change necessary to reduce HIV transmission. By leveraging behavioural science to develop HIV prevention campaigns, the Global Strategy emphasized rights-based access to information, education, and services as a means to support personal responsibility among vulnerable individuals (Mann 1987a). Through this Global Strategy, human rights framed the international HIV/AIDS response, with the Global Strategy serving as a normative basis for the development of international guidelines, national policies and non-governmental action.

From non-governmental advocacy to international health policy, the states of the World Health Assembly unanimously endorsed the Global Strategy as a political framework for 'urgent and vigorous globally directed action' to address HIV/AIDS (World Health Assembly 1987). Taking up this call for action in the UN General Assembly, UN delegates debated issues of infectious disease for the first time, with presentations from both the WHO Director-General and GPA Director conceptualizing HIV prevention and control as a human rights imperative (Mann 1987c). Confirming the role of interconnected human rights in speaking to intersectoral determinants of HIV, the UN General Assembly resolved 'to ensure ... a coordinated response by the United Nations system to the AIDS pandemic,' directing all UN agencies to assist in WHO's efforts (UN General Assembly 1987). With WHO continuing to draw on political collaborations with non-governmental advocates, the GPA sought to develop international guidelines to discourage national policies that infringed on human rights, including international travel restrictions (WHO 1987d), mandatory HIV testing (WHO 1987e) and HIV-based employment discrimination (WHO 1988b). In upholding WHO's rights-based authority, the World Health Assembly reaffirmed in May 1988 that 'respect for human rights and dignity of HIV-infected people, people with AIDS and members of population groups is vital to the success of national AIDS prevention and control programs and of the global strategy' (World Health Assembly 1988). Providing global leadership under the World Health Assembly's directive 'to issue guidance on the prevention and control of AIDS on a continuing basis,' the WHO Secretariat worked with international, national, and non-governmental stakeholders to develop evidence-based guidelines to ensure global collaboration against this unprecedented threat (Mann and Tarantola 1998).

To support national HIV/AIDS policy, WHO operationalized universal rights-based frameworks to coordinate national plans, prevention programmes, and resource mobilization for HIV (Gruskin *et al*. 2007), bridging non-governmental organizations and national governments in developing health legislation, training programme staff, and coordinating international donors (Mann and Kay 1991). Despite tensions between WHO staff and national ministries, with national governments often hesitant to report AIDS cases, WHO's GPA persevered in working with the vast majority of states to support the adoption of national policies based on rights-based principles of dignity, equality, and non-discrimination. Complemented by financial support to build governmental capacity and non-governmental involvement, these policy reforms overcame the iniquitous legislation that had limited individual rights, promoting rights to realize disease prevention goals (Gostin 2004). Creating a dialogue by which states could share rights-based practices, WHO brought together representatives from 148 nations in 1988 for a World Summit of Ministers of Health on Programmes for AIDS Prevention (WHO 1988a). The resulting London Declaration on AIDS Prevention encapsulated a rights-based political consensus to catalyze national policy, with WHO authority supporting international coordination and cooperation in the design, implementation, and monitoring and assessment of these national HIV/AIDS programmes (Mann and Kay 1991).

In this effort and in the years to come, evolving conceptions of human rights continued to frame policy for the prevention, treatment, and care of HIV. Although a shift in the WHO leadership diminished the Secretariat's ability to promote a rights-based approach to health – leading the director of the GPA to resign in protest, stymieing WHO authority for furthering human rights, and leaving WHO's entire AIDS programming in a state of disarray (Garrett 1994) – this focus on a rights-based approach to health persisted (Gruskin *et al*. 2007). Even as WHO lost programmatic authority for HIV/AIDS, overtaken by the 1994 establishment of the Joint United Nations Programme on HIV/AIDS (UNAIDS), the human rights framing of public health continued through this transition and remains to the present day – galvanizing political attention to create a human rights basis for global health.

Conclusion

As various actors have taken up human rights as a basis for health policy, they have conceptualized human rights in new and different ways to meet their political needs. This unsteady evolution – throughout the foundation, development, implementation and operationalization of human rights – has highlighted the politically contingent nature of the human rights imperative in public health. With international institutions, national governments and non-governmental organizations continuing to reconceptualize human rights for global health, human rights have been extended over a wide range of communicable and non-communicable disease threats, transforming human rights to set universal norms for social, political and economic determinants of health. To ensure that these human rights efforts continue to frame public health under international law, it will be necessary to understand the role of politics in conceptualizing rights to realize the highest attainable standard of health.

Acknowledgments

In the development of this research, the author is grateful to Maya Mahin for her research assistance, to Gerald Oppenheimer for his comments on previous drafts of this chapter, and to Alex Mold and David Reubi for their editorial guidance.

Abbreviations

AIDS   Acquired Immune Deficiency Syndrome
CIOMS   Council for International Organizations of the Medical Sciences
ECOSOC   UN Economic and Social Council
GPA   World Health Organization's Global Programme on AIDS
HIV   Human Immunodeficiency Virus
ICESCR   International Covenant on Economic, Social, and Cultural
                Rights
UDHR   Universal Declaration of Human Rights
UN   United Nations
UNAIDS   Joint United Nations Programme on HIV/AIDS
UNESCO   United Nations Educational, Scientific, and Cultural Organization
UNICEF   United Nations Children's Fund
WHO   World Health Organization

Bibliography

Alfredsson, G. and Eide, A. (1999). *The Universal Declaration of Human Rights: A Common Standard of Achievement*, Boston, MA: Martinus Nijhoff Publishers.
Alston, P. (1979). 'The United Nations' specialized agencies and implementation of the International Covenant on Economic, Social, and Cultural Rights,' *Columbia Journal of Transnational Law* 18:79–118.
Bayer, R. (1991). 'Public health policy and the AIDS epidemic. An end to HIV exceptionalism?,' *New England Journal of Medicine* 324:1500–504.
Beveridge, W. (1942). *Social Insurance and Allied Services: Report by Sir William Beveridge*, London: Inter-Departmental Commission on Social Insurance and Allied Services.
Borowy, I. (2009). *Coming to Terms with World Health: The League of Nations Health Organization 1921–1946*, Berlin: Peter Lang.
Bourne, P. (1978). *New Directions in International Health Cooperation: A Report to the President*, Washington, DC: US Government Printing Office.

Candau, M.G. (1954). 'WHO – prospects and opportunities: The road ahead,' *American Journal of Public Health* 44(12):1499–1504.

Chorev, N. (2012). *The World Health Organization Between North and South*, Ithaca, NY: Cornell University Press.

Claude, R.P. and Issel, B.W. (1998). 'Health, medicine and science in the Universal Declaration of Human Rights,' *Health and Human Rights* 3(2):126–42.

Commission on Human Rights (1950). 'Sixth Session. Compilation of the Comments of Governments on the Draft International Covenant on Human Rights and on the Proposed Additional Articles,' E/CN.4/365. March 22, 1950.

——(1951). Seventh Session, E/CN.4/SR.223. June 13, 1951.

——(1952). Eighth Session, Draft International Covenant on Human Rights and Measures of Implementation: Provisions Concerning Economic, Social and Cultural Rights. E/CN.4/650. March 10, 1952.

——(1973). *The Widening Gap: A Study of the Realization of Economic, Social and Cultural Rights.* (Compiled by Manouchehr Ganji, Special Rapporteur of the Commission on Human Rights.) E/CN.4/1108. February 5, 1973.

Committee of Advisers on Essential Human Rights (1946). 'American Law Institute. Statement of essential human rights,' *Annals of the American Academy of Political and Social Science* 243:18–26.

Cueto, M. (2004). 'The origins of primary health care and selective primary health care,' *American Journal of Public Health* 94:1864–74.

Dietrich, P. (1988). 'WHO's budget "crisis",' *Wall Street Journal* May 5:32.

——(1948). Report of the Third Session of the Commission on Human Rights. E/800.

Eide, A. (1993). 'Article 25.' In Eide, A., Alfredsson, G., Melander, G., Rehof, L.A., and Rosas, A., *The Universal Declaration of Human Rights: A Commentary*, Oslo: Scandinavian University Press.

Evang, K. (1967). *Health of Mankind: Ciba Foundation*, London: Churchill.

——(1973). 'Human rights: Health for everyone,' *World Health* 3–11.

Eze, O.C. (1979). 'Right to health as a human right in Africa.' In *The Right to Health as a Human Right: Workshop, The Hague, 27–29 July 1978*, Alphen aan den Rijn: Sijthoff & Noordhoff.

Farley, J. (2008). *Brock Chisholm, the World Health Organization, and the Cold War*, Vancouver: UBC Press.

Fee, E. and Parry, M. (2008). 'Jonathan Mann, HIV/AIDS, and human rights,' *Journal of Public Health Policy* 29:54–71.

Garrett, L. (1994). *The Coming Plague: Newly Emerging Diseases in a World Out of Balance*, New York: Penguin.

Glendon, M.A. (2003). 'The forgotten crucible: The Latin American influence on the universal human rights idea,' *Harvard Human Rights Journal* 16:27–40.

Goodman, N.M. (1952). *International Health Organizations and Their Work*, London: Churchill.

Gostin, L.O. (2004). *The AIDS Pandemic: Complacency, Injustice and Unfulfilled Expectations*, Chapel Hill: University of North Carolina Press.

Green, J.F. (1956). *The United Nations and Human Rights*, Washington, DC: Brookings.

Gruskin, S., Mills, E.J., and Tarantola, D. (2007). 'History, principles, and practice of health and human rights,' *Lancet* 70:449–54.

Gruskin, S. and Tarantola, D. (2005). 'Health and human rights.' In Gruskin, S., Grodin, M.A., Annas, G.J., and Marks, S.P. (eds), *Perspectives on Health and Human Rights*, New York: Routledge.

Gunn, S.W.A. (1983). 'The right to health through international cooperation.' In *Il Diritto alla Tutela della Salute: Acts of the International Colloquium on the Right to Health Protection*, Torino, Italy, May 20–21.

Howard-Jones, N. (1976). 'Health and human rights,' *World Health* 3–7.

International Health Conference (1946). 'Proceedings and final acts of the International Health Conference,' *WHO Official Records*. 2: 67.

Jenks, C.W. (1946). 'The five economic and social rights,' *Annals of the American Academy of Political and Social Science* 243:40–46.

Konstitutsiia SSSR (1936). Art. 120; reprinted in Georgadze, M. (ed.) (1982) *USSR, SixtyYears of the Union 1922–1982: A Collection of Legislative Acts and Other Documents*, Moscow: Progress Publishers.

Lambo, T.A. (1979). 'Towards justice in health,' *World Health* 25:4.

Litsios, S. (1969). 'A program for research in the organization and strategy of health services,' Paper presented at the WHO Director General's Conference, Geneva, Switzerland.

Mahler, H. (1973). 'Born to be healthy,' A message from Dr. H. Mahler, Director-General of the World Health Organization. Reprinted in Secretary-General's progress report. A/9133.

——(1978). 'Justice in health,' *WHO Magazine* May:3.

Manela, E. (2010). 'A pox on your narrative: Writing disease control into Cold War history,' *Diplomatic History* 30:299–323.

Mann, J. (1987a). 'AIDS – A global perspective: The World Health Organization's global strategy for the prevention and control of AIDS,' *Western Journal of Medicine* 147:732–34.

——(1987b). 'AIDS. World Health Forum,' 8:361–72.

——(1987c). 'Address to Special Session of the Fortieth World Health Assembly on AIDS: The Global Strategy for AIDS Prevention and Control,' WHO/SPA/INF/ 87.2. Geneva: WHO, May 5.

Mann, J.M. and Carballo, M. (1989). 'Social, cultural and political aspects: Overview,' *AIDS* 3:S221-S223.

Mann, J.M. and Kay, K. (1991). 'Confronting the pandemic: The World Health Organization's Global Program on AIDS, 1986–89,' *AIDS* 5:S221-S229.

Mann, J.M. and Tarantola, D. (1998). Responding to HIV/AIDS: A historical perspective,' *Health and Human Rights* 2:5–8.

Masters, R.D. (1947). *International Organization in the Field of Public Health*, Washington, DC: Carnegie Endowment.

Meier, B.M. (2010). 'Global health governance and the contentious politics of human rights: Mainstreaming the right to health for public health advancement,' *Stanford Journal of International Law* 46:1–50.

Meier, B.M., Brugh K.N., and Halima Y. (2012). 'Conceptualizing a human right to prevention in global HIV policy,' *Public Health Ethics* 5:263–82.

Morgan, M.C. (2010). 'The seventies and the rebirth of human rights.' In Ferguson, N. *et al.* (eds) *The Shock of the Global: The 1970s in Perspective*, Cambridge, MA: Belknap Press.

Morsink, J. (1999). *The Universal Declaration of Human Rights: Origins, Drafting, and Intent*, Philadelphia: University of Pennsylvania Press.

Mower, A.G. (1985). *International Cooperation for Social Justice: Global and Regional Protection of Economic/Social Rights*, Westport, CT: Greenwood Press.

Organization of American States (1948). 'American Declaration of the Rights and Duties of Man. Resolution XXX,' Art. XI. OEA/Ser.L/V/II, 23 doc., 21 rev. 6.

Pannenborg, C.O. (1979). *A New International Health Order: An Inquiry into the International Relations of World Health and Medical Care*, Alphen aan den Rijn: Sijthoff and Noordhoff.

Parran, T. (1946). 'Chapter for world health,' *Public Health Reports* 61:1265–68.

Reubi, D. (2011). 'The promise of human rights for global health: A programmed deception?,' *Social Science and Medicine* 73:625–28.

Roosevelt, F.D. (1941). *President Franklin Roosevelt's 6 January 1941 State of the Union Address*, The Public Papers of Franklin D. Roosevelt, Vol. 9.

Roscam Abbing, H.D.C. (1979). *International Organizations in Europe and the Right to Health Care*, Deventer: Kluwer.

Ryle, J.A. (1948). *Changing Disciplines: Lectures on the History Method and Motives of Social Pathology*, London: Oxford University Press.

Sipilä, H. (1979). 'Women, health and human rights,' *World Health* July:6–9.

Stampar, A. (1949). 'Suggestions relating to the Constitution of an International Health Organization,' *WHO Official Records* 1(Annex 9).

Taylor, A.L. (1991). *The World Health Organization and the Right to Health*, New York: Columbia Law School.

——(1992). 'Making the World Health Organization work: A legal framework for universal access to the conditions for health,' *American Journal of Law and Medicine* 18:301–46.

Tobin, J. (2012). *The Right to Health in International Law*, New York: Oxford University Press.

Toebes, B.C.A. (1999). *The Right to Health as a Human Right in International Law*, Antwerp: Intersentia.

Torelli, M. (1980). *Le Medecin et les Droits de L'homme*, Paris: Berger-Levrault.

UDHR (1948), 'Universal Declaration of Human Rights,' Art 7, G.A. Res. 217A(III), U. N. GAOR, 3d Sess., at 71, U.N. Doc. A/810.

UN (1945). 'United Nations Charter,' signed at San Francisco, June 26, 1945, entered into force on October 24, 1945.

——(1952). 'Letter from UN Division of Human Rights Director John Humphrey to UN Division of Human Rights Lin Mousheng,' January 3.

——(1968). *The United Nations and Human Rights*, New York: United Nations.

UN ESCOR (1947). 'Draft Outline of the International Bill of Rights,' prepared by the Division of Human Rights. E/CN.4/AC.1/3/Add.1, July 1.

UN General Assembly (1950). 'Resolution 421(V),' December 4.

——(1952). 'Resolution 3031 (XI),' January 21.

——(1955). Official Records. 'Annotations on the text of the draft International Covenants on Human Rights,' Prepared by the Secretary-General. A/2929, July 1.

——(1957). Official Records. 743rd Meeting. 'Agenda Item 31. Draft International Covenants on Human Rights,' January 28.

——(1966). International Covenant on Economic, Social and Cultural Rights. 'Resolution 2200A (XXI),' December 16.

——(1987). Res. 42/8, 'Prevention and control of acquired immune deficiency syndrome (AIDS),' New York: UN, October 26.

United Nations Conference on Food and Agriculture (1943). 'Declaration, Hot Springs. May 1943' *American Journal of International Law [Supp]* 37(4):159–92.

Vaughan, J.P., Mogedal, S., Walt, G., Kruse, S.-E., Lee, K., and de Wilde, K. (1996). 'WHO and the effects of extrabudgetary funds: Is the Organization donor driven?,' *Health Policy and Planning* 11(3):253–64.

Verdoodt, A. (1964). *Naissance et Signification de la Déclaration Universelle des Droits de l'Homme*, Louvain: Nauwelaerts.

Vigne, C. (1979). 'Droit à la santé et coordination,' in *The Right to Health as a Human Right: Workshop, The Hague, 27–29 July 1978*, Alphen aan den Rijn: Sijthoff and Noordhoff.

World Health Assembly (1977). Res. 30.43.

——(1987). Res. 40.26, '*Global Strategy for the Prevention and Control of AIDS*,' May 5.

——(1988). 'Res. 41.24. Avoidance of discrimination in relation to HIV-infected people and people with AIDS.'

WHO (1946). 'Constitution of the World Health Organization.'

——(1951a). 'Letter from WHO Director-General Brock Chisholm to UN Assistant Secretary-General H. Laugier,' SOA 317/1/01(2), January 12.

——(1951b). 'Executive Board. Eighth Session,' EB8/39, June 2.

——(1956). 'Letter from WHO Director of the Division of External Relations and Technical Assistance P.M. Kaul to UN Deputy Under-Secretary for Economic and Social Affairs Martin Hill,' September 26.

——(1959). 'Memorandum from WHO Liaison Office with United Nations Director to WHO Deputy-Director General,' Report on the Fifteenth Session of the Commission on Human Rights, April 21.

——(1968). *The Second Ten Years of the World Health Organization*, Geneva: World Health Organization.

——(1973). *Interrelationships between Health Program and Socioeconomic Development*, Geneva: WHO.

——(1974). *Protection of Human Rights in the Light of Scientific and Technological Progress in Biology and Medicine*, Proceedings of a Round Table Conference Organized by CIOMS with the Assistance of UNESCO and WHO. WHO Headquarters, Geneva, 14, 15, and 16 November 1973. Geneva: WHO.

——(1975). 'Working paper by WHO to the Inter-Agency Meeting on the Implementation of the Human Rights Covenants,' 3.

——(1978). *Primary Health Care: Report of the International Conference of Primary Health Care Alma-Ata*, USSR, September 6–12 1978, Geneva: World Health Organization.

——(1980). 'First Report on the right to health in Article 12 ICESCR,' UN doc E/1980/24, February 22.

——(1981). *Global Strategy for Health for All by the Year 2000*, Geneva: World Health Organization.

——(1983). *Progress in Primary Health Care: A Situation Report*, Geneva: World Health Organization.

——(1985). 'AIDS and the WHO Collaborating Centres: Memorandum from a WHO Meeting,' *Bulletin of the World Health Organization* 6: 330–36.

——(1987a). 'Social aspects of AIDS prevention and control program' (brochure), Geneva: Special Program on AIDS, WHO, December 1.

——(1987b). 'Memorandum from GPA Coordinator J. Mann to Director-General H. Mahler.'

——(1987c). 'Global Strategy for the Prevention and Control of AIDS,' Geneva: World Health Organization.

——(1987d). 'Report of the consultation on international travel and HIV infections,' WHO/SPA/GLO/87.1, Geneva: World Health Organization, March 2–3.

——(1987e). 'Report of the Meeting on Criteria for HIV Screening Program,' WHO/ SPA/GLO/ 87.2, Geneva: World Health Organization, May 20–21.

——(1988a). *AIDS Prevention and Control: Invited Presentations and Papers from the World Summit of Ministers of Health on Programs for AIDS Prevention*, Geneva: World Health Organization; Oxford: Pergamon Press.

——(1988b). 'Statement from the consultation on AIDS and the workplace,' WHO/GPA/ INF/ 88.7 Rev. 1, Geneva: World Health Organization, June 27–29.

World Medical Association (1951). 'Letter from World Medical Association Secretary-General Louis H. Bauer to UN Secreatry-General Trygvie Lie,' October 9.

5 Health right or human right?

Changing tides in the international discussion of female genital mutilation, 1970–2010[1]

Marion A. Hulverscheidt

Today, female genital mutilation (FGM), as practised on girls and women, is recognized internationally as a violation of human rights. As the World Health Organization (WHO) explains in its Fact Sheet on FGM:

> It [FGM] reflects deep-rooted inequality between the sexes, and constitutes an extreme form of discrimination against women. It is nearly always carried out on minors and is a violation of the rights of children. The practice also violates a person's rights to health, security and physical integrity, the right to be free from torture and cruel, inhuman or degrading treatment, and the right to life when the procedure results in death.
>
> (WHO 2012)

This statement illustrates clearly the international community's position on FGM, and serves as the basis for its ongoing efforts to put an end to this practice. In this chapter, I will discuss how a global campaign against FGM emerged, which arguments were used in order to receive international attention and who carried them in the last 40 years. The movement against FGM was subject to changing tides, expressed not only by different protagonists, but also by changing arguments and understandings. But, it was seldom a clear-cut change, more a variation in the mixture of arguments and understandings. Different actors held various views and brought up different arguments or even the same arguments, but at different times, to reach diverse goals.

This paper draws attention to the different perspectives and intentions in constructing the notion of FGM, drawing public attention to it and turning it into a human rights issue. As it shows, anthropologists in the nineteenth and twentieth centuries were among the first to bring this custom to the attention of the western world. Later, physicians involved in medical development aid in African countries in the late 1960s, and western feminists in the 1970s played a critical role in drawing the attention of the western world to the problems and suffering inherent to FGM and generating international action to eliminate this practice. As this chapter also shows, the construction and reconstruction of FGM continued in the 1990s with the framing of the practice as a human rights issue. More recently, there has been an increasing medicalization of FGM, whereby the practice is mostly understood as a threat to the health of women as determined by physicians. Before analysing the changing and often overlapping understandings of FGM as the practice was made and remade, the chapter describes the practice of FGM as it is understood today.

An overview of FGM

Today, the term FGM is defined as comprising all procedures that involve partial or total removal of the external female genitalia or other injury to the female genital organs, whether for cultural or other non-therapeutic reasons. The age at which girls undergo FGM varies widely and depends on the ethnic group practising it. The procedure may be carried out immediately after birth, during childhood, adolescence, at marriage or during the first labour. In some cultures practising FGM, women are routinely re-infibulated (re-stitched) after childbirth. The WHO estimates that worldwide about 100–140 million girls and women have undergone this practice, mainly in 28 African countries, but due to globalization and migration, also in industrialized countries. FGM covers a range of different practices. The WHO, for example, identifies four overlapping types of FGM:

Type I: Involves the removal of the prepuce with or without excision of all or part of the clitoris (rare).
Type II: Excision of the clitoris with partial or total excision of the labia minora (this type constitutes more than 60 per cent of female genital mutilation performed worldwide).
Type III: Excision of part or all of the external genitalia (clitoris, labia minora and labia majora) with stitching/narrowing of the vaginal opening (infibulation). This is the most extreme form of FGM, involving removal of almost two-thirds of the female genitalia. Type III constitutes 15 per cent of mutilations performed worldwide and has the highest rate of complications, often (estimated rate 20 per cent) resulting in death.
Type IV: Unclassified: includes pricking, piercing, incising of the clitoris and/or labia; cauterisation by burning of clitoris and surrounding tissue; scraping of the tissue surrounding the vaginal orifice or cutting into the vagina, introduction of corrosive substances or herbs into the vagina to cause bleeding or for the purposes of tightening or narrowing it, and any other procedure which falls under the definition of FGM given above.

These operations are performed mainly by traditional circumcisers. In most cases, these are old women who are highly respected for their role. While their intention is to do good, from a human rights perspective, they can only be seen to cause harm.

The origins of FGM are complex and numerous and its justifications and reasons are manifold and not easy to understand (Schnüll and Terre des Femmes 1999). They reflect the ideological and historical context of the societies in which the practice developed and generally relate to tradition, power inequality and the ensuing compliance of women to the dictates of their communities. The reasons why people undertake FGM that can be found in the literature include: tradition and custom; role expectation; religion; preservation of virginity and chastity; social acceptance; hygiene and cleanliness; family honour and economy; enhancing fertility; increasing sexual pleasure for the male; ensuring the acceptance within society; and making the gender distinct by removing the 'male' parts of the female body (Schnüll 2003: 39–47). The outcome of FGM, on the one hand, is a normal life, acceptance and, in the majority of cases, a feeling of belonging to society. On the other hand, the practice can cause physical as well as psychological complications, difficulties during delivery, sexual problems (often overestimated by westerners) and implications for society and gender relationships.

Development and shaping of knowledge of FGM

Anthropologists

In the nineteenth century ethnographers compiled existing knowledge about different people and their customs and traditions in the world. In general, their theories were not based on their own fieldwork, but on the reports published by other scientists or travellers. At the time, this was regarded as a respected and legitimate scientific method. The quality or reliability of these travel accounts was not verified or even doubted. The Leipzig-based physician and gynaecologist Hermann Heinrich Ploss established a branch of anthropology, which he termed *anthropological-ethnological gynaecology and paediatrics*. On the basis of travelogues and responses to questionnaires he had sent to other travellers, he compiled not only an anthropology of childhood (*Das Kind in Brauch und Sitte der Völker* [Manners and Customs of Children among Primitive People]) but also an anthropology of women (*Das Weib in der Natur-und Völkerkunde – Anthropologische Studien* [Woman in Natural History and Ethnography: Anthropological Inquiries], first edition 1885, followed by numerous extended editions; 11th edition by Reitzenstein in 1926/27).[2] The term anthropology here refers to nineteenth-century German anthropology, a scientific practice that stands in stark contrast to current forms of Anglo-Saxon social and cultural anthropology. For Ploss and his fellow anthropologists, the object of anthropological inquiry was mankind, from his physical and biological characteristics to his customs and social traditions. They sought to describe, measure and classify these characteristics and traditions as well as explain their variability and development along racial and ethnic categories across time and space (Hulverscheidt 2002).

As a typical product of this nineteenth-century German anthropology, Ploss' *Das Weib in der Natur-und Völkerkunde* contained a richly illustrated and detailed description of FGM, which differentiated between circumcision and infibulation. According to Ploss, the custom of circumcision had originally been based on a specific purpose, which had, however, been lost to the tribes (ethnicities), while infibulation served the purpose of maintaining absolute sexual abstinence. Ploss (1891: 156) considered infibulation to be a 'gross degradation of the female sex'.[3] The detailed descriptions of this custom, illustrated by drawings of circumcised and infibulated female genitals deepened the separation between 'us' and 'them', a common way of thinking in nine-teenth-century anthropology. There was, of course, no place for any sort of reflexive analysis in Ploss' work – indeed, the critical, reflexive turn in anthro-pology was still far away. Thus, for a nineteenth-century anthropologist such as Ploss, who did not report first-hand observations but compiled his story from other books, the position and actions of the observer did not at all affect the findings. Ploss described female circumcision as a custom, comparable to foot binding in China, and did not focus on the potential burden of suffering and sorrow – a value-neutral position still common in much of contemporary anthropology and which holds that the role of the anthropologist is solely to describe and not judge and intervene in others' cultural traditions (cf. Babatunde 1998).

The eyes of others – the physicians' approach

In the late 1960s the development of humanitarian aid programmes led to a second 'discovery' of the practice of FGM – this time by physicians. Articles written by the Austrian doctor and founder of child and adolescent gynaecology in Europe, Alfons Huber (Lauggas 2007: 52–53), are a good example. Huber spent 12 years in medical development aid in Ethiopia, as Director and Senior Doctor of the Garde Hospital in Addis Ababa (1949–61), before returning to Austria in 1962 to open his own gynaecological practice. He published two articles in 1966 and 1969 on female circumcision in tropical medicine journals in which he referred to his own experiences in Ethiopia (Huber 1966, 1969). In the 1966 article, he gave an extensive description of female circumcision and infi-bulation and also cited anthropological sources. The reasons for the practice, however, remained unclear to Huber. He wrote that: 'It has not yet been pos-sible to establish the origin or even the significance of this practice, which is widespread especially in Ethiopia. Generally most natives remain silent about it towards strangers' (Huber 1966: 88). Nevertheless, Huber linked specific gender roles and gender relations with the custom:

> Female circumcision, particularly infibulation, is an invasion of [a woman's] personality that is only possible in a social system that keeps women on the lowest rung [of the hierarchical ladder] and values them practically only for their sexual characteristics. This mutilation is not linked to any religious or ritual ideas and not even hygienic reasons can be cited. It can only be hoped that with the help of increased education and

hygiene we will be successful in making these barbaric traditions disappear amongst the different ethnic groups in Ethiopia.

(Huber 1966: 90)

Interestingly, even though physicians working in development realized the implications of FGM for the health of women, they never advocated – or were never able to advocate – its elimination in international forums such as the WHO. Thus, in his 1969 article, Huber only mentions that 'international organizations' should do something about it but it is not clear which ones he has in mind or what they should be doing. One explanation for this lack of advocacy could be the fact that these physicians did not have the right contacts among the international community. Another explanation is that most physicians working in medical aid did not have the knowledge, skills or support networks to conduct an effective advocacy campaign against FGM. Other physicians with similar experiences to Huber's expressed comparable views in articles published in international medical journals (e.g. Longo 1964; Shandall 1967). But, like Huber's articles, these did not receive much attention.

In the eyes of feminists – solidarity with the other

It was not physicians but feminists who brought the issue of FGM to the attention of the public. Fran Hosken, Hanny Lightfoot-Klein, Herta Haas and Tobe Levin offer four excellent examples of such activists who had strong links to the international feminist movement and were committed in combating FGM. This section examines the work of each of these four women in turn. Fran Hosken (1920–2006) came across FGM during a trip through Africa in the 1970s. She was instrumental in raising awareness about FGM within the WHO and temporarily served as advisor to the WHO's First Seminar on Harmful Traditional Practices in Khartoum, Sudan. For her, genital mutilation was inextricably linked with medical concerns, feminist theory and human rights issues (Shannon 2012: 289). In particular, she argued that FGM was the 'most horrific form of male oppression' (quoted in Shannon 2012: 289) and sought to frame it as a violation of human rights and bodily integrity. She did not remain unchallenged. Some argued that FGM was a practice that belonged to the private sphere in which the state could and should not intervene. Similarly, anthropologists accused Hosken of committing cultural genocide when criticising Africans who promoted or tolerated female circumcision. This did not stop her, however, but drew her to concentrate on the collection of data on FGM. It was Hosken who, together with the Boston Women's Health Movement, made the first estimations of the worldwide distribution of FGM and the numbers of girls and women it affected (Hosken 1978). In 1975 she began to publish the *Hosken Report*, with a growing bibliography on the subject in collaboration with the Women's International Network *WIN News*. She seemed, however, to have had a somewhat difficult personality that made her unable to cooperate and her controversial manner alienated others who had similar aims (Kahn 2006, Shannon 2012).[4]

A group of very committed women in Munich translated Hosken's papers and publications and published them in 1979 (Braun, Levin and Schwarzbauer 1979). One of these women was Tobe Levin, an American literary scholar born in 1948 and married to a German citizen, who attempted to explain the reasons for FGM in a separate article that was appended to the published collection of Hosken's papers (Levin 1979). This explanation is less a declaration of solidarity with the women in Africa than a depiction of the mutilation as a particularly drastic example of the oppression of women and the suppression of their sexuality by men. Aside from publishing Hosken's papers, Levin also created the German branch of the Foundation for Women's Health, Research and Development (FORWARD), a UK-based African Diaspora Women's Campaign founded in 1983. With FORWARD, Levin succeeded in building solidarity between Europeans and Africans and enabling those concerned with and those threatened by FGM to work and discuss together how to put an end to female circumcision. They used exhibitions, plays and other artistic means to express their outrage at FGM, rather than mere factual information and education (Levin and Shibuogwu 2000). Levin's main activity, however, was the translation of feminist texts from English, German, French and Italian into other languages in order to disseminate feminist ideas and bring about change. As part of this work, she also edited the journal *Feminist Europe* (Levin 2001) with reviews and essays on feminist subjects.

Herta Haas (1907–2007) was as multilingual as Tobe Levin; she spoke four languages fluently. Born to a Jewish family in Frankfurt, she studied history, earning her doctorate in 1934, before leaving Germany and moving to Italy. There she worked as a nanny and nurse. In 1938, as a 'stateless' person, she managed to emigrate to Great Britain, where she found employment as a bookseller, in charge of the foreign orders department at Blackwell's in Oxford. In 1947 she married Willy Haas, a literature critic and publisher of the 'Literarische Welt', whom she had come to know as a customer. Haas was a German-speaking Jewish resident of Prague, who had been forced to emigrate to India. In 1953 the by then married couple moved to Hamburg. The decision to move back to Germany was a difficult one for her as the Nazis had murdered her parents and grandparents. After her husband's death in 1973, Hertha Haas focused on her husband's lifetime achievements and on reviving the 'Literarische Welt' and was also recognized for her translations of Henry James, Bernard Malamud and Philip Roth. After having read a newspaper article about FGM, she channelled her anger and outrage into action. She corresponded with politicians, activists and public figures to draw attention to the topic. Haas was a founding member of the German non-governmental women's organization Terre des Femmes and had good connections to experts on sexual medicine and gynaecology. As an external expert, she contributed to the drafting of the 1985 British Prohibition of Female Circumcision Act. She also wrote a book on FGM (which was never published) and was a keen networker, communicating and collaborating with, among others, Fran Hosken and Hanny Lightfoot-Klein.

Like Hosken, Hanny Lightfoot-Klein (born in 1927) began research on FGM after she had come across the subject during her travels in Africa in the late 1970s. Born in Hamburg to a Jewish family, she left for the United States of America in 1938. She gained an MA in social psychology from the American University in Washington, DC, got married, had two children and worked as a high school English teacher in New York. After her children had grown up and her marriage had broken apart, she went to Africa in order to spend time travelling on her own. Lightfoot-Klein first heard of the custom of FGM on her way from Egypt to Sudan and the topic remained important for her since that time. She later returned to Egypt, Kenya and Sudan as a researcher and lived with a number of African families, from different social backgrounds. She conducted more than 400 interviews with midwives, women and men, with and without experience of FGM in these countries and asked her interviewees about their sexual experiences and anxieties. She worked with the medical psychologist and sexologist John Money and focused on the impact FGM had on female sexuality. She also published three books on female circumcision. Her first book, *Prisoners of Ritual: An Odyssey into Female Genital Circumcision in Africa* (1989), was even more successful in Germany than in the USA. Indeed, first published in 1992 under the title *Das grausame Ritual* (The Cruel Ritual), the German translation was reprinted numerous times. She also worked as a consultant, in particular in hearings of African asylum seekers in the USA.

These four women had many characteristics in common. Except Hanny Lightfoot-Klein, they all founded NGOs on FGM. All of them knew and interacted with one another. All four of them were of Jewish origin and had a German-language background. Both Fran Hosken and Hanny Lightfoot-Klein began travelling in the 1970s, after their children had grown up and they had separated from their husbands, while Herta Haas began her campaign after her husband's death, following a prolonged illness. Furthermore, they were all academically trained, spoke two or more languages fluently and had a strong sense of mission. They also combined their feminist dedication to the emancipation of women worldwide with a special interest for women in Africa. Their fight against FGM was framed as a mission against what they perceived to be a misogynist, patriarchal world. For them, FGM was one of the most horrific expressions of injustice in relation to existing gender relations.

When feminists gained influence in the late 1970s, they regarded FGM as violence against women and as an attempt to suppress female sexuality. They called on international organizations, such as the WHO, to act and to collect data on the extent of FGM and the immediate and subsequent consequences for women's health and to force the international community to implement laws against FGM. Feminists were very active in Europe and the USA. However, they did not always act in collaboration with African women, who in turn felt patronized by their western alter egos. To quote Nawal el Saadawi, the famous Egyptian feminist:

> Women in Europe and America may not be exposed to the surgical removal of the clitoris. Nevertheless, they are victims of cultural and psychological

clitoridectomy. 'Lift the chains off my body, put the chains on my mind.' Sigmund Freud was perhaps the most famous of all those men who taught psychological and physiological circumcision of women when he formulated his theory on the psychic nature of women, describing the clitoris as a male organ, and how sexual activity relates to the clitoris as an infantile phase, and when he maintained that maturity and mental health in a woman requires that sexual activity to the clitoris related cease and be transferred to the vagina. No doubt, the physical ablation of the clitoris appears a much more savage and cruel procedure than its psychological removal. Nevertheless, the consequences can be exactly the same, since the end result is the abolition of its function so that its presence or absence amount to the same thing.

(Saadawi 1980: XXXV)

Both Hosken and Lightfoot-Klein started to raise awareness at home and on an international level, but continued as lone 'feminist crusaders'. Their work had an impact in the USA as well as in Germany and in other European countries. Their articles were published in British, Swedish, Norwegian and German magazines and newspapers. With Hosken and Lightfoot-Klein at the forefront, the feminist movement took up the issue of FGM as a severe form of violation of women's rights. In accordance with feminist ideology at the time, FGM was regarded as an exclusively female issue and was brought under the same umbrella as rape and domestic abuse (Keck and Sikkink 1998). Men were not included in the struggle to end FGM, as they were considered to be perpetrators, or those on whose behalf this tradition was kept alive. The feminist movement in Europe and the USA had established the struggle for women's rights, which were clearly separate from general human rights. This initially served to strengthen solidarity among women and create awareness in relation to violence specifically directed at women. But, as Shannon pointed out, the feminist argument was not used as the primary argument at the international level. Indeed, health arguments were seen as so much 'more palatable to governments and practitioners, for whom the custom was deeply tied to issues of culture and religion' (Shannon 2012: 293). With a medically focused campaign it was possible to attract the support of international leaders. Interestingly, among the international organizations lobbied by feminists, the WHO was one of the quickest to react to the issue of FGM, organising one of the first international seminars on the topic in Khartoum in 1979 at which Fran Hosken acted as advisor to the WHO.

FGM as a women's rights issue

Representing FGM as a human rights issue is a rather recent development. While it is true that the UN's 1948 Universal Declaration of Human Rights proclaims a right not to be tortured and a right to health, it would be anachronistic to deduce that it also covered FGM. Indeed, when the Declaration was formulated its focus was mainly the white western male and not a poor, disadvantaged and illiterate African woman. An important milestone in framing FGM as a human rights issue was thus the adoption of the UN Convention on the Elimination of All Forms of Discrimination Against Women (CEDAW) in 1979, which purported to protect the human rights of women in particular. Although the CEDAW did not explicitly mention FGM, its adoption was important in constructing violence against women as a human rights issue. The CEDAW did not, however, offer any solution to another key obstacle in using human rights to stop violence against women: the then widely held belief that the state should not intervene within the private sphere. The problem with this belief was that what was defined as the private sphere or the home was exactly the area in which women were most at risk of attacks, including domestic violence and conjugal rape. Indeed, it was this very way of reasoning that prevented the criminalization of both rape in wedlock and domestic violence in the west until the 1990s. As Kurt Merkel from Amnesty International (AI) explained in 1979 to Herta Haas who had inquired about what AI was doing in relation to FGM:

> [M]y attention was drawn to an article in the [feminist] magazine EMMA … in which clitoral circumcisions was described as torture. I wholeheartedly agree with this description. I would like to point out an AI internal problem at this point which will surely play a role during a possible future discussion: according to statute and mission AI only deals with human rights issues that occur within the framework of the state. In the case of torture for example only with armed forces, police, security forces and so on, i.e. with state-run institutions that carry out torture. The area you mention is obviously limited to the cultural sphere. It might therefore be somewhat difficult to find a workable way in (who can be accused as 'responsible'? Which government bodies need to be approached? What shape should work in this area take?). New paths of intervention would need to be found for AI.[5]

Violence against women in the private sphere and, especially domestic violence was first addressed explicitly by the UN in the 1993 Vienna Declaration and Program of Action. This was further corroborated two years later, at the Fourth World Conference on Women in Beijing in 1995, where a declaration was made that explicitly recognized FGM as a human rights violation that had to be tackled in order to achieve equal freedom and opportunities for women. African delegates, in particular, called for an end to deeply entrenched attitudes and practices perpetuating the inequality of the sexes and discrimination against women. They asked for help and support in their struggle against the traditional practice of FGM that many young African girls were still forced to undergo (Büchner 2004: 93–95).

The official acceptance of FGM as a human right violation resulted in the involvement of international bodies such as the WHO and UNICEF, research and projects at a grassroots level and the implementation of new laws. This included research on the psychological effects of FGM on circumcised women living in Europe (Behrendt 2011), the establishment of new counselling institutions in Europe or projects to tackle FGM funded by European NGOs (such as by the German Agency for Technical Cooperation – GTZ). The Beijing Declaration also led to the adoption of new laws against FGM in several European and African countries, such as Norway (1995), Egypt (1996), Ivory Coast (1998), Sweden (1998), Tanzania (1998), Senegal (1999), Belgium (2000), Austria (2001), Chad (2002), Kenya (2002), Benin (2003), Burkina Faso (2007) and Switzerland (2012) (Kalthegener 2003).

Medicalising FGM: from the right to bodily integrity to the right to health

After 1995 there was also a wave of scientific, cultural and medical studies addressing the health consequences resulting from FGM. A keyword search for the term 'clitoridectomy' (female circumcision) in the Medline database illustrates this trend. For the period from 1966 to 1994 there were 11 articles, whereas for the period from 1995 to 1999 a total of 111 articles were published, so publication decupled (Hulverscheidt 2002: 9). The focus shifted away from violence against women and their right to bodily integrity to the health effects of FGM and women's right to health. This was the case even though the majority of published studies showed that in three out of four types of FGM medical complications were the exception rather than the rule (Obermeyer, 1999, 2003, 2005). The new, medical approach quickly gathered momentum and, in the first 10 years after the Beijing Conference, medical interventions to curtail the health aspects of FGM gained progressively more attention than programmes aimed at empowering women and addressing the violence associated with FGM. This reconfiguration of FGM seems to have been characterized by an increased emphasis on the right to health rather the right to bodily integrity. In 2000, for example, the UN Committee on Economic, Social and Cultural Rights expressed this attitude in its Comment on the Right to Health:

> It is also important to undertake preventive, promotive and remedial action to shield women from the impact of harmful traditional cultural practices and norms that deny them their full reproductive rights.
>
> (United Nations 2000)

Thus, FGM was now framed as a right to health issue. This was different to saying that FGM was a question of violence against women and bodily integrity as feminists had tried to do up to the mid-1990s.

Focusing on health consequences while omitting human, moral, social or economic consequences of FGM led to a somewhat narrowed perception of the practice, limiting its effects to health aspects or even to a 'genital' issue. Overemphasizing the possible physical consequences and the focus on the supposedly diminished capacity for sexual pleasure served to attract media attention. The movie *Wüstenblume* (Desert Flower) is a good illustration of this trend. Based on an autobiography of Waris Dirie, the film was a huge popular success in both North America and Europe. Waris Dirie grew up as a young nomad girl in Somalia. In her early teens, after she was circumcised and threatened with forced marriage, she fled to London where she later became a very successful model. It was only after she emigrated that she became aware of her 'mutilation' and started campaigning against FGM. This story subtly blended the sexualized reality in Europe with the ostensibly archaic practice in Africa. The attention created for FGM as a human rights violation is created by a sense of shock and pity, thus deepening the rift between 'us' and 'them', rather than narrowing it, as would be desirable in the interest of universal human rights.

For those taking a medical approach to FGM, the most important aspect was to reduce the physical complications associated with this practice. This, it was thought, could be done if FGM was carried out under improved conditions and, especially, was performed by a medical professional who had anatomical knowledge, worked under sterile conditions and used anaesthesia. Thus, immediate complications such as infections or fractures caused by resistance of the girls or women circumcised could be minimized. Such a view was, of course, incompatible with a feminist approach articulated around the right to bodily integrity, not least because it made it justifiable to perform FGM under clinical conditions if there was no medical risk (Kentenich and Utz-Billing 2006). For a feminist approach, there was little difference between FGM performed by a midwife in a rural area and FGM performed by a surgeon in a hospital under aseptic conditions and with anaesthesia. Many medical professionals share this view. Thus, the WHO clearly condemned participation in FGM by medically trained personnel as unethical in 1982. And, one year later, following the intervention of the physician and founder of Terre des Hommes, Edmond Kaiser, the Swiss Academy of Medical Sciences (1983) released a declaration on FGM, arguing that participation in such a procedure for reasons of 'misunderstood sympathy or other ill-judged motives' consisted of grievous bodily harm even if 'it is carried out under clinical conditions; it is a violation of basic human rights to carry out a cruel and humiliating procedure on a person who is under age, unable to assess the situation and unable to defend her personal right to physical integrity'(Central Medical Ethics Commission of the Swiss Academy of Sciences 1983).

Conclusion

In this chapter, I have discussed the framing of FGM as a feminist argument, a human rights violation and a health rights issue by exploring the history of the movement against this traditional practice. Knowledge about FGM has changed and grown over time and, more importantly, it has been shaped and reshaped by the different actors who promoted, talked about and discussed it. Anthropologists were among the first to discuss FGM. They sought to describe meticulously FGM and framed it as a particular cultural practice that existed among certain tribes. For them, cultural differences between races and ethnicities were something to be respected, observed and explained rather than changed. Physicians active in development work in the 1960–70s further contributed to our knowledge of FGM. In particular, they stressed the medical risks and psychological suffering brought about by FGM without, however, really challenging anthropologists' cultural relativism. Like these physicians, feminists also emphasized the medical risks associated with FGM. But, unlike anthropologists, they associated FGM with the misogyny that dominated medicine and society, a misogyny that they, of course, sought to eliminate. In particular, they emphasized how FGM denied women their right to sexual satisfaction and orgasm (Groult 1985: 85; Lightfoot-Klein 1992: 23, 109–11). They also sought to frame FGM as a human right issue and, more specifically, as a type of violence against women and a violation of their right to bodily integrity. Some have criticized feminist readings of FGM as overly Euro-American. African activists, for example, have argued that western feminists' obsession with FGM was itself a product of male diktats on what female sexuality should be and, in particular, Freud's idea that vaginal orgasm was superior to clitoral orgasm. Others criticized feminist readings of FGM for being over reliant on western notions of individual autonomy and disregarding the importance of the group and being integrated in a community in which one can grow up, work and live.

More recently, activists fighting against FGM have sought to medicalize the discussion. Emphasizing the right to health instead of the right to bodily integrity put forward by feminists, they have focused on the elimination of the medical risks associated with FGM, arguing that it can only be carried out when there is no medical counterindications and by a qualified surgeon. Many have argued that this view of FGM is much to narrow. Indeed, while the medicalisation of FGM has reduced the rates of morbidity and mortality associated with this practice, they point out that it still leads to the conduct of serious surgical interventions on women who are perfectly healthy. Furthermore, they also point out that the medicalization of FGM disregards women's right to determine what happens to their own bodies. As this chapter has shown, it is this knowledge of FGM that was shaped and reshaped over time that informs current laws, campaigns and programmes that seek to eliminate female circumcision today. And, so too, the tensions inherent within this complex, layered knowledge, such as arguments between cultural relativism and universal human rights and between an emphasis on medical risks and one on bodily integrity, remain with us and inform the discussions and debates about FGM today.

Abbreviations

AI	Amnesty International
FGM	Female genital mutilation
FORWARD	Foundation for Women's Health, Research and Development
IAC	Inter-African Committee on Traditional Practices Affecting the Health of Women and Children

UN   United Nations
UNICEF   United Nations International Children's Emergency Fund
WHO   World Health Organization

Notes

1 I would like to thank the editors of this volume for their patience and their comments, as well as Isabelle Ihring, Nina Staehle and Stefani Ross for their valuable advice and comments. If not otherwise mentioned, all quotes were translated by the author.
2 An English-language edition entitled *Femina Libido Sexualis Compendium of the Psychology, Anthropology and Anatomy of the Sexual Characteristics of the Woman*, by Herman Heinrich Ploss, Max Bartels and Paul Bartels, was edited by Eric John Dingwall, arranged by J. R. Brosslowsly, published by Medical Press, New York, 1965.
3 The original German version reads: 'Überall dort, wo die Infibulation praktiziert werde, sei das weibliche Geschlecht auf das Tiefste herabgewürdigt'.
4 Terre des Femmes Archive, Berlin, Legacy Herta Haas, File Correspondence 1979–80, Haas to Huber on 3 November 1980.
5 Terre des Femmes Archive, Berlin, Legacy Herta Hass, File Correspondence 1979–80, Kurt Merkel to Haas on 12 October 1979.

Bibliography

Babatunde, E. D. (1998) *Women's Rites vs Women's Rights: A Study of Circumcision Among the Ketu Yoruba of South Western Nigeria*, Asmara (Eritrea): Africa World Press, Inc.

Behrendt, A. (2011) *Listening to African voices. Female Genital Mutilation/Cutting Among Immigrants in Hamburg: Knowledge, Attitudes and Practice*, Hamburg: Plan International.

Braun, I., Levin, T. and Schwarzbauer, A. (1979) *Materialien zur Unterstützung von Aktionsgruppen gegen Klitorisbeschneidung*, Munich: Frauenoffensive.

Büchner, A. C. (2004) *Weibliche Genitalverstümmelung. Betrachtungen eines traditionellen Brauchs aus Menschenrechtsperspektive*, Oldenburg: Paulo Freire Verlag.

Central Medical Ethics Commission of the Swiss Academy of Sciences (1983) 'Erklärung zur Vornahme ritueller, verstümmelnder Eingriffe bei Frauen', *Schweizerische Ärztezeitung*, 64: 1274.

Groult, B. (1985) *Ödipus Schwester. Zorniges zur Macht der Männer über Frauen*, Munich: Knaur.

Hosken, F. (1978) 'Klitorisbeschneidung' (transl. Susan Patton), *Courage*, 3: 20–28.

——(1979) *The Hosken Report: Genital and Sexual Mutilation of Females*, Lexington, MA: Women's International Network News.

Huber, A. (1966) 'Weibliche Zirkumzision und Infibulation in Äthiopien', *Acta Tropica*, 23: 87–91.

——(1969) 'Die weibliche Beschneidung', *Zeitschrift für Tropenmedizin und Parasitologie*, 20: 1–9.

Hulverscheidt, M. (2002) *Weibliche Genitalverstümmelung. Diskussion und Praxis in der Medizin während des 19. Jahrhunderts im deutschsprachigen Raum*, Frankfurt am Main: Mabuse-Verlag.

Kahn, J. P. (2006) 'Obituary Fran P. Hosken, 86; activist for women's issues globally', *Boston Globe*, February 12, 2006. Available at: www.boston.com/news/globe/

obituaries/articles/2006/02/12/fran_p_hosken_86_activist_for_womens_issues_globally/ ?page=full (accessed 14May 2012).

Kalthegener, R. (2003) 'Strafrechtliche Regelungen in europäischen Staaten', in Schnüll, P. and Terre des Femmes e.V. (eds) *Schnitt in die Seele. Weibliche Genitalverstümmelung – eine fundamentale Menschenrechtsverletzung*, Frankfurt am Main: Mabuse-Verlag.

Keck, M. E. and Sikkink, K. (1998) *Activists Beyond Borders*, Ithaca, NY: Cornell University Press.

Kentenich, H. and Utz-Billing, I. (2006) 'Weibliche Genitalverstümmelung: Lebenslanges Leiden', *Deutsches Ärzteblatt*, 103: A842–45.

Lauggas, M. (2007) '"Mädchen" und wissenschaftliche Tatsachen. Geschlechter-und wissenschaftshistorische Annäherungen an Kinder-und Jugendgynäkologie', unpublished thesis, University of Vienna.

Levin, T. (1979) 'Warum geschehen all diese Greueltaten an Frauen? Versuchen wir eine Erklärung, suchen wir nach den Begründungen – und Gründen', in Braun, I., Levin, T. and

Schwarzbauer, A. (eds) (1979) *Materialien zur Unterstützung von Aktionsgruppen gegen Klitorisbeschneidung*, Munich: Frauenoffensive.

Levin, T. (2001) 'Female genital mutilation: recent contributions in German', *Feminist Europa. Review of Books*, 1: 8–29.

Levin, T. and Shibuogwu, J. K. (eds) (2000) *Weibliche Genitalverstümmelung. Künstlerinnen und Künstler aus Nigeria klagen an* [Female genital mutilation: Nigerian artists protest a rite], Exhibition Catalogue, Frankfurt am Main.

Lightfoot-Klein, H. (1992) *Das grausame Ritual. Sexuelle Verstümmelung afrikanischer Frauen*, Frankfurt am Main: Fischer Verlag.

Longo, L. D. (1964) 'Sociocultural practices relating to obstetrics and gynaecology in a community in West Africa', *American Journal of Obstetrics and Gynaecology*, 89: 470–75.

Obermeyer, C. M. (1999) 'Female genital surgeries: the known, the unknown and the unknowable', *Medical Anthropology Quarterly*, 13: 79–106.

——(2003) 'The health consequences of female circumcision: science, advocacy, and standards of evidence', *Medical Anthropology Quarterly*, 17: 394–412.

——(2005) 'The consequences of female circumcision for health and sexuality: an update on the evidence', *Culture, Health & Sexuality*, 7: 443–61.

Ploss, H. H. (1891) *Das Weib in der Natur-und Völkerkunde*, 3rd edn, Leipzig: Grieben.

Saadawi, N. E. (1980) *The Hidden Face of Eve: Women in the Arab World*, London: Zed Books.

Schnüll, P. (2003) 'Weibliche Genitalverstümmelung in Afrika', in Terre des Femmes (ed.) *Schnitt in die Seele. Weibliche Genitalverstümmelung – eine fundamentale Menschenrechtsverletzung*, Frankfurt am Main: Marbuse-Verlag.

Schnüll, P. and Terre des Femmes (eds) (1999) *Genitalverstümmelung – eine fundamentale Menschenrechtsverletzung*, Göttingen: Terre des Femmes.

Shandall, A. A. (1967) 'Circumcision and infibulation of females: a general consideration of the problem and a clinical study of the complications in Sudanese women', *Sudanese Medical Journal*, 5: 178–212.

Shannon, K. J. (2012) 'The right to bodily integrity: women's rights as human rights and the international movement to end female genital mutilation, 1970s–1990s', in Iriye, A., Goedde, P. and Hitchcock, W. I. (eds) *The Human Rights Revolution: An International History*, Oxford & New York: Oxford University Press.

UNICEF (2009) *Social dynamics of abandonment of harmful practices: a new look at the theory*. Available at: www.unicef-irc.org/publications/558 (accessed 14 May 2012).

United Nations (2000) 'The right to the highest attainable standard of health', *General Comment* 14.Available at: www.unhchr.ch/tbs/doc.nsf/%28symbol%29/E.C.12.2000.4. En (accessed 6 August 2012).

WHO (2012) 'Female Genital Mutilation', *Fact Sheet No. 241*. Available at: www.who. int/mediacentre/factsheets/fs241/en/ (accessed 6 August 2012).

6 Constructing tobacco control as a human rights issue

Smoking, lawyers and the judicialization of the right to health

David Reubi

Over the last 20 years, there have been an increasing number of initiatives and efforts to use the language, institutions and practices of human rights in the field of global health (Reubi 2011). HIV/AIDS was one of the first global health issues in relation to which human rights approaches were articulated, generally to protect those with HIV/AIDS from stigma and discrimination. The establishment, by Jonathan Mann, of a Human Rights Office within the WHO's Global Programme on AIDS is a typical illustration of such efforts (Fee and Parry 2008; Rushton 2010, forthcoming). Global health activists have also employed the human rights rhetoric in relation to access to medicines. Indeed, from the celebrated South African HIV/AIDS medicines access campaign led by large, international NGOs such as Oxfam and Médecins Sans Frontières to efforts by Brazilian patient groups to obtain free drug treatment for rare genetic diseases, all have explicitly appealed to the values and norms of international human rights (Olesen 2006; Petryna 2009). More recently, public health advocates have sought to frame maternal and child health as a human right issue with the hope of generating public interest and political action (Yamin and Maine 2005; Shiffman and Smith 2007).

The present chapter addresses this proliferation of human rights discourses in international public health by examining recent attempts at framing the global smoking epidemic as a human rights problem. Rather than advocating in favour or against human rights-based approaches like much of the literature on human rights and global health has done (e.g. Gruskin *et al.* 2005; Ferraz 2009; Schrecker *et al.* 2010; Reubi 2011), this chapter purports to understand how and why such approaches are being articulated and disseminated. Drawing on the literature on 'thought collectives', 'epistemic communities' and 'advocacy networks' (e.g. Fleck 1979; Hass 1992; Keck and Sikkink 1998; Mirowski and Plehwe 2009), the chapter first argues that the identification and description of the global smoking epidemic as a human rights issue have been the product of a small, international network of public health experts and lawyers that I term the human rights and tobacco control collective or community (HTC). The chapter describes in particular the HTC's membership, its style of thinking and its efforts to articulate and disseminate human rights-based approaches to tobacco control over the last 10 years.

Second, this chapter argues that the HTC's use of human rights as a frame did not purport to generate attention for and a will to address a global health issue like the smoking epidemic, as much of the literature on framing and human rights tends to assume (e.g. Keck and Sikkink 1998; Jacobson and Banerjee 2005; Shiffman and Smith 2007; Rushton 2010). Instead, as the chapter shows, the HTC framed tobacco control as a human rights problem in order to tap into the powerful, judicial monitoring and enforceability mechanisms that make up the international human rights framework. As the chapter further shows, the HTC's view of human rights as powerful, judicial monitoring and enforceability mechanisms has led the network to adopt a legal definition of the right to health and give lawyers an important role within the network, thus contributing to the judicialization of the right to health and marginalizing alternative, non-legal understandings of what human rights could be (Gloppen 2008; Biehl *et al.* 2009; Ferraz 2009; Reubi 2011).

Before presenting this twofold argument, the chapter first discusses the research methods used in this study and then traces the development of human rights-based approaches to tobacco control over the last 10 years.

Methodology

The study presented in this chapter is based on the meticulous collection and analysis of a large corpus of texts. The collection of this corpus followed a three-pronged approach modelled on the method developed by Bruno Latour (1988) in his analysis of the development and diffusion of pasteurization in late nineteenth-century France. First, all the relevant articles were gathered from a literature search on human rights and tobacco control. The search was conducted using a range of keywords (tobacco, smoking, rights, litigation, etc.) on five different online databases (PubMed, Hein Online, IBSS, JStore and Web of Knowledge). Special attention was paid to three of the main journals in the fields of human rights and tobacco control: *Human Rights Quarterly*, *Health and Human Rights* and *Tobacco Control*.

Second, all the relevant documents (reports, guidelines, directives, pamphlets, manuals, articles, websites, minutes from meetings, etc.) were collected from key organizations in both tobacco control and human rights. These included: the World Conference on Tobacco or Health; the WHO Tobacco Free Initiative; the WHO Health and Human Rights Unit; the Pan-American Health organization (PAHO); the Campaign for Tobacco Free Kids; the Framework Convention Alliance; the American Cancer Society; the Human Rights and Tobacco Control Network (HRTCN); the UN High Commissioner for Human Rights; the UN Special Rapporteur on the Right to Health; the UN Committee on Economic, Social and Cultural Rights (UN-CESCR); the Francois-Xavier Bagnoud Centre for Human Rights and Health, Harvard University; and the O'Neill Institute for National and Global Health Law, Georgetown University.

Third, in-depth, semi-structured interviews were conducted with over 70 experts and advocates in the fields of tobacco control and human rights.

In addition, the author also took part in a Witness Seminar on the WHO Framework Convention on Tobacco Control (FCTC) organized by both the Wellcome Trust Centre for the History of Medicine at University College London and the WHO in February 2010 (Reynolds and Tansey 2012). Interviewees were identified on the basis of both the literature search and the collection of documents from key institutions in tobacco control and human rights. They were also identified on the basis of the Witness Seminar as well as through the snowballing method (Bauer and Gaskell 2000).

The corpus of texts thus assembled was analyzed using standard content analysis methods (Latour 1988; Bauer and Gaskell 2000). The articles, documents and interviews, among other things, were examined in detail to: identify the main institutions and actors involved; understand the emergence pattern of human rights approaches in the field of tobacco control; determine the different understandings of human rights at work among the main institutions and actors; and ascertain the reasons, advantages and disadvantages for using human rights-based approaches put forward by the main institutions and actors. The analysis was streamlined and organized through the use of QSR International's NVivo 10 software for qualitative research.

The recent development of human rights-based approaches to tobacco control

From the 1970s onwards, tobacco control has been primarily framed as a public health issue (Berridge 2007; Brandt 2007). A critical aspect of this way of problematising smoking is, of course, epidemiological and biomedical. Smoking has been repeatedly portrayed as a key causal factor, both statistically and biologically, of an ever growing number of diseases. Furthermore, tobacco use has also increasingly been portrayed as one of the single, highest causes of preventable morbidity and mortality worldwide, killing more than tuberculosis, HIV/AIDS and malaria combined (Mathers and Loncar 2006; WHO 2009a, 2012). Another significant element of identifying and describing smoking as a public health issue has been the emphasis on the enormous costs associated with smoking in terms of medical care, loss of productivity and fire damages. Last, but not least, the framing of tobacco as a problem of public health has also involved strong moral overtones, with the smoking epidemic consistently described as the product of the greed and deceitful strategies of the transnational tobacco industry (Larsen 2008; Studlar 2008). It was this way of portraying smoking that so successfully informed the 2003 FCTC, the first public health treaty drafted and adopted under the aegis of the WHO (WHO 2009b; Mamudu *et al.* 2011; Reynolds and Tansey 2012).

Until the early 2000s public health advocates did not use human rights and, specifically, the right to health together with their existing monitoring and enforceability mechanisms to advance tobacco control. At least, they did not do so in any systematic or concerted way.[1] The FCTC provides a good illustration of this dearth of human rights-based approaches in global tobacco control until recently. Indeed, aside from the preamble's reference to the right to health found in the WHO Constitution and UN treaties, human rights were absent from both the FCTC negotiation process and its final text (Taylor 2005; Dresler and Marks 2006). As Richard Daynard (2011), a prominent tobacco control advocate who participated in the negotiations, remembers:

> It is certainly true that nobody was thinking about human rights when the FCTC was being negotiated. It was simply not the vocabulary ... There was of course the customary reference in the preamble to some human rights treaties ... but that was not something most of us even noticed.

Today, in contrast, human rights have started to make inroads in the field of global tobacco control. Indeed, while it is too early to make any definite judgements on the extent of this transformation,[2] it is clear that the language of human rights is increasingly complementing and combining with the already established public health discourses on smoking (Daynard 2012). First, a growing number of key organizations in the fight against the smoking epidemic have adopted, funded and encouraged human rights-based approaches. Both the WHO and PAHO, for example, now endorse and promote the use of human rights norms, institutions and procedures in relation to tobacco control through the organization of workshops and the publications of factsheets (PAHO 2006, 2008; Roses 2006; Vestal 2010). Similarly, the largest source of funding for tobacco control in developing countries, the Bloomberg Initiative for the Reduction in Tobacco Use, currently finances the work of the O'Neill Institute for National and Global Health Law on human rights and smoking (Myers 2010; Cabrera 2011; O'Neill Institute 2011a). Furthermore, in its recently published 20th anniversary issue, *Tobacco Control*, the leading academic journal in the field of global tobacco control, identified the 'human rights-based approach to tobacco control' as a 'strategic direction and emerging issue' in the field and included three papers on the topic (Daynard 2012; Dresler *et al.* 2012; Marks 2012). Second, there is an increasing number of both human rights and tobacco control advocacy groups that are currently testing whether existing human rights monitoring and enforceability mechanisms can be successfully used to advance anti-smoking policies. For example, local coalitions of lawyers and tobacco control activists have recently filed lawsuits against the governments of both India and Mexico for violation of their human right to health, arguing that they have so far failed to adopt the necessary tobacco control policies to protect their health (Cabrera and Madrazo 2010; Myers 2010; O'Neill Institute 2011b). Similarly, local human rights and health activists groups in Argentina and Brazil have started submitting reports to both the UN-CESCR and the UN Committee for the Elimination of All Forms of Discrimination Against Women (UN-CEDAW), in which they accuse these states of violating their right to health by not implementing strong anti-smoking policies (O'Neill Institute 2009, 2010a, 2010b; HRTCN 2011b).

The HTC and the representation of tobacco control as a human rights problem

What I term the HTC is best understood as a hybrid between an epistemic community or thought collective and an advocacy network (cf. Fleck 1979; Hass 1992; Keck and Sikkink 1998; Mirowski and Plehwe 2009). Such collectives, communities or networks are groups of professionals with a recognized expertise in a specific domain. What makes these networks distinctive is that their members, who can come from a variety of backgrounds and disciplines, develop and share a same 'style of thinking' – a distinctive apparatus of knowledge, values, language, practices and devices, which allows the network's members to identify problems that need addressing and suggest particular explanations, analyses and solutions.

The HTC understood as such a collective, community or network began to emerge from the early 2000s onwards, but it is only more recently that efforts were made to formalise its existence and structure. A critical moment in that respect was the creation of the HRTCN in Lausanne, Switzerland, in 2008 – an organization that 'works to advance a human rights-based approach to tobacco control' (HRTCN 2011a). The HRTCN's hundred or so members comprise most of the professionals who make up the HTC.[3] These professionals are, for the most part, either global tobacco control advocates or international human rights lawyers. Many of the tobacco control advocates work for American and international organizations active in the fight against smoking, including the American Cancer Society, the Campaign for Tobacco Free Kids, the Framework Convention Alliance and the WHO Tobacco Free Initiative. Some also work for North American universities and public health schools, including the O'Neill Institute for National and Global Health Law at Georgetown University, the Masonic Cancer Center at the University of Minnesota and the Public Health Advocacy Institute at Northeastern University. It is interesting to note that many of these advocates have been active for a decade or more in the field of global tobacco control (Mamudu and Glantz 2009; Mamudu *et al.* 2011).[4] For them, human rights is a discourse that has been highly successful in other areas of global health, such as HIV/AIDS and access to medicines, which they are keen to tap into. Most of the human rights lawyers who are members of the HTC work for American universities and international organizations specializing in human rights and law, including: the François-Xavier Bagnoud Centre for Human Rights and Health at Harvard University opened by Jonathan Mann in the early 1990s; the Wellesley College's Centres for Women; and both the WHO's and the PAHO's Human Rights and Health Units. Many of these lawyers are seasoned human rights professionals.[5] For them, tobacco control is yet another area in which they can apply the legal expertise they have developed in relation to other issues from discrimination against women and people with AIDS to the protection of children and biomedical research subjects.

The HTC's thought style is characterized by a will to frame smoking as a human rights issue associated with a belief that human rights-based approaches to tobacco control will help strengthen anti-smoking efforts. An excellent illustration of this way of conceptualizing the relation between human rights and tobacco control can be found on the HRTCN (2011a) website:

> [We] believe that tobacco control is a human right and can be advanced by using a human rights-based approach.

Human rights lawyers and HTC members Carolyn Dresler and Stephen Marks' (2006) article *The Emerging Human Right to Tobacco Control* and tobacco control pioneer Judith Mackay's (2009) keynote address at the HRTCN's Mumbai meeting provide two more good examples of this style of reasoning:

> Our claim is that a human rights framework implies both norms and potential remedies that may reinforce tobacco control regulation.
>
> (Dresler and Marks 2006: 602)

> [There is] the need for a human rights approach to tobacco control ... to advance tobacco control.
>
> (Mackay 2009)

In principle, HTC members acknowledge that human rights-based approaches to tobacco control can be based on any relevant human rights norms (e.g. Crow 2004; McIntyre 2008; Dresler *et al.* 2012). In practice, however, they generally focus on the right to health as recognized in international human rights treaties such as the International Convention on Economic, Social and Cultural Rights (ICESCR), the Convention on the Elimination of all Forms of Discrimination Against Women (CEDAW) and the Convention on the Rights of the Child (CRC). So, for example, Oscar Cabrera, a human rights lawyer at the O'Neill Institute and a HRTCN member, explains that 'the right to health must play a central role in any strategy that deploys human rights in advancing tobacco control' (Cabrera and Madrazo 2010: S291). Similarly, Dresler and Marks argue that what they call the 'human right to tobacco control' is, for the most part, 'derived from ... the right to health' (2006: 631; cf. Dresler *et al.* 2012). The centrality given by the HTC to the right to health is because the latter is the human rights norm that is most relevant to tobacco control efforts. Indeed, according to the HTC, the right to health can be invoked: (a) to forbid states to actively contribute to the tobacco epidemic by directly or indirectly supporting the production and sale of cigarettes; and (b) to oblige states to set up and implement comprehensive tobacco control policies including prevention campaigns, public smoking bans and smoking cessation programmes. As Cabrera explains:

> The right to health can provide significant support to tobacco control policies. First and foremost, the State must respect the right to health by refraining from spreading the tobacco epidemic ... State ownership of

tobacco companies [for example] is problematic from this perspective ... The State also has an obligation to protect people's right to health from the threat of tobacco ... his obligation requires the State to regulate private parties if their activities infringe on human rights. Clear examples of measures oriented at realising this obligation are: smoking bans in public places ... [and] bans on advertising and promotion of tobacco products ... The state must also fulfil the right to health by implementing all the relevant measures, legislation, regulation and budgetary allocation that will be conducive to effective tobacco control regulation ... [This includes:] providing health services for people afflicted by diseases stemming from tobacco use, facilitating smokers' access to cessation programmes; and prevention campaigns that inform ... the ... population ... about the dangers associated with tobacco use.

(Cabrera and Madrazo 2010: S291–S292)

As the literature on thought collectives, epistemic communities and advocacy networks has suggested (Fleck 1979; Hass 1992; Keck and Sikkink 1998; Mirowski and Plehwe 2009), such groups play a critical part in the production of many of the political truths that prevail today. The same can be said about the HTC in relation to the framing of smoking as a human rights problem over the last 10 years. To start with, its members have contributed decisively to the articulation of human rights-based approaches to tobacco control. They have mostly done so through intellectual reflection, research and debates carried out in academic or similar settings. Much of this work has involved the preparation and publication of numerous scholarly articles in which HTC members outline how human rights and, in particular, the right to health could be used to improve tobacco control. Examples include: Melissa Crow's (2005) *The Human Rights Responsibilities of Multinational Tobacco Companies*; Oscar Cabrera and Alejandro Madrazo's (2010) *Human Rights as a Tool for Tobacco Control in Latin America*; Ragnita De Silva de Alwis and Richard Daynard's (2011) *Defining Tobacco Control as an Important Human Right and Development Goal*; and Carolyn Dresler, Harry Lando, Nick Schneider and Hitakshi Sehgal's (2012) *Human Rights-based Approach to Tobacco Control*. It has also involved the organization of seminars and colloquiums at which HTC members and others examined and discussed human rights-based approaches to tobacco control. One example is a 2003 seminar, on human rights and health at the Harvard School of Public Health where Carolyn Dresler, Stephen Marks and others discussed the idea of a right to tobacco control (Dresler 2011). Another illustration is the 2004 seminar funded by the Robert Wood Johnson Foundation, at which scholars, many of whom were linked to the HTC, debated the 'opportunities, problems and prospects involved in having rights arguments play a significant role in efforts to reduce the harm associated with tobacco' (Fox and Katz 2005: ii1). A further two examples are the HRTCN meetings organized at both the University of Lausanne's Institute of Social and Preventive Medicine and the Tata Institute for Social Sciences in Mumbai (HRTCN 2008, 2009).

HTC members have also made important efforts to disseminate the human rights-based approaches, which they helped articulate. First, they have organized numerous workshops on the use of human rights to improve tobacco control for both human rights and anti-smoking advocates. The O'Neill Institute, for example, has conducted many workshops on 'shadow reporting' and 'human rights-based litigation strategies for tobacco control' in cities throughout Latin America such as Mexico City, Buenos Aires and Santiago de Chile (Cabrera 2011; O'Neill Institute 2011a). Richard Daynard's Public Health Advocacy Institute did similar work across Asia and Africa (De Silva de Alwis and Daynard 2011; De Silva de Alwis *et al.* 2011; Daynard 2012). As Daynard explains:

> We have been to something like 15 countries talking with human rights people and trying to push human rights and tobacco control people together to … get them to include tobacco control issues in their shadow reports … In Bangladesh, … Vietnam … or Beijing … we would have these conferences and we would invite local tobacco control people there.
>
> (Daynard 2011)

Second, HTC members have also sought to disseminate human rights-based approaches by producing manuals in which they explain how to organize and conduct shadow reporting or litigation strategies. One example is the O'Neill Institute's (2011b) *Litigation Guide on Tobacco Industry Strategy in Latin American Courts*. Another example is human rights lawyer Ragnita De Silva de Alwis's (2008a) *Basic Guidelines for Shadow Reporting Preparation* written for the HRTCN. Third, HTC members have also disseminated their human rights-based strategies by lobbying relevant national and international human rights bodies. For example, the HRTCN organized a series of meetings in Geneva with the UN Special Rapporteur on the Right to Health, the UN-CESCR, the UN-CEDAW and the CRC Committee where it outlined why tobacco control was an important issue (Vestal 2010; Dresler 2011; Dresler *et al.* 2012).

Lawyers and the promise of powerful tools

For much of the literature on framing and human rights (e.g. Keck and Sikkink 1998; Jacobson and Banerjee 2005; Shiffman and Smith 2007; Rushton 2010, forthcoming), the aim of representing a specific issue as a human rights issue is to attract attention and encourage action. For example, Keck and Sikkink (1998: ch. 5) suggest that the use of a human rights frame rather than a 'development' or 'discrimination' frame was critical in drawing attention to and generating the political will to address women's rights. Similarly, Rushton (forthcoming) argues that a human rights framework was employed with the intention of attracting attention to and changing existing travel restrictions against people living with HIV/AIDS. While a human rights framework can be exploited to generate awareness and encourage action, the HTC's use of such a framework suggests that it would be wrong to assume that this is the only possible aim when presenting an issue as a human rights one.

Indeed, for most HTC members the attraction of human rights-based approaches to tobacco control was not to attract attention to and encourage action to tackle the global smoking epidemic but to tap into the powerful, judicial monitoring and enforceability mechanisms that make up international human rights. A good illustration can be found on the HRTCN's (2011a) website, where it is explained that a 'human rights-based approach to tobacco control' is about 'utilizing the legal remedies and reporting requirements of current [human rights] treaties and conventions'. Similarly, when introducing a new forum about human rights on the major online tobacco control advocacy network Globalink, tobacco control advocate Doreen McIntyre (2008) claimed that what is 'most important' about human rights is that they 'have enforceable legal protection mechanisms that could be pursued to advance tobacco control'.

For HTC members, these monitoring and enforceability mechanisms are conceptualized as 'powerful' or 'effective tools' for the advancement of tobacco control. For example, in a speech on the importance of human rights for public health, PAHO director Mirta Roses (2006) argued that:

> Human rights instruments ... [are] effective tools for the promotion and protection of health ... PAHO's newest initiative in health and human rights is the issue of exposure to second hand smoke and ... in this area international human rights instruments have been an underutilized but powerful mechanism that can help diminish deaths and diseases in the Americas.

Similarly, in a posting on Globalink's Human Rights Forum, Ragnita De Silva de Alwis (2008b) explained that UN human rights monitoring procedures and, in particular, the Human Rights Council's Universal Periodic Review (HPR) were 'very powerful'. This understanding is shared by Oscar Cabrera who asserts that 'human rights law is one of the most powerful legal tools that can be used' to advance tobacco control (Cabrera and Madrazo 2010: S288).

These powerful human rights tools praised and promoted by HTC members are of two types. The first one comprises the monitoring and reporting procedures for the UN human rights treaties that assert the right to health such as the ICESCR, the CEDAW and the CRC (e.g. Crow 2004; Dresler and Marks 2006; De Silva de Alwis 2008a; HRTCN 2008, 2009; Cabrera and Madrazo 2010; Dresler *et al.* 2012; Marks 2012). These procedures oblige states to regularly submit official reports on how they fulfil their human rights obligations – including their obligation to protect everyone's health – to the relevant treaty bodies. With the help of alternative, shadow reports submitted by civil society groups, the treaty bodies assess these official reports and make recommendations to states on what they can and should do to better fulfil their obligations. If states ignore these recommendations, the treaty bodies can attempt to force their hand by publicly condemning and shaming them. For HTC members, these procedures offer the possibility to submit shadow reports on how states have fulfilled and how they could better fulfil their human rights obligation to protect everyone's health in relation to tobacco control. They have used this possibility by submitting shadow reports about Brazil and Argentina to the UN-CESCR and about Argentina and Egypt to the UN-CEDAW (O'Neill Institute 2009, 2010a, 2010b; HRTCN 2011b). Each time, the treaty bodies have responded favourably, identifying tobacco as a critical issue and strongly recommending that these countries set up and implement comprehensive tobacco control policies (O'Neill Institute 2011a).

The second type of powerful tools praised and promoted by the HTC are human rights litigation strategies (e.g. Crow 2004; Dresler and Marks 2006; Gostin 2007; Cabrera and Madrazo 2010; Dresler *et al.* 2012; Marks 2012). These strategies allow individuals and civil society groups to claim their right to health against a government in a court of law. Relevant jurisdictions include both international courts like the European and Inter-American Courts of Human Rights and higher level national courts. For HTC members, these strategies are an opportunity to advance tobacco control. Litigation can either be passive/defensive or active (Cabrera and Madrazo 2010; O'Neill Institute 2011b). Passive litigation allows individuals and civil society groups to use their right to health to defend existing tobacco control policies that the tobacco industry is challenging in a court of law on the grounds that they violate its rights to economic freedom or of speech. Active litigation allows individuals and civil society groups to use their right to health to ask a judge to force a government to pass and implement comprehensive tobacco policies. Members of the HTC have increasingly been involved in both passive and active litigation strategies in countries such as Argentina, Guatemala, India, Mexico and Uruguay (Crow 2004; Cabrera and Madrazo 2010; O'Neill Institute 2011b). As the Campaign for Tobacco Free Kids director Matthew Myers (2010) explains:

> We are supporting lawyers who have filed suits in Mexico ... Arguing that the right to health is a fundamental right, therefore the Mexican government's failure to fully implement the FCTC violates not only its international obligations under the FCTC but the constitutional right [to health] of citizens. We are supporting some litigation in India that is also looking at the issue of the right to health ... Fundamental human rights issues. India should be obligated, in our mind, to comply under both its constitution and its international obligations. We are looking at other opportunities like those around the world.

The HTC's reasons for conceiving the human rights framework as a way to access powerful monitoring and enforceability mechanisms rather than as a way to attract attention and encourage political action are threefold. First, there is an understanding that there is no real need to employ human rights to draw awareness and promote action to tackle the global smoking epidemic. Indeed, as already alluded to, the public health frame that has been used from the 1970s onwards has been very successful at doing that over the last 15 years, as demonstrated by the adoption of the FCTC and the increasing funding from philanthropists including Bloomberg and Gates (Brandt 2007; WHO 2009b; Mamudu *et al.* 2011; Reynolds and Tansey 2012). Second, there is a certain scepticism as to whether the use of human rights can really be efficient in terms of raising awareness and encouraging action about tobacco control. Indeed, there is a sense among many HTC members that, when compared to famine, war, genocide or rape, tobacco control will never be among the most urgent and compelling human rights issues. As Patricia Lambert (2010), a human rights lawyer and tobacco control advocate, explains:

> There is a growing movement to see tobacco control as a human right and I think that is a good thing ... But when you compare [tobacco control] to ... food and water ... the wars of the future ... climate change ... The most urgent human rights debates are not around a right to tobacco control. So we should move beyond debate and into direct action through, for example, litigation.

Third, there is a perceived need for monitoring and enforceability mechanisms in relation to tobacco control. As HTC members repeatedly argue, the FCTC does not have procedures through which states party to the convention can be forced to comply with their obligations. Already existing human rights monitoring and enforceability mechanisms, they suggest, can offer a practical alternative. As Melissa Crow, one of the first human rights lawyers to discuss the use of human rights in tobacco control, explains:

> In their present form, neither the FCTC's reporting requirements nor its dispute resolution procedures are likely to influence the conduct of governments ... [The use] of implementation mechanisms employed by existing human rights institutions – including reporting requirements, individual petition procedures and advisory opinions – would enhance the likelihood of promoting compliance by [governments]. Confronted with heightened scrutiny of their conduct, [they] would have greater incentives to take their FCTC commitments seriously.
>
> (Crow 2004: 220, 249)

Similarly, Carolyn Dresler, Harry Lando and other fellow HRTCN members (Dresler *et al.* 2012: 208) explain that the FCTC does not have any 'enforcement mechanisms'. One way of addressing this problem, they suggest, is by 'construct[ing] legal claims to [human] rights related to tobacco' (Dresler *et al.* 2012). Indeed, this would allow 'citizens from across the globe [to] demand effective action for tobacco control' by using the enforcement mechanisms contained in international human rights conventions (Dresler *et al.* 2012).

Interestingly, the way most HTC members conflate human rights-based approaches with the use of existing monitoring and enforceability mechanisms has led them to take a legal view of the right to health and thus gives lawyers a critical role within the network. Indeed, when using these mechanisms one needs to use the right to health as defined in human rights law and jurisprudence as only this understanding of the right to health will be recognized by UN treaty bodies, international human rights courts and national courts of law. There are many signs of HTC's legal understanding of the right to health. One is the way in which the members of the network have sought to ground the right to health in both internationally recognized legal norms such as article 12 IESCR and the jurisprudence of international human rights bodies such as the UN-CESCR's (2000) *General comment 14* on the right to health. Both Crow's (2004) paper, *Using human rights to promote global tobacco control*, and Dresler and Marks's (2006) essay, *The emerging human right to tobacco control*, are excellent illustrations of such attempts. Another sign of HTC's legal understanding of the right to health is the importance given to trained lawyers within the network – a pattern that, interestingly, seems to be common to a large number of transnational regulatory fields (Dezalay and Garth 2011, 2012). One example is the prominence accorded to highly technical presentations given by lawyers such as Rangita de Silva de Alwis, Yehenew Walilegne and Benjamin Meier on the 'Human Rights Framework', 'Rights Holders' and 'Duty Bearers' at the HRCTN's first conference in Lausanne (HRTCN 2008). Another example is how HTC members explicitly recognize the importance of lawyers within the network. So, Oscar Cabrera (2011) explains that: 'You need to have the lawyers in the group so they can interpret what are the rights and what are the obligations.'

The key role given by the HTC to judicial monitoring and enforceability mechanisms, lawyers and a legal definition of the right to health is not without important consequences. First, it has led to the marginalization of other, alternative understandings of this right within HTC and beyond. For example, the use of anthropological films to denounce the exploitative working conditions of tobacco farmers in Africa proposed by Marty Otanez (2010) or the abstruse concept of 'breathing [as] a human rights issue' put forward by tobacco control activist Robert Starkey (2009) have received very little attention. Indeed, these alternative understandings of human rights have never really been taken up in HTC publications or discussed at HTC meetings (e.g. Crow 2004; Dresler and Marks 2006; HRTCN 2008, 2009; Daynard 2012; De Silva de Alwis *et al.* 2011). Neither have they attracted any interest or funding from the major players in the field of global tobacco control such as the WHO and the Bloomberg Initiative (Myers 2010; Vestal 2010). Second, the importance given by the HTC to judicial mechanisms, lawyers and legal definitions is also contributing to what many authors have termed the judicialization of the right to health (Gloppen 2008; Biehl *et al.* 2009; Ferraz 2009; Petryna 2009). Following the celebrated South African HIV/AIDS medicines access campaign, there has been an increasing tendency to view the right to health as a legal concept to be defined by lawyers and enforced by judicial or quasi-judicial institutions. This has especially been the case across Latin America in relation to access to medicines, from anti-retroviral therapies to drugs for rare genetic diseases. The work of the HTC in articulating a right to tobacco control around judicial mechanisms and lawyers further reinforces this tendency and extends it from access to medicines to the field of tobacco control.

Conclusion

As mentioned, human rights have increasingly been used to label and interpret a variety of global health issues such as HIV/AIDS to maternal health over the last two decades (Reubi 2011). The present chapter addressed this proliferation of human rights discourses in international public health by examining recent efforts to frame the tobacco epidemic as a human rights problem. More specifically, it has sought to contribute to our understanding of how and why such approaches are being articulated and disseminated.

To start with, the chapter stressed the critical role played by networks of expertise and advocacy in the proliferation of human rights discourses in the field of global health (Fleck 1979; Hass 1992; Keck and Sikkink 1998). More specifically, it argued that recent efforts to frame tobacco control as a problem of human rights was the product of a small, international collective, which I termed the HTC. The chapter described how the HTC comprises principally tobacco control advocates and human rights lawyers who believe that invoking the right to health will help strengthen anti-smoking efforts. It also described the ways in which the HTC has helped articulate and disseminate human rights-based approaches to tobacco control, from the publication of scholarly articles and how-to-do manuals to the organization of meetings and workshops.

Furthermore, the chapter also emphasized the role of human rights frameworks in providing access to powerful, legal and quasi-legal tools. The existing literature on framing usually assumes that human rights-based approaches are used to draw attention to and encourage political action on a particular issue (e.g. Keck and Sikkink 1998; Jacobson and Banerjee 2005; Shiffman and Smith 2007). The chapter showed that this assumption can be restrictive by outlining how the HTC viewed human rights mainly as a judicial monitoring and enforcement mechanism. It also showed how this has led the HTC to privilege a legal definition of the right to health and grant lawyers a critical role. An important consequence of the HTC's efforts to elaborate and promote such an understanding of human rights in relation to smoking has been to reinforce the current judicialization of the right to health and further extend it to the issue of tobacco control.

Acknowledgements

This chapter is a revised version of an article that I published in *Global Public Health*, volume 7, supplement 2, in December 2012, under the title 'Making a human right to tobacco control: expert and advocacy networks, framing and the right to health'. My thanks to Taylor & Francis Ltd for granting me the permission to do so. I would also like to thank the tobacco control advocates and human rights experts interviewed for this research for their interest and the time spent answering my queries. Furthermore, I thank Alex Mold for her helpful comments on an earlier draft of this chapter. I also gratefully acknowledge the financial support from the European Research Council under the European Community's Seventh Framework Programme (Ideas Grant 230489 GHG). All views expressed remain mine.

Notes

1 This assertion comes with three caveats. First, there have been instances over the last 40 years when both the tobacco industry and the anti-smoking movement have used a rhetoric or language of rights, i.e. have used linguistic expressions like 'the right to smoke' and 'the right to a smoke-free environment' as arguments in policy debates about smoking (cf. Jacobson and Soliman 2002; Berridge 2007; Brandt 2007). This, however, is quite different from the HTC's efforts to use a legally recognized and defined human right to health together with the existing national and international human rights monitoring and enforceability mechanisms. Second, some international human rights institutions had already made a link between human rights and tobacco control in the late 1990s and early 2000s (Crow 2004). In particular, the UN-CESCR has, from 1999 onwards, sometimes mentioned, both in its *General Comment 14* on the right to health and in its reviews of states' reports, that information campaigns on the dangers of smoking are a measure through which states can fulfil the right to health found in article 12 ICESCR. These few mentions did not, however, amount to any systematic or concerted effort to use the right to health to improve tobacco control. Third, in 1999, the WHO Tobacco Free Initiative sought to ally with UNICEF and use the 1989 UN CRC to support its call for increased efforts in tobacco control. A two-day workshop was held and a report entitled 'Tobacco and the rights of the child' was published (WHO 2001), but neither had any impact and the attempt to frame tobacco control as a children's rights issue was not pursued further (Yach 2010).

2 Some tobacco control advocates are still uncertain as to whether the language of human rights will become important in their field. As Matthew Myers (2010), the current President of the Campaign for Tobacco Free Kids which currently funds the work of human rights lawyers on smoking, explains:

> I think it is too early to know whether human rights will become a powerful tool or not (…) We are testing them out (…) It's too early to know (…) Up to this time with a couple of exceptions it has not been as successful as we had hoped, but that does not mean it won't be (…) It is still a nascent discussion.

3 Members of the HRTCN include: Douglas Bettcher, Chris Bostic, Pascal Bovet, Oscar Cabrera, Richard Daynard, Rangita de Silva de Alwis, Carolyn Dresler, Tom Glynn, Patricia Lambert, Harry Lando, Judith Mackay, Hadii Mamudu, Stephen Marks, Benjamin Meier, Kathy Mulvey, Helena Nygren-Krug, Marty Otanez, Gemma Vestal and Yehenew Walilegney (HRTCN 2011a).

4 HTC members who have been involved in the field of global tobacco control for a decade or more include: Douglas Bettcher, Chris Bostic, Pascal Bovet, Richard Daynard, Patricia Lambert, Tom Glynn, Judith Mackay and Kathy Mulvey.

5 HTC members with a previous experience of the field of international human rights include: Oscar Cabrera, Rangita de Silva de Alwis, Stephen Marks, Helena Nygren-Krug and Yehenew Walilegney.

Bibliography

Bauer, M.K. and Gaskell, G. (eds), 2000. *Qualitative Research with Text, Image and Sound. A Practical Handbook*. London: Sage.

Berridge, V., 2007. *Marketing Health: Smoking and the Discourse of Public Health in Britain, 1945–2000*. Oxford: Oxford University Press.

Biehl, J., Petryna, A., Gertner, A. and Picon, P.D., 2009. 'Judicialisaiton of the right to health in Brazil', *The Lancet*, 373(9682), 2182–84.

Brandt, A., 2007. *The Cigarette Century: The Rise, Fall and Deadly Persistence of the Product that Defined America*. New York: Basic Books.

Cabrera, O.A., 2011. Phone interview with the author.

Cabrera, O.A. and Madrazo, A., 2010. 'Human rights as a tool for tobacco control in Latin America', *Salud Publica de Mexico*, 52 (Suppl. 2), S288–S297.

Crow, M.E., 2004. 'Smokescreens and state responsibility: using human rights strategies to promote global tobacco control', *Yale Journal of International Law*, 29, 209–50.

——, 2005. 'The human rights responsibilities of multinational tobacco companies', *Tobacco Control*, 14 (Suppl. II), ii14–ii18.

Daynard, R., 2011. Phone interview with the author.

——, 2012. 'Allying tobacco control with human rights: invited commentary', *Tobacco Control*, 21, 213–14.

De Silva de Alwis, R., 2008a. *Human Rights Reporting: Basic Guidelines for Shadow Report Preparation*. Available at: www.globalink.org (accessed 1 August 2011).

——, 2008b. *HR Reporting*. Available at: www.globalink.org (accessed 1 August 2011).

De Silva de Alwis, R. and Daynard, R., 2011. 'Defining tobacco control as an important human right and development goal', *Turkish Policy Quarterly*, 10 (1), 113–19.

De Silva de Alwis, R., Daynard, R. and Oniang'o, R., 2011. 'Tobacco control as a human right and development goal in Kenya', *African Journal of Food, Agriculture, Nutrition and Development*, 11 (3), 1–7.

Dezalay, Y. and Garth, B., (eds), 2011. *Lawyers and the Rule of Law in an Era of Globalization*. Oxford: Routledge.

——, 2012. *Lawyers and the Construction of Transnational Justice*. Oxford: Routledge.

Dresler, C., 2011. Phone interview with the author.

Dresler, C., Lando, H., Schneider, N. and Sehgal, H., 2012. 'Human rights-based approach to tobacco control' *Tobacco Control*, 21, 208–11.

Dresler, C. and Marks, S., 2006. 'The emerging human right to tobacco control', *Human Rights Quarterly*, 28 (3), 599–651.

Fee, E. and Parry, M., 2008. 'Jonathan Mann, HIV/AIDS, and human rights', *Journal of Public Health Policy*, 29, 54–71.

Ferraz, O.L.M., 2009. 'The right to health in the courts of Brazil: worsening health inequalities?', *Health and Human Rights*, 11 (2), 33–45.

Fleck, L., 1979. *Genesis and Development of a Scientific Fact*. Chicago: University of Chicago Press.

Fox, B.J. and Katz, J.E., 2005. 'Individual and human rights in tobacco control: help or hindrance?', *Tobacco Control*, 14 (Suppl. II), ii1–ii2.

Gloppen, S., 2008. 'Litigation as a strategy to hold governments accountable for implementino the right to health', *Health and Human Rights*, 10(2), 21–36.

Gostin, L.O., 2007. 'The "tobacco wars" – global litigation strategies', *Journal of American Medical Association*, 298 (21), 2537–39.

124   *David Reubi*

Gruskin, S., Grodin, M., Anna, G., and Marks, S. (eds), 2005. *Perspectives on Health and Human Rights*. New York: Routledge.

Hass, P., 1992. 'Epistemic communities and international policy coordination', *International Organization*, 46 (1), 1–35.

HRTCN, 2008. *Summary of the First HRTCN Meeting, Lausanne, Switzerland, 1–2 August 2008*. Available at: http://hrtcn.net/ (accessed 20 July 2011).

——, 2009. *Summary of the Second HRTCN Meeting, Mumbai, India, 13–14 March 2009*. Available at: http://hrtcn.net/ (accessed 20 July 2011).

——, 2011a. 'The human rights and tobacco control network'. Available at: http:// hrtcn.net/ (accessed 20 July 2011).

——, 2011b. *Tobacco Control and the Right to Health: Submission to the Committee on Economic, Social and Cultural Rights, Pre-sessional Working Group, 46th session, 23–27 May 2011*. Available at: http://hrtcn.net/ (accessed 20 July 2011).

Jacobson, P.D. and Banerjee, A., 2005. 'Social movements and human rights rhetoric in tobacco control', *Tobacco Control*, 14 (Suppl. II), ii45–ii49.

Jacobson, P.D. and Soliman, S., 2002. 'Co-opting the health and human rights movement' *Journal of Law, Medicine and Ethics*, 30, 705715.

Keck, M.E. and Sikkink, K., 1998. *Activists Beyond Borders: Advocacy Networks in International Politics*. Ithaca, NY: Cornell University Press.

Lambert, P., 2010. Interview with the author, Campaign for Tobacco Free Kids, Washington, DC.

Larsen, L.T., 2008. 'The political impact of science: is tobacco control science-or policy driven?', *Science and Public Policy*, 35 (10), 757–69.

Latour, B., 1988. *The Pasteurization of France*. Cambridge, MA: Harvard University Press.

Mackay, J., 2009. Keynote address, second HRTCN meeting, Tata Institute, Mumbai, 3–14 March 2009.

Mamudu, H.M. and Glantz, S.A., 2009. 'Civil society and the negotiation of the framework convention on tobacco control', *Global Public Health*, 4 (2), 150–68.

Mamudu, H.M., Gonzalez, M.E. and Glantz, S.A., 2011. 'The nature, scope and development of the global tobacco control epistemic community', *American Journal of Public Health*, 101 (11), 2044–54.

Marks, S., 2012. 'Invited commentary', *Tobacco Control*, 21, 212.

Mathers, C.D. and Loncar, D., 2006. 'Projections of global mortality and burden of disease from 2002 to 2030', *Public Library of Science Medicine*, 3 (11), e442, 2011–30.

McIntyre, D., 2008. *Globalink forum*. Available at: www.globalink.org (accessed 1 August 2011).

Mirowski, P. and Plehwe, D. (eds), 2009. *The Road to Mont-Pèlerin: The Making of the Neo-liberal Thought Collective*. Cambridge, MA: Harvard University Press.

Myers, M., 2010. Interview with the author, Campaign for Tobacco Free Kids, Washington, DC.

Olesen, T., 2006. '"In the court of public opinion": transnational problem construction in HIV/ AIDS medicine access campaign', *International Sociology*, 21 (1), 5–30.

O'Neill Institute, 2009. *Preventing and Reducing Tobacco use in Brazil: Pending Tasks, Shadow Report to the Periodic Report by the Government of Brazil, UN Committee on Economic, Social and Cultural Rights, 42nd session*. Available at: www.law. georgetown.edu/ oneillinstitute/documents/2009–05_Shadow-Report-Brazil.pdf (accessed 20 July 2011).

——, 2010a. *Women and Tobacco in Egypt: Preventing and Reducing the Effects of Tobacco Consumption Through Information, Implementation and Non-discrimination,*

Shadow Report to the Combined Sixth and Seventh Periodic Reports by the Government of Egypt, UN Committee on the Elimination of All Forms of Discrimination Against Women, 45th session. Available at: www.law.georgetown.edu/oneillinstitute/ global-health-law/ global-tobacco_control.cfm accessed 20 July 2011).

——, 2010b. *Challenges in the Prevention and Reduction of Women's Tobacco Use in Argentina, Shadow Report to the Sixth Periodic Report by the Government of Argentina, UN Committee on the Elimination of All Forms of Discrimination against Women, 46th session.* Available at: www.law.georgetown.edu/oneillinstitute/global-health-law/ global-tobacco_control.cfm (accessed 20 July 2011).

——, 2011a. *O'Neill Institute.* Available at: www.law.georgetown. edu/oneill institute/ global-health-law/global-tobacco_control.cfm (accessed 20 July 2011).

——, 2011b. *Tobacco Industry Strategy in Latin American Courts: A Litigation Guide.* Washington, DC: O'Neill Institute for National and Global Health Law.

Otanez, M., 2010. *Video on What it is Like to be a Pregnant Woman Farming Tobacco in Kenya.* Available at: www.globalink.org (accessed 1 August 2011).

PAHO, 2006. *Exposure to Second Hand Smoke in the Americas: A Human Rights Perspective.* Washington, DC: PAHO.

——, 2008. *Human Rights and Health: Persons Exposed to Second Hand Tobacco Smoke.* Washington, DC: PAHO.

Petryna, A., 2009. *When Experiments Travel: Clinical Trials and the Global Search for Human Subjects.* Princeton, NJ: Princeton University Press.

Reubi, D., 2011. 'The promise of human rights for global health: a programmed deception?', *Social Science and Medicine*, 73, 625–28.

Reynolds, L.A. and Tansey, E.M. (eds), 2012. *WHO framework convention on tobacco control: transcript of witness seminar organized by the Wellcome Trust Centre for the History of Medicine at UCL, in collaboration with the Department of Knowledge Management and Sharing, WHO, held in Geneva, on 26 February 2010.* London: Queen Mary, University of London.

Roses, M., 2006. *Human Rights Instruments and Standards as Effective Tool for the Promotion and Protection of Health.* Presentation at Georgetown University Law Centre, Washington, DC, 13 October 2006. Available at: www.paho.org/English/D/ Georgetown_CCenter_MRoses.htm (accessed 20 June 2011).

Rushton, S., 2010. 'Framing AIDS: securitization, development-ization, rights-ization', *Global Health Governance*, IV (1).

——, forthcoming. 'The global debate over HIV-related travel restrictions: framing and policy change', *Global Public Health*.

Schrecker, T., Chapman, A., Labonte, R. and de Vogli, R., 2010. 'Advancing equity on the global market place: how human rights can help', *Social Science & Medicine*, 71, 1520–26.

Shiffman, J. and Smith, S., 2007. 'Generation of political priority for global health initiatives: a framework and case study of maternal mortality', *The Lancet*, 370, 1370–79.

Starkey, R., 2009. *Breathing is a Human Rights Issue.* Available at: www. globalink.org (accessed 1 August 2011).

Studlar, D., 2008. 'US tobacco control: public health, political economy, or morality policy?', *Review of Policy Research*, 25 (5), 393–410.

Taylor, A., 2005. 'Trade, human rights and the WHO framework convention on tobacco control: just what the doctor ordered?' In T. Cottier, J. Pauwelyn and E. Burgi (eds), *Human Rights and International Trade.* Oxford: Oxford University Press, 322–33.

UN Committee on Economic, Social and Cultural Rights, 2000. *General Comment 14: The Right to the Highest Attainable Standard of Health*. Geneva: UN High Commissioner for Human Rights.

Vestal, G., 2010. Interview with the author, Tobacco Free Initiative, WHO, Geneva.

WHO, 2001. *Tobacco and the Rights of the Child*. Geneva: WHO.

——, 2009a. *Global Health Risks: Mortality and Burden of Disease Attributable to Selected Major Risks*. Geneva: WHO.

——, 2009b. *History of the WHO Framework Convention on Tobacco Control*. Geneva: WHO.

——, 2012. *Mortality Attributable to Tobacco*. Geneva: WHO.

Yach, D., 2010. Interview with the author.

Yamin, A.E. and Maine, D., 2005. 'Maternal mortality as a human rights issue: measuring compliance with international treaty obligations.' In S. Gruskin, M. Grodin, G. Annas and S. Marks (eds), *Perspectives on Health and Human Rights*. New York: Routledge, 400–438.

Part III

Resistance, contestation and translation

7 From isolation to 'living together'

Human rights in Japanese HIV/AIDS discourse

Hannah Waterson

Introduction

HIV/AIDS in Japan

There are currently estimated to be around 10,000 people living with HIV/AIDS (hereafter PLWHA) in Japan (UNAIDS 2009a), in comparison to around 80,000 in the UK (UNAIDS 2009b). However, new diagnoses of both HIV and AIDS have been steadily rising in Japan over the last 25 years. In 2007 new HIV diagnoses exceeded 1000 for the first time, and have remained above this threshold in subsequent years (Kōseirōdōshō Eizu Dōkō Iinkai 2012). Around one-third of new HIV/AIDS cases are only diagnosed once symptoms of AIDS become evident and Japan is one of the few high-income countries in which AIDS cases have not fallen dramatically since the introduction of new anti-retroviral therapies in 1996 (Kihara 2008). This would suggest that people do not attend HIV testing even if they have engaged in high-risk behaviour. Epidemiologists, therefore, estimate that the actual number of PLWHA may be considerably higher than is reflected in the official statistics (Hashimoto *et al.* 2004; Shirasaka 2005). The epidemiology of Japan's HIV/AIDS epidemic has also followed a different trajectory from other high-income nations. While in the early stages of the global epidemic attention focused on the gay community, in Japan haemophiliacs infected through blood products dominated HIV/AIDS statistics and media attention. However, in the twenty-first century, new infections have been overwhelmingly a result of sexual contact, particularly among men who have sex with men (MSM), who now account for over two-thirds of new diagnoses (Kōseirōdōshō Eizu Dōkō Iinkai 2012), raising new challenges for public health experts and policy makers.

This epidemiological profile combines with a cultural context in which the prevention and treatment of HIV/AIDS is hampered by a general lack of awareness about the disease and a prevailing stigma that prevents PLWHA from speaking openly about their condition. A nationwide household survey in 2007 found basic knowledge of HIV and methods of prevention to be lacking (Kihara 2008) and recent UNAIDS data reveals that only 18 per cent of respondents were personally worried about HIV; still fewer considered it to be an issue in their community. Furthermore, less than half of those questioned would be prepared to continue working with someone diagnosed with HIV (UNAIDS 2010).

In this chapter, I elucidate the evolution of HIV/AIDS policy in Japan, from an initial focus on containment, to a more inclusive approach that specifically emphasizes the human rights of the patient. I discuss why Japan has adopted a rights-based approach to HIV/AIDS prevention, arguing that non-governmental organizations (NGOs) and political entrepreneurs have played an integral role in facilitating this shift, adapting international health rights discourses and practices associated with HIV/AIDS to suit local needs and employing a range of strategies, including lobbying, research and education, to ensure the recognition of these in national HIV/AIDS policy. First, however, it is necessary to contextualize both the link between HIV/AIDS and human rights in the international context and Japanese understandings of rights and, in particular, rights relating to health.

HIV/AIDS and human rights

As Reubi and Mold (2013) argue, the combination of human rights discourses and biomedical knowledge about HIV/AIDS is best understood as an assemblage of concepts, policies and practices including testing techniques, informed consent procedures, public education programmes and strategies to eliminate stigma and discrimination. The Joint United Nations Programme on HIV/AIDS (UNAIDS) exemplifies the way of thinking associated with this assemblage of rights and biomedicine (UNAIDS 2007). In instances in which the human rights of PLWHA are not protected, the programme argues, stigma and discrimination will prevail, leading to social exclusion, the inability to work and support families and, if access to medicine is denied, illness and death. Members of marginalized populations in which rights are not protected, it further argues, are especially vulnerable to these dangers. According to the programme, the right to the highest standard of health demands not only that governments make appropriate care and treatment available, but also that they provide prevention and education programmes to prevent epidemics, which must be accessible to all sections of society. Other fundamental rights, such as the right to work, to privacy, to education and freedom of movement hold implications for HIV/AIDS care and prevention, not least the right to live free from discrimination. Furthermore, according to the programme, discrimination on account of someone's HIV status is not only a direct violation of their human rights, but also obstructs public health methods, preventing those potentially at risk from attending testing for fear of the consequences of a positive result, and inhibiting PLWHA from speaking out about their condition, reinforcing the taboo nature of HIV/AIDS.

This way of thinking where human rights inform and structure HIV/AIDS care and prevention, was pioneered by Jonathan Mann in his capacity as the inaugural director of the World Health Organization's (WHO) Global Programme on AIDS (GPA), the predecessor to UNAIDS. Given the emergence of

AIDS among the gay communities in the developed world, HIV/AIDS not only stimulated debate over individual rights to confidentiality, but also incorporated wider issues of discrimination, stigma and prejudice. Measures to combat the stigmatization of HIV/AIDS were linked to epidemiology, as it was understood that forcing those infected underground would hamper prevention (Mann 1999). Mann categorized the social, cultural, economic and political responses to AIDS as a third epidemic (after HIV infection and the appearance of AIDS), considering the stigma and discrimination associated with the epidemic as central to the global AIDS Challenge (Mann, quoted in Parker and Aggleton 2003). By the late 1980s, the WHO had established a discrimination reduction programme for HIV/ AIDS – the first time such an initiative had been applied to a pandemic (Mann 1999).

These ideas were embraced by HIV/AIDS organizations in a range of countries in which HIV/AIDS was particularly prevalent in minority communities and successful prevention initiatives were built around the key concepts (Piot and Seck 2001). However, this approach to HIV prevention was not universally embraced and a number of barriers have hindered its successful application. There were challenges from within the WHO leadership itself (Fee and Parry 2008), while a number of governments preferred a traditional public health approach and were particularly resistant to the changes to social structures necessary to implement the WHO framework (Heywood and Altman 2000). As the scale of the HIV/AIDS epidemic in the developing world has become clear, questions have been raised over the practical application of a rights-based approach to HIV/AIDS first conceived of in developed Western societies. Some have asserted that such an approach legitimizes pressure on indigenous communities to adopt a specific set of behaviours (such as monogamy and condom use) at odds with their culture or promotes a particular type of PLWHA who is empowered to speak openly about their status (Heywood and Altman 2000; London 2002; Nguyen 2005). Others draw attention to the potential of a rights-based approach to increase existing inequalities when services do not prioritize those most in need (London 2002).

In the absence of a biomedical solution to the epidemic, UNAIDS has continued to promote the incorporation of human rights into HIV/AIDS prevention initiatives. The UN obliges states to protect the rights of PLWHA and provide a right to health for all citizens and so rights remain central to HIV/AIDS prevention discourse in the international context, although the extent to which these ideas can be implemented on a local and practical level varies widely. This chapter assesses the extent to which the rights-based approach promoted in the international context has been adopted by Japan, how human rights have been understood in relation to HIV/AIDS, and how these understandings have changed as the epidemic has progressed.

Human and health rights in the Japanese context

Whether human rights as a Western construct can be applied in East Asian contexts, where traditional Confucian values emphasize deference to authority and group harmony over individualism has been a topic of much debate (Bauer and Bell 1999). Certainly, Western notions of rights and human rights are not unknown in Japan. For example, after the Meiji restoration, Japan adopted a range of Western legal practices (Port 1991). Similarly, after World War Two, human rights were incorporated in the new Japanese Constitution drafted during the immediate post-war allied occupation. In 1979, Japan ratified the two first major UN rights covenants – the International Covenant on Economic, Cultural and Social Rights and the International Covenant on Civil and Political Rights. More recently, as Japan sought to embrace globalization and play a more significant role in the international arena in the 1990s, it was forced to clarify its position on a number of human rights issues, resulting in the ratification of more UN treaties and greater efforts to promote human rights in the public domain (Neary 2002). At the same time, domestic NGOs also began to look to international rights legislation and push for individual civil rights in this context (Chan-Tiberghien 2004).

However, the introduction of these Western notions of rights and human rights has not taken place without some difficulty and resistance. Feldman (2000:16–37), for example, describes how the translation of the Western concept of rights proved difficult for Meiji intellectuals. Likewise, during Japan's rapid economic growth in the 1960s and 1970s, the country's leaders hesitated to ratify international covenants proposed by the United Nations (in which Japan was not a major force), fearing it would interfere with internal politics and negatively impact on its economic development (Peek 1992). Furthermore, as Neary (2002) has shown with reference to racial minorities, Japan has preferred to focus on social welfare rights, promoting the improvement of conditions for those groups with a grievance rather than providing legal mechanisms through which citizens can demand the recognition of individual civil rights. It has also been argued that Japan's strong bureaucracy can suppress rights assertions and excludes interest groups from policy making, while the conservative and hierarchical judicial system, characterized by a dearth of lawyers, makes it difficult for citizens to make rights claims through the courts even when the appropriate legislation is in place (Feldman 2000).

The same tension and ambivalence about rights has existed in relation to health and medicine in Japan. Although Japan's national health insurance scheme ensures comparatively equitable access to healthcare, a traditionally highly paternalistic medical system assumes deference to the physician with patients often denied an explanation of their treatment and access to their medical records. Furthermore, it is not uncommon for a terminal diagnosis to be withheld from the patient. Historically, attitudes towards infectious disease in Japanese society have been strongly stigmatizing and the state has typically favoured strategies of confinement and compulsory treatment, prioritizing the protection of the public over the individual rights of the patient (Ōtani, 1993; Fukuda, 1994). In response, Japanese patients' rights movements have focused on the issues of informed consent and patient autonomy as well as the protection of the rights of individual patient (Morikawa, 1994). One patients' rights movement that gained particular popular support was the fight for compensation by haemophiliacs infected with HIV through blood products, addressed later in this chapter.

Evolving HIV/AIDS policy – from isolation to 'living together'

Privacy versus protection: early HIV/AIDS prevention measures

In 1985 the Ministry of Health and Welfare (MHW)[1] announced Japan's first official AIDS patient to be a gay artist, who had spend several years living in the United States (Japan Times 1985). This portrayal, in keeping with the stereotypical HIV/AIDS patient familiar from coverage of the developing overseas epidemic, caused little public alarm and the government took no action. Given that it was strongly suspected there had been several prior infections in haemophiliac patients, gay activists perceived the announcement as an attempt by the government to make the gay community a scapegoat for HIV/AIDS and were angered by the construction of AIDS as a gay disease (Nami 1987) but this anger did not manifest itself in community mobilization. Although homosexuality has never been legally restricted in Japan, a strong expectation of conformation to societal norms deters gay men from disclosing their sexuality (McLelland 2005) and although some activists attempted to establish support and information services, the undercover nature of the community, and the reluctance of its members to expose themselves to further marginalization through association with a deadly disease, resulted in the lack of a strong gay voice in HIV/AIDS discourse.

Haemophiliac support groups were equally antagonized by the government's characterization of Japan's 'patient zero' as a gay man, believing the move to be part of a strategy by the MHW to obscure the extent of infection through blood products (Yasuda 1987). Monitoring the situation overseas, these groups pressed their physicians for information but were told repeatedly that there was no problem (Akase 1991). However, it later became clear that a large number of infections had taken place and in some instances physicians had chosen not to inform these patients of their HIV status (Kingston 2004). Patient groups believed that the MHW should have withdrawn the infected blood products sooner and that the delay led to their infection (Kikuchi 1996). In 1989 haemophiliacs affected by HIV instigated court proceedings against the MHW and the directors of a number of pharmaceutical companies for compensation, in what became known as the *yakugai eizu* (iatrogenic AIDS) trials. Feldman (1999) has discussed in detail the use of the concept of rights employed by the haemophiliac plaintiffs throughout the trials. While the court battle focused on the right to compensation, the wider haemophiliac campaign drew attention to issues such as informed consent, patient privacy, access to medical care and stigma and discrimination.

HIV/AIDS did not become a priority for the government until a series of female diagnoses in quick succession in late 1986 and early 1987 caused a media frenzy known as 'AIDS Panic' and the possibility of widespread domestic heterosexual transmission became apparent. The MHW established the AIDS Countermeasures Subcommittee, consisting of politicians, bureaucrats and physicians, who were tasked with the development of HIV/AIDS policy. The committee discussed the possibility of quarantine and compulsory testing and examined the policies established overseas (Ōhama 1988), but, with little time to negotiate new legislation, they were forced to look to existing laws governing infectious disease dating back as far as the Communicable Diseases Prevention Law (1897) and the Venereal Diseases Prevention Act (1948), which were combined to form the basis of the AIDS Prevention Law (APL) (Feldman and Yonemoto 1992). While the WHO framework put forward by Mann considered the protection of rights as a prerequisite to successful HIV prevention, discussions held between subcommittee members show that Japanese policy makers instead saw the protection of individual rights as an impediment to public health measures and therefore striking a balance between public health and human rights was a serious point of contention (Ōhama 1988: 117). The subcommittee believed that they had paid sufficient attention to rights by proposing penalties for doctors or civil servants who violated the privacy of people diagnosed with HIV but the first draft of the law met with considerable opposition from groups such as the National Haemophiliac Association, the Tokyo Bar Association and the Japan Civil Liberties Union when it was leaked to the press in February 1987 (Swinbanks 1987). The draft required notification of HIV/ AIDS diagnosis to the local authorities, along with names and addresses should they be suspected of spreading the disease. Punishments for engaging in dangerous activities such as unsafe sex or donating blood ranged from financial penalties to imprisonment. Public health officials were given the authority to enforce HIV tests on those they suspected to be infected and penalties were also awarded for failure to comply. Additionally, the Ministry of Justice demanded a clause that afforded immigration officials the power to refuse entry to anyone they suspected of carrying the virus (Feldman and Yonemoto 1992). Soon after, the Tokyo Bar Association issued a statement of objection to the proposals, citing infringement of fundamental human rights and violations of privacy as its main concerns but the subcommittee defended the law by insisting that the right of the majority population to live outweighed the concerns of infringements of individual rights (Ōhama 1988). When the final bill was passed the more draconian aspects, such as the threat of imprisonment, had been removed and haemophiliacs were excluded from some of the notification clauses, but the majority of the draft stood (Feldman 2000).

Towards an inclusive HIV/AIDS policy

In the mid-1990s a number of factors combined to stimulate a change in direction for HIV policy. First, in 1994 the city of Yokohama hosted the 10th International Conference on AIDS. The conference placed Japanese HIV/AIDS strategies under the international microscope and provided the opportunity for a large delegation of Japanese ministers, bureaucrats, researchers and public health staff to interact with international organizations such as the WHO, International AIDS Society and Global Network of PLWHA (Shiokawa 2004).

Simultaneously, the *yakugai eizu* movement gained momentum and public support for haemophiliac groups mounted, to the embarrassment of the MHW who were under pressure to introduce policy measures to ensure the quality of life for PLWHA. In 1994 the Stop AIDS Seven Year Plan was instigated, which stressed the importance of medical care, facilitated through the establishment of specialized block hospitals in each prefecture specifically geared towards the treatment of HIV/AIDS and its related conditions. The Chair of the programme made it clear that the government was prioritizing the needs of PLWHA (Ōuchi 1994). During the early stages of the plan, HIV/AIDS spending increased dramatically and while funds for prevention and education remained steady, the majority of resources were distributed to the provision of medical care (AIDS Report 1997).

On the conclusion of the *yakugai eizu* trials in 1996, the settlement not only awarded plaintiffs a compensatory stipend, but also required the government to improve medical provision and ensure that the rights of PLWHA were adequately protected (Kingston 2004). The MHW agreed to fund the establishment of the AIDS Clinical Centre, which opened in 1997 and was at the forefront of developing best practice for the care of PLWHA (AIDS Report 1997). In contrast to the combative approach they had previously employed, *yakugai eizu* campaigners entered discussions with the MHW to ensure that new HIV/AIDS policy was based on the reality of living with HIV – an early example of the greater involvement of people with HIV/AIDS (GIPA) movement in Japan. Their advocacy was instrumental in gaining PLWHA eligibility for disability allowance to cover the high cost of medication (AIDS Report 1998).

In 1999 infectious disease legislation underwent a major overhaul. The century-old Communicable Disease Prevention Law (1897) was no longer effective in an era of globalization with new threats such as ebola (Nomura *et al.* 2003). The new legislation reflected the international human rights covenants, which Japan had ratified in the intervening period, and WHO declarations on the right to health, such as 'health promotion in the 21st century' (1998) (Sase and Gruskin 2007). As already discussed, during this period Japan was seeking to expand its international influence, participating in international conferences on global health and promoting human rights education for the general public and was, therefore, keen to demonstrate its compliance with international norms.

The *yakugai eizu* trial had drawn attention to human rights issues in relation to public health and popular opinion also demanded the adoption of a rights-based approach to infectious disease control. Prime Minister Obuchi acknowledged this when the law was introduced to the Diet in 1998:

> In Japan, it is important to acknowledge the fact that discrimination and prejudice against the patients of Hansen's disease or Acquired Immunodeficiency Syndrome (AIDS) existed in the past and to make use of the lessons we learnt from those experiences. Based on the changing situation concerning infections and the circumstances surrounding the patients of

infections, we are now required to ensure effective medical treatment for these patients and to deal with infections promptly and appropriately, while respecting the human rights of the patient.

(Obuchi 1998)

Under the new legislation, HIV/AIDS was no longer considered a unique disease requiring its own legislation, but rather ranked alongside measles and influenza.

To coincide with the introduction of the new legislation in 1999, MHW established a subcommittee to discuss future HIV/AIDS prevention strategies and, in keeping with the spirit of the new law, PLWHA as well as representatives from groups most affected by HIV/AIDS were invited to participate (AIDS Report 1999a). By this time, the overwhelming majority of new infections occurred through sexual transmission and surveillance statistics showed that the virus was spreading most quickly in particular subsets of the population, particularly MSM (Kōseirōdōshō Eizu Dōkō Iinkai 2000). Acting in accordance with the subcommittee findings, the MHW announced new HIV prevention guidelines in October 1999. Respect for human rights was stated explicitly as official policy and the need for cooperation between the state, local government, medical professionals, NGOs and researchers was emphasized (AIDS Report 1999b). Cooperation with NGOs formed part of a wider trend in social welfare provision during the 1990s to outsource public services to private groups and served to open channels through which representatives from minority communities could become involved in the policy-making process and make clear their specific health needs. As a result the new guidelines stressed extra provisions for 'groups requiring special measures', which took into account social backgrounds.

By the turn of the century, national HIV/AIDS policies had evolved from legislation that was widely believed to infringe the human rights of PLWHA, violating their privacy and prompting discrimination against both those infected and populations associated with HIV/AIDS, to one that explicitly stressed respect for human rights and allocated resources for the most vulnerable populations. These ideas were reinforced when the guidelines were renewed in 2006 (Akino 2008). International pressure to conform to UN and WHO standards on health and human rights, as well as increased exposure to international HIV prevention strategies through participation in international conferences were important factors contributing to this change. This chapter argues that a further vital factor has been the influence of NGOs and patient groups, as the following section discusses.

Developing a rights-based approach to HIV/AIDS prevention for the twenty-first century

The previous section demonstrated how a combination of international and domestic pressures led to the explicit recognition of human rights in both infectious disease and HIV/AIDS policy by the end of the twentieth century. However, specifically which rights were to be recognized, and in what way, was not made clear. This section argues that since the introduction of the new leg-islation domestic NGOs have continued to influence HIV/AIDS policy and that it is these organizations that have determined the rights-based agenda for HIV/AIDS prevention. *Yakugai eizu* campaigners used the courts to assert their right to compensation and drew on the political gains to insist on the incorporation of rights for PLWHA into policy, achieving the establishment of a comprehen-sive medical system and welfare benefits making the cost of treatment afford-able. Subsequently, as new HIV diagnoses continued to rise, particularly in minority populations such as MSM, NGO attention shifted to tackle the pre-vailing stigma and discrimination hampering HIV prevention, drawing on the international human rights-based approach advocated by the WHO and UNAIDS, including concepts such as community empowerment and GIPA.

These ideas were introduced to Japan through domestic NGOs, which, I argue here, have successfully framed HIV/AIDS as a human rights issue and have acted as mediators, translating international rights-based approaches to HIV to suit local understandings and needs, developing effective initiatives for their target audiences. This process has often taken place under the leadership of charismatic activists, or 'political entrepreneurs' (Keck and Sikkink 1998; Reubi and Mold 2013) who have positioned themselves as experts in the field and employed a range of advocacy strategies to ensure that their favoured approach is reflected in national HIV policy. Although NGOs working in the Japanese HIV sector are much smaller than comparable organizations in the UK, with access to considerably fewer resources, the following examples demonstrate where they have been successful in promoting a rights-based approach to HIV/AIDS.

From isolation to 'living together': stigma reduction in HIV/AIDS awareness campaigns

As HIV/AIDS policy evolved, so too did the nature of national awareness campaigns. Early campaigns were accused of excluding PLWHA from the dia-logue, except to portray them as a threat and met with criticism for reinforcing existing stereotypes of HIV/AIDS (Miller 2002). For example, an educational booklet, *Laughing AIDS,* was withdrawn in 1992 after complaints about its portrayal of foreigners and homosexuals as the cause of HIV/AIDS (Mainichi Shimbun 1992). The design of these early campaigns was outsourced by the MHW to marketing agencies, with little or no input from either public health specialists or people affected by HIV/AIDS. In subsequent years national awareness campaigns took a less controversial approach, simply importing the international World AIDS Day theme proposed by the WHO, with little attempt to adapt the message to address specific Japanese concerns.[2] However, from 2006 to 2010 the MHW introduced awareness campaigns based on the concept of stigma reduction and adopted the slogan 'living together', which, it felt, 'provided an opportunity for the entire public to contemplate on what each individual can do to prevent the spread of AIDS and eliminate discrimination and prejudice against AIDS patients' (Hashimoto 2008: 36).

The 'living together' theme was originally devised by the NGO Place (Positive Living and Community Empowerment) Tokyo as the theme for a gay men's HIV/AIDS prevention event. Place Tokyo is one of the oldest and largest HIV/AIDS NGOs in Japan, established in 1994 by Ikegami Chizuko on her return from a period of residence in Hawaii, where she was heavily involved in HIV/AIDS support and prevention (Ikegami 2009). Finding the Japanese approach exclusionary and discriminatory, and immediately aware of the lack of service provision for PLWHA in Japan, she attempted to implement similar schemes to those she had been involved with overseas, including a buddy support programme and the provision of social spaces for PLWHA (Ikegami 2009). Place Tokyo has put particular emphasis on the links between stigma, discrimination and prevention and, together with other local NGOs, developed the 'Living Together Programme' in order to raise awareness of the realities of life with HIV/AIDS among Tokyo's gay community. The theme proved popular and spawned a series of live events and publications in which PLWHA were able to share their experiences. Place Tokyo was awarded a MHW research grant to investigate the merits of 'living together' as a prevention strategy through which it became clear that the concept was not only useful as an awareness raising tool in the gay community, but also signified the link between support and prevention, which had hitherto been considered separate aspects of HIV/AIDS service provision (Ikegami 2004).

The 'living together' concept took on still broader meaning in 2006, when Ikegami was given the responsibility of organizing the annual Japan Society for AIDS Prevention conference and selected it as the conference theme. In this context, it also came to represent the need for collaboration between researchers, NGOs and community-based groups, the media and government for effective HIV/AIDS prevention. In keeping with the theme, PLWHA were fully incorporated into the conference proceedings. Members of the Japan Network for People Living with HIV/AIDS (JaNP+) were invited to sit on the organizing committee and a scholarship was established to enable the full participation of PLWHA (Ikegami 2006). To coincide with the conference the MHW adopted the slogan as part of its World AIDS Day campaign.

Place Tokyo drew on international frameworks promoting stigma reduction as a HIV prevention strategy and successfully introduced the concept to its target community through a series of awareness-raising events. Through continued lobbying, the production of research reports demonstrating the efficacy of the approach, and its wider dissemination through national conferences, the merit of a stigma reduction approach to HIV/AIDS, as advocated by an NGO, was recognized by the MHW and became a central component of national awareness-raising strategies. In contrast to early campaigns, which played on stereotypes of PLWHA and could be said to legitimize the association of HIV with particular sections of society, the incorporation of the 'living together' slogan was a significant step towards a more inclusive, rights-based approach to HIV prevention by the MHW. However, discrepancies between the NGO and government understanding of the slogan are still evident. For example, in 2007, the subtitle 'to protect the ones you love' was added to the national awareness programme, changing the nuance of the message and, once again, invoking images of PLWHA as a threat.

Subsequently, the involvement of PLWHA and representatives from affected communities has increased still further, through the 'Making the Campaign' initiative in which interested parties are invited to discuss their requirements and ideas for forthcoming campaigns through a series of focus groups, before a theme is decided on democratically (Eizu and Sosaeti Kenkyūkai 2010). The greater involvement of NGO representatives in this process is one way in which HIV prevention messages felt to be discriminatory can be eliminated and a rights-based approach to national HIV prevention can be promoted.

Community empowerment and HIV/AIDS prevention

The shift towards a rights-based approach to HIV/AIDS prevention in the international context coincided with wider developments in public health that acknowledged the success of local level interventions, where marginalized communities became empowered to define and tackle their own health concerns (Minkler and Wallerstein 1997). The prompt response of American gay communities in areas worst affected by HIV/AIDS exemplified the benefits of prevention initiatives carried out at community level, where the specific barriers to changing sexual behaviour were well understood (Wohlfeiler 1997; Lune 2007). A secondary effect of these grassroots initiatives was the political empowerment of previously marginalized populations and often HIV/AIDS prevention activities acted as a catalyst for the community to assert the rights of its members in different contexts (Wallerstein 1992).

Japanese NGOs have been instrumental in adopting and developing notions of community empowerment, particularly with reference to minority groups affected by HIV/AIDS. Here I use the example of MASH (Men and Sexual Health) Osaka, a collaborative project between local government, an epidemiological research group and local activists, to demonstrate this process in the gay community.

Although the programme is now widely accepted to have made considerable progress in raising awareness of HIV/AIDS among gay men, and in the provision of a range of HIV-related services that meet the specific needs of the community, initial attempts by epidemiologists to tackle the issue were met with hostility and accusations of exploitation and violation of the rights of gay men. Keen to investigate the prevalence of HIV/AIDS in *hatenba* (saunas in which gay men often engage in sex with multiple partners), but unable to gain the cooperation of the establishments themselves, a research group led by epidemiologist and AIDS Surveillance Committee member Ichikawa Seiichi attempted to determine the information through the analysis of tissues taken from the waste bins of individual rooms (Ichikawa *et al.* 1997). It was hoped that the results, which indicated a high rate of infection, would stimulate HIV/AIDS awareness in the community, but instead, the unorthodox methodology alienated its target audience. The feeling at the time, articulated by one prominent activist, was that 'the power of the state had entered their hidden away space and selfishly removed their property' (Fushimi, quoted in Hasegawa *et al.* 2006). Recalling the early days of the epidemic when it was felt that the government was attempting to frame HIV/AIDS as a gay issue, the survey was belittled by the community and the possibility of future collaboration seemed slim.

Surprisingly, however, the incident became a catalyst for the development of community-specific HIV/AIDS prevention strategies. Ichikawa persisted with the study, but in subsequent projects insisted on the formation of closer links with the gay community. He envisaged a community-based response to HIV/AIDS such the well-regarded initiatives carried out by the Australian gay community (Ichikawa 2003), but as Japan lacked strong community links, these needed to be put in place before any intervention could be effective. Ichikawa found a receptive outlet for his ideas in Osaka, where by the mid-1990s new HIV/AIDS cases were rising rapidly. Local activists were attempting awareness activities, but with scarce resources it was difficult for small volunteer groups to put their ideas into practice. With the local government acting as an intermediary, the two sides were introduced and after a complex period of negotiation a mutually beneficial relationship was established between key gay community members and the research team (Onitsuka 2007). Community cooperation facilitated the collection of fundamental data, such as population size, sexual behaviours, knowledge of HIV and attitudes towards safe sex, which had hitherto not been investigated and from which evidence-based interventions could be planned (Ichikawa 2007).

Whereas previous national prevention campaigns had neglected minority groups, this collaborative project generated original ideas specific to the needs of Osaka's gay community, ranging from the production of a condom range designed by popular gay illustrators, to live events that combined music and entertainment with HIV/AIDS prevention information and the opportunity for HIV testing in a gay-friendly environment (Ichikawa 2007). The involvement of respected local activists encouraged previously reticent bar owners to participate in awareness raising activities and HIV/AIDS gradually became a talking point in the community. This approach to HIV prevention showed encouraging results. Between 1999 and 2003 participation in HIV testing in Osaka's gay community increased from 16 per cent to 34 per cent, while knowledge of the connection between HIV and other sexually transmitted infections improved considerably, from 25 per cent to 68 per cent. By 2004 over half the bars in the Dōyama area of Osaka, where the programme was based, had signed up to help distribute condoms to their clientele (MASH Osaka 2005).

With the success of the collaboration proven, representatives from several NGOs and gay advocacy groups nationwide were invited by the MHW to discuss further targeted prevention strategies. The committee proposed additional investment for MSM-specific prevention material, improvements in the HIV testing environment to meet the needs of MSM and an insistence that anti-discrimination measures were taken to avoid the characterization of HIV/AIDS as an exclusively gay issue (AIDS Report 2003). As the project expanded, MASH Osaka planned a community centre from which research results could be disseminated, volunteers could meet to exchange ideas and members of the public could call in for safe sex advice. Funding for these centres was secured from the MHW, which was concerned with rising HIV rates and had been convinced by MASH's initial results (Ichikawa 2007). Similar initiatives were rolled out in the capital and have achieved comparable levels of success.

The central involvement of gay activists and volunteers has helped to vocalize the community, empowering them to take control of their own health issues, while the reciprocal relationship with researchers has allowed them to influence the type of research that takes place, ensuring that the rights of community members are not violated and to develop effective strategies. The impressive results of initial prevention strategies, reported scientifically by the research group, has alerted the MHW to the merits of targeted prevention and the movement has resulted in the first allocation of government funds ring-fenced for use specifically in the gay community. As an epidemiologist and member of the AIDS Surveillance Committee, Ichikawa was ideally placed to advocate for funding on behalf of the community, translating the results of the community-based projects into scientific reports and interacting with MHW bureaucrats on a number of advisory committees. The merits of this advocacy technique were again demonstrated in 2006 when Ichikawa was successful in an application for a one-off MHW strategic research grant, awarded to implement further research into health issues deemed to be a particular concern, significantly boosting MASH Osaka's budget (Ichikawa and Kimura 2007). Additionally, mobilization over HIV/AIDS prevention has resulted in the establishment of networks, forums and events through which gay men can address other issues of concern and press for their needs to be recognized in other contexts.

Greater involvement of PLWHA

The increasing presence of PLWHA in the policy-making process has been apparent on several occasions throughout this chapter, most notably through the efforts of those groups involved in the *yakigai eizu* movement whose high-profile advocacy forced the MHW to make several improvements to conditions for all PLWHA, such as the establishment of a specialized medical system and allocation of disability welfare benefits. The admittance of representatives of these groups into the policy-making process paved the way for greater participation of PLWHA on government advisory committees after the epidemiology of the disease shifted and sexual infection became the primary concern. For example, representatives from a range of NGOs, including PLWHA, sat on the AIDS Prevention Measures Advisory Subcommittee, which considered the direction of future HIV policy in the aftermath of the new infectious disease legislation

(AIDS Report 1999a). Subsequently, a small number of organizations have attempted to foster a HIV community and to advance GIPA in Japan, endeavouring to collate the voices of PLWHA and ensure that their opinions are reflected adequately in HIV/AIDS policy and prevention.

Haemophiliac activists have maintained their commitment to patient rights after the conclusion of the *yakugai eizu* trials, establishing new support groups to ensure government promises are upheld. Habataki Fukushi, for example, was established using a portion of the money awarded in the *yakugai eizu* settlement and continues to advocate on behalf of PLWHA from all backgrounds, mostly in disputes over access to medical or dental care and workplace discrimination. Additionally, they survey their members regularly to identify where improvements could be made and lobby the appropriate organizations for change, ensuring the highest standards of support are in place for PLWHA (Habataki Fukushi 2011).

Haemophiliac advocacy and the GIPA initiatives of international organizations have inspired like-minded activists to form their own patient groups, which advocate for the rights of all PLWHA, regardless of the route of infection. The Japan Network for People Living with HIV/AIDS (JaNP+) was established by activist Hasegawa Hiroshi in time for the International Congress on AIDS in the Asia Pacific (ICAAP) held in Japan in 2005. The network models itself on the Global Network of PLWHA (GNP+) and Asia and Pacific Network of PLWHA (APN+) and aims to create a stronger voice for PLWHA in society by creating links between members and providing a forum for the exchange of ideas and opinions. Due to the stigma associated with HIV/AIDS in Japan, it has been rare for PLWHA, particularly those infected sexually, to come out as HIV+ and therefore community empowerment has been problematic. Prior to ICAAP a nationwide network of PLWHA was not in existence and patient groups more commonly acted at local level and in a private fashion, rarely engaging in advocacy. Drawing inspiration from its international counterparts, JaNP+ has developed a range of mechanisms through which PLWHA can connect with one another, including an annual general meeting and other smaller local symposia and the development of an online community. Since ICAAP, the network has grown such that 1000 people now subscribe to the mailing list and over 2000 take advantage of the social networking services. The online forum can also be used by members to exchange ideas and respond to surveys on particular issues of concern. The organization encourages members to become more involved in all aspects of HIV service provision and policy issues and coordinates a scholarship, which allows PLWHA to participate in the Japan Society for AIDS Research annual conference (JaNP+ 2010). JaNP+ is also heavily involved in lobbying for the rights of its members. For example, in the most recent general election the organization wrote to all major parties asking why HIV/AIDS was not included in their respective manifestoes and for them to clarify their HIV/AIDS policy. The responses were then made available to members through the JaNP+ website. In addition to lobbying, JaNP+ also works to tackle stigma and discrimination in society as a whole, through the positive speakers scheme in which PLWHA are trained and dispatched to a wide range of institutions including schools, media institutions and other NGOs to share their experiences and promote understanding of HIV/AIDS (JaNP+ 2010).

As the examples examined here demonstrate, NGOs and their members have been successful in advocating for a rights-based approach to HIV in Japan. They have not developed such strategies independently, but have instead formed domestic and transnational networks that have informed their approach to HIV and through which knowledge, values and practices have been shared and adapted to suit the local situation. Given the lack of resources available to Japanese NGOs, collaboration with other domestic groups has facilitated the provision of a comprehensive HIV service and the groups discussed in this chapter work together on a number of initiatives, including the Living Together Programme. While the particular priorities of the organizations and individuals involved varies, they share a common aim – to ensure the rights of PLWHA and those groups most vulnerable are reflected adequately in HIV measures.

In addition to the links that have been established between domestic groups, the opportunity to interact with international organizations has also influenced the Japanese NGO response to HIV/AIDS. Place Tokyo's Ikegami Chizuko, for example, was involved in community liaison at the Yokohama International Conference on AIDS in 1994, where her interaction with international NGOs alerted her to the lack of a community-based response to HIV in Japan (Ikegami 2001). Similarly, as a result of links formed at ICAAP in 2005, JaNP+ now acts as the Japanese link to APN+ and aims to forge stronger links between PLWHA across Asia, actively participating in APN+ programmes and maintaining a presence at international conferences (JaNP+ 2010). MASH Osaka frequently publishes research results in international journals in which it draws attention to the need for further funding for minority health issues in Japan (Koerner and Ichikawa 2011).

In comparison to MHW or local authority bureaucrats, who are often only involved in HIV issues for a short period, the activists discussed in this chapter have developed effective strategies as a result of a long-term presence in the HIV sector and, as such, have become recognized as experts in the field, allowing them to enter the policy-making arena. For example, Place Tokyo's Ikegami, MASH Osaka's, Ichikawa, JaNP+'s Hasegawa and the director of Habataki Fukushi, Ōhira Katsumi, are all members of the MHW's Assessment and Review Committee on HIV/AIDS measures, which meets twice a year to monitor the implementation of HIV/AIDS strategies at both local and national levels, providing an ideal opportunity for them to put across the views of their members (Hasegawa 2008).

Conclusion

National HIV/AIDS policy in Japan has evolved from an initial contain and control strategy reflected in the AIDS Prevention Law, to an approach that emphasizes respect for the rights of PLWHA and vulnerable groups. Incorporation of a rights-based rhetoric into HIV/AIDS policy has been the result of pressure to conform to international norms and state obligations to recognize the rights related to health as set forward by the WHO and UN, but was also due to the influence of NGOs and the political entrepreneurs that make up the domestic HIV sector. The *yakugai eizu* court case bought by haemophiliac campaigners placed patient rights, including ideas such as informed consent, access to medical records and the right to compensation for medical negligence in the public eye and pressured the MWH to emphasize the rights of PLWHA. Having gained public support and political influence, these campaign groups participated directly in HIV policy making, ensuring that steps were taken to improve the quality of life for PLWHA. This early form of GIPA set a precedent for the NGOs that followed and, as the epidemiology of the epidemic shifted, NGOs representing groups most vulnerable to HIV/AIDS, such as MSM, were also able to participate in policy making.

This chapter argues that it is these NGOs that have determined specifically how rights are to be incorporated into HIV/AIDS policy. Inspired by international frameworks governing rights related to HIV, the personal experiences of members, and their interactions with overseas organizations at international conferences, I argue that domestic NGOs have pioneered a rights-based approach to HIV, adapting these concepts to suit local needs so that in the twenty-first century HIV rights discourse has focused on the elimination of stigma and discrimination, community empowerment and GIPA. Through community building initiatives, education and public outreach schemes NGOs have slowly built up a rights consciousness among PLWHA and vulnerable communities, particularly among gay men.

Having developed these concepts in their target communities, NGOs and the political entrepreneurs that lead them have established themselves as experts, carrying out research and producing evidence to demonstrate the benefits of their chosen approach and feeding research reports back to the MHW in a bid to win further funding for HIV measures. Increased participation in policy making at both local and national level has allowed NGOs to lobby for the incorporation of these ideas into policy and they have been successful in promoting a stigma reduction-based approach to awareness campaigns, gaining funding for HIV prevention in vulnerable minority communities (MSM) and continuing to build a network of PLWHA who campaign for further improvements.

While there is much to be done before the stigma and discrimination directed at PLWHA can be eradicated from Japan, and recent funding cuts have called into question Japan's commitment to HIV/AIDS prevention, NGOs have introduced a rights-based framework into national HIV policy on which future initiatives can be built.

Notes

1 In 2001 the Ministry of Health and Welfare merged with the Ministry of Labour to become the Ministry of Health, Labour and Welfare. To avoid confusion, the acronym MHW has been used throughout this chapter

2 Previous MHW awareness campaigns can be viewed via the Japan Foundation for AIDS Prevention website: http://api.net.jfap.or.jp/event/aidsday/aidsday_poster_poster.htm (accessed 2 December 2012).

Bibliography

AIDS Report (1997) 'Atarashi eizu iryō taisei ga sutāto', 26:6 Tokyo Chūō Hōki.

——(1998) 'HIV kansensha no shōgainintei ni tsuite', 31:4 Tokyo Chūō Hōki.

——(1999a) 'Kansenshō shinhō ni motozuku eizu taisaku', 37:2 Tokyo: Chūō Hōki.

——(1999b) 'Yobō shishin ni tsuite', 41:2 Tokyo: Chūō Hōki.

——(2003) 'Dōseikan no seitekisesshoku ni kan suru kansen yobō kentōkai chukan hōkoku', 60:2 Tokyo: Chūō Hōki.

Akase, N. (1991) *Atarimae de ikitai: Aru eizu kansensha no hansei.* Tokyo: Mokuba Shokan.

Akino, K. (2008) 'Various policies for HIV/AIDS control after the revision of AIDS Prevention Guideline', *Challenging Practices on HIV/AIDS in Japan, 2008.* Tokyo: JFAP.

Bauer, J.R. and Bell, D.A. (eds) (1999) *The East Asian Challenge for Human Rights.* Cambridge: Cambridge University Press.

Chan-Tiberghien, J. (2004) *Gender and Human Rights Politics in Japan: Global Norms and Domestic Networks.* Stanford, NJ: Stanford University Press.

Eizu and Sosaeti Kenkyūkai (2010) 'Making the AIDS Campaign: Eizu kyanpēn fōramu hōkoku'. Available at: http://asajp.at.webry.info/201006/article_3.html (accessed 14 October 2010).

Fee, E. and Parry, M. (2008) 'Jonathan Mann, HIV/AIDS, and human rights', *Journal of Public Health Policy* 29: 54–71.

Feldman, E.A. (1999) 'HIV and blood in Japan: Transforming private conflict into public scandal', in Feldman E.A. and Bayer R. (eds) *Blood Feuds: AIDS, Blood, and the Politics of Medical Disaster.* Oxford: Oxford University Press.

——(2000) *The Ritual of Rights in Japan: Law, Society and Health Policy.* Cambridge: Cambridge University Press.

Feldman, E.A. and Yonemoto, S. (1992) 'Japan: AIDS as a non-issue?', in Kirp, D. and Bayer, R. (eds) *AIDS in the Industrial Democracies: Passion, Politics and Policies.* New Brunswick, NJ: Rutgers University Press.

Fukuda, M.H. (1994) 'Public health in modern Japan: From regimen to hygiene', in Porter D. (ed.) *History of Public Health and the Modern State.* Amsterdam: Rodopi.

Habataki Fukushi (2011) *Shakai fukushi hōjin Habataki Fukushi jigyōdan: Jigyō hokokusho heisei.* 22 nendo.

Hasegawa, H. (2008) 'Progress in AIDS measures in Japan to be submitted to the UNAIDS country report', in Kashiwazaki, M. (ed.) *Challenging Practices on HIV/AIDS in Japan 2008.* Tokyo: JFAP.

Hasegawa, H., Ichikawa, S., Ikushima, J. and Fushimi, T. (2006) 'Nihon no gei komyuniti to HIV/eizu', *Q. Jr* 2: 102–17.

Hashimoto, S., Kawado, M., Murakami, Y., Ichikawa, S., Kimura, H., Nakamura, Y., Kihara, M. and Fukutomi, K. (2004) 'Numbers of people with HIV/AIDS reported and not reported to surveillance in Japan', *Journal of Epidemiology* 14(6): 182–86.

Hashimoto, Y. (2008) 'Providing the right message and information for general population: World AIDS Day event 2006', in *Challenging Practices on HIV/AIDS in Japan, 2008.* Tokyo: JFAP.

Heywood, M. and Altman, D. (2000) 'Confronting AIDS: Human rights, law and social transformation', *Health and Human Rights* 5(1): 149–79.

Ichikawa, S. (2003) 'MSM ni okeru HIV kansen yobō kainyū: Purojekuto MASH Ōsaka ni tsuite', *Journal of Japanese Society for AIDS Research* 5: 174–81.

——(2007) 'Waga kuni no danseidōseikan no HIV kansen taisaku ni tsuite: Gei NGO to no kyōdō ni yoru ekigaku kenkyūwo tōshite', in *Ōsaka chiiki ni okeru danseidōseikan no HIV kansen yobō taisaku to sono suishin ni kan suru kenkyū*. Tokyo: JFAP.

Ichikawa, S. and Kimura, T. (2007) *Eizu yobō no tame no senryaku kenkyū shūtohan oyobi hanshinhan no danseidōseiaisha wo taishō to shita HIV kōtaikensa no fukyū kyōka puroguramu yūkōsei ni kan suru chiiki kainyū kenkyū*. Tokyo: Kōseirōdōshō.

Ichikawa, S., Ohya, H., Kihara, M., Sankary, T., Kihara, M., Imai, M. and Kondo, M. (1997) 'The prevalence of HIV and STD in condom semen samples', *AIDS Research Newsletter (Japan Society for AIDS Research)* 10: 65.

Ikegami, C. (2001) 'CBO konnan de minoriōki basho' in *Eizu wo shiru* (ed.) *AIDS and Society Kenkyūkai*. Tokyo: Kadokawa.

——(2004) *HIV kansen yobō taisaku no kōka ni kan suru kenkyū: Heisei 15 nendo sōkatsu buntan hōkokusho*. Tokyo: Kōseirōdōshō.

——(2006) 'Dai 20 kai nihon eizu gakkai gakujyutsu shūkai kuru!', *Place Tokyo Newsletter* 50: 4.

——(2009) Altman Award Lecture, 23rd Annual Meeting of the Japan Society for AIDS Research, 27 November 2009, Nagoya.

JaNP+ (2010) Japanese Network of People Living with HIV/AIDS 2009, nendo katsudō hōkokusho.

Japan Times (1985) 'Group identifies man as 1st Japanese AIDS sufferer', March 23: 1.

Keck, M.E. and Sikkink, K. (1998) *Activists Beyond Borders: Advocacy Networks in International Politics*. Ithaca, NY: Cornell University Press.

Kihara, M. (2008) *AIDS Data Book Japan 2007*. Kyoto: Study Group for the Trends and Impact of HIV Epidemic and Monitoring of HIV/AIDS Policy.

Kikuchi, O. (1996) *Tsukareta eizu panniku: Giwaku no eizu yobōhō*. Tokyo: Kiri Shobō.

Kingston, J. (2004) *Japan's Quiet Transformation: Social Change and Civil Society in the Twenty-first Century*. Abingdon: Routledge Curzon.

Koerner, J. and Ichikawa, S. (2011) 'The epidemiology of HIV/AIDS and gay men's community-based pesponses in Japan', *Intersections: Gender and Sexuality in Asia and the Pacific* 26: August.

Kōseirōdōshō Eizu Dōkō Iinkai (2000) *Heisei 11 (1999). nen eizu hasshō dōkō*. Tokyo: Kōseirōdōshō.

——(2012) *Heisei 23 (2011). nen eizu hasshō dōkō*. Tokyo: Kōseirōdōshō.

London, L. (2002) 'Human rights and public health: Dichotomies or synergies in developing countries? Examining the case of HIV in South Africa', *Journal of Law, Medicine and Ethics* 30: 677–91.

Lune, H. (2007) *Urban Action Networks: HIV/AIDS and Community Organising in New York City*. Lanham, MD: Rowman & Littlefield.

Mainichi Shimbun (1992) 'Manga [Eizu ha Warau] no hatsubai chūshi motomeru', 27 November: 26.

Mann, J. (1999) 'Human rights and AIDS: The future of the pandemic', in Mann, J., Gruskin S., Grodin, M.A. and Annas, G.J. (eds) *Health and Human Rights: A Reader*. New York: Routledge.

MASH Osaka (2005) 'Background to the Organization's HIV/STI Prevention Intervention programs for MSM in the Osaka Area.' Osaka: JFAP.

McLelland, M.J. (2005) *Queer Japan from the Pacific War to the Internet Age.* Lanham, MD: Rowman & Littlefield.

Miller, E. (2002) 'What's in a condom? HIV and sexual politics in Japan', *Culture, Medicine and Psychiatry* 26: 1–32.

Minkler, M. and Wallerstein, N. (1997) 'Improving health through community organization and community building: A health education perspective', in Minkler, M. (ed.) *Community Organising and Community Building for Health.* New Brunswick, NJ: Rutgers University Press.

Morikawa, I. (1994) 'Patients' rights in Japan: Progress and resistance', *Kennedy Institute of Ethics Journal* 4: 337–43.

Nami, T. (1987) 'Dōseiaisha ga eizu panniku no naka de kangaeta koto', in Iwai, S. (ed.) *Eizu no Bunkajinruigaku: Eizu genshō wo dō yomu ka?* Tokyo: JICC.

Neary, I. (2002) *Human Rights in Japan, South Korea and Taiwan.* Abingdon: Routledge.

Nguyen, V.K. (2005) 'Antiretroviral globalism, Biopolitics and therapeutic citizenship', in Ong, A and Collier, S (eds) *Global Assemblages: Technology, Politics and Ethics as Anthropological Problems.* Malden, MA: Blackwell.

Nomura, T., Takahashi, H. and Takeda, Y. (2003) 'Changes in measures against infectious diseases in Japan and proposals for the future', *Journal of the Medical Association of Japan* 46: 390–400.

Obuchi, K. (1998) 'Law concerning the prevention of infections and medical care for patients of infections', *Law No.114*, 143rd Extraordinary Diet Session, 2 October 1998.

Onitsuka, T. (2007) 'Rinji kensa ebento SWITCH 2000–2002 ni miru sekutā kan no pātonāshippu', in *Ōsaka chiiki ni okeru danseidōseikan no HIV kansen yobō taisaku to sono suishin ni kan suru kenkyū.* Tokyo: JFAP.

Ōhama, H. (1988) *Nihon no Eizu.* Tokyo: Simul Press.

Ōtani, F. (1993) *Gendai no Sutiguma.* Tokyo: Keisoshobo.

Ōuchi, K. (1994) 'Kantōgen', *AIDS Report* 7:1.

Parker, R. and Aggleton, P. (2003) 'HIV and AIDS-related stigma and discrimination: A conceptual framework and implications for action', *Social Science and Medicine* 57: 13–24.

Peek, J.M. (1992) 'Japan, the United Nations, and human rights', *Asian Survey* 32(3): 217–29.

Piot, P. and Seck, A. (2001) 'International response to the HIV/AIDS epidemic: Planning for success', *Bulletin of the World Health Organization* 79: 1106–12.

Port, K. (1991) 'The Japanese international law "revolution": International human rights law and its impact in Japan', *Stanford Journal of International Law* 28: 139–72.

Reubi, D. and Mold, A. (2013) 'Global assemblages of virtue and vitality: Genealogies and anthropologies of rights and health' in Reubi, D. and Mold, A. (eds) *Health Rights in Global Context: Contemporary and Historical Perspectives.* London: Routledge.

Sase, E. and Gruskin, S. (2007) 'A human rights perspective on infectious disease laws in Japan', *Japan Medical Association Journal* 50: 443–55.

Shiokawa, Y. (2004) *Watashi no Nihon no Eizu Shi.* Tokyo: Hyōronsha.

Shirasaka, T. (2005) 'National responses to AIDS in Japan: More action needed', *Iryō* 59: 635–36.

Swinbanks, D. (1987) 'Doubts voiced in Japan over controversial AIDS legislation', *Nature* 327 (14 May): 95.

UNAIDS (2007) *Handbook on HIV and Human Rights for National Human Rights Institutions.* Geneva: UNAIDS.

——(2009a) *Epidemiological Factsheet: Japan.* Geneva: UNAIDS.

——(2009b) *Epidemiological Factsheet: United Kingdom.* Geneva: UNAIDS.

——(2010) *The Benchmark: Japan.* Geneva: UNAIDS.

Wallerstein, N. (1992) 'Powerlessness, empowerment and health: Implications for health promotion programmes', *American Journal of Health Promotion* 6: 197–205.

Wohlfeiler, D. (1997) 'Community building and community organising in gay and bisexual men: The Stop AIDS Project', in Minkler, M. (ed.) *Community Organizing and Community Building for Health.* New Brunswick, NJ: Rutgers University Press.

Yasuda, Y. (1987) 'Ketsuyūbyō kanja ga eizu panniku ni tsuite omō koto', in Iwai, S. (ed.) *Eizu no Bunkajinruigaku: Eizu no genshō wo dō yomu ka?* Tokyo: JICC.

8 Evidence-based advocacy and the reconfiguration of rights language in safe motherhood discourse

Katerini T. Storeng and Dominique P. Béhague

Introduction

Health rights are not a static concept; as set out in this book's introduction, they vary across time and place and have been constructed, deconstructed and reconstructed in a variety of ways. This chapter analyses the historical, cultural and social context of public health activists' use of rights discourse, drawing on an ethnographic study of the international safe motherhood movement (Béhague and Storeng 2008; Storeng 2010; Storeng and Béhague 2014).[1] This movement emerged in the mid-1980s, when public health activists within UN agencies, public health institutes and international NGOs launched the Safe Motherhood Initiative (SMI). The aim of this initiative was to galvanize international action on high levels of maternal mortality or pregnancy-related deaths in poor countries. Over the years the SMI has expanded to incorporate new actors and has become one of the many 'transnational advocacy networks' (Keck and Sikkink 1998) or coalitions that advocate for specific diseases and issues within the emerging, and highly competitive, global health field.

During the decades since the SMI's launch, human rights discourse has played an important role in the promotion of maternal health as an international health priority (Gruskin *et al.* 2008: 589). According to one commentator, the application of human rights in safe motherhood is now 'so widely accepted that human rights have been named as central to achieving the goal and targets of the Millennium Declaration', which include reducing maternal mortality by two-thirds by 2015 (Cottingham *et al.* 2010: 551). We argue, however, that during the past two decades the use of rights in safe motherhood – particularly in global-level advocacy – has often been highly contentious. Indeed, our ethnography shows that that there has been retreat from the explicit reference to rights that was so central in global safe motherhood advocacy in the years when this initiative was established. Since the creation of the SMI in 1987, moral and social justice arguments – rooted principally in liberal egalitarian discourses – have become progressively eclipsed by an 'evidence-based' approach to advocacy. This approach relies extensively on scientific evidence, particularly epidemiological evidence and health statistics, to justify the importance of prioritizing maternal health. Although morally imbued social justice arguments have become less prominent, rights-based language and argumentation have not been completely marginalized. Rather, the growing reliance on 'evidence' in safe motherhood discourse has modified the very notion of rights as applied to maternal health, both displacing it by making it narrower and reconfiguring it by making human rights claims more solid through the use of numerical tools and appeals to the authority of scientific evidence. What historical, social and political specificities account for the reconfiguration of rights language?

In addressing this question, our ethnography contributes to a burgeoning anthropological literature on the emergence of a powerful global health field and global forms of expertise as socio-cultural fields in their own right (Adams 2010; Janes and Corbett 2009; Lakoff 2010; Pfeiffer and Nichter 2008). Such global forms are characterized by their ability to 'assimilate themselves to new environments [and] to code heterogeneous contexts and objects', although they are also limited by specific technical infrastructures, administrative apparatuses, or value regimes (Collier and Ong 2005: 11). We have adopted a multifaceted approach for understanding the broader institutional contexts in which networks such as the SMI operate and through which specific perspectives, forms of knowledge and practices are shaped and reproduced (Mosse 2011). This approach included a review of international policy documents, scientific papers, and commentaries to identify trends in global policy debates; participant observation within the safe motherhood research and policy spheres (conducted between 2004 and 2009); and formal, open-ended in-depth interviews with 72 individuals from the main organizations involved in the SMI. These organizations are located in London, Geneva, New York, Washington, DC, and Oslo and include multi-lateral agencies; donor development agencies; prominent research institutes and schools of public health; professional organizations for obstetricians and mid-wives; and international research and advocacy NGOs. We have at times had to sacrifice ethnographic details ideally needed to properly locate informants in time, place and within specific social relationships in order to ensure our informants' anonymity within contentious developments and debates.

In what follows, we describe how advocacy specialists have, over the past two decades, gradually modified the SMI's original construction of maternal health as an inherent right and adopted an 'evidence-based' approach to safe motherhood advocacy. We then consider some of the factors that help to account for this trend. Finally, we analyze some of the more problematic and unexpected aspects of these developments and reflect on the emergence of a new, but distinct, kind of 'rights-based approach' to maternal health that incorporates the emerging discourses of evidence-based policy-making.

The position of rights in global safe motherhood advocacy

Women's social rights and early safe motherhood discourse

A commitment to women's health rights was central to early safe motherhood advocacy. Many of the SMI's founding members – several of whom were our key informants – belonged to the generation of women who participated in the anti-war and civil rights movements of the 1960s and 1970s and worked in humanitarian roles in their early twenties, often as Peace Corps volunteers. Although some went on to train as doctors and statisticians, most retained their politicized interest in women's rights and saw poor women's health as a main arena for this struggle. Their feminist identity was coupled with an ideological commitment to health equity and rights, as expressed both in the World Health organization's founding Constitution and in the 1978 Alma-Ata Declaration, which pronounced 'health for all' a universal human right (WHO and UNICEF 1978).

For these early activists, international action on maternal health was a matter of gender equality, international solidarity and social justice. High levels of maternal mortality in poor countries was not inevitable, but rather the result of discrimination against women. Poor women were dying, they claimed, because they lacked access to emergency obstetric care and professionalized delivery care (Rosenfield and Maine 1985). It was such care that had virtually eliminated pregnancy-related deaths in high-income countries by the 1930s (Loudon 1992). Poor women's continued lack of access to care was said to be underpinned by a 'chain of poor nutrition, illiteracy, lack of income and employment opportunities, poor environmental conditions, inadequate health and family planning services, and low social status' (Starrs 1987: 4–5). The report of the first Safe Motherhood Conference, held in Nairobi, Kenya, in 1987, thus concluded that both the international community and national governments had neglected maternal mortality because those affected by it 'have the least power and influence in society' (Starrs 1987: 4–5).

At the time, the SMI's key recommendations for tackling maternal mortality were multifaceted, rejecting the 'vertical' approaches that had become popular in the fields of child survival and family planning (Storeng 2010). Early safe motherhood proponents were influenced by the Alma-Ata Declaration's comprehensive primary healthcare strategy, and insisted that reducing maternal mortality would require, on the one hand, functioning health systems capable of providing good-quality delivery care (including emergency care) and, on the other, policies to address the underlying social and economic determinants of maternal mortality (Rosenfield and Maine 1985; Starrs 1987). Indeed, at the Nairobi conference, Halfdan Mahler, the WHO's Director General at the time, advised the public health community to resist the urge to search for 'a single magic bullet that could slay this dragon' (Mahler 1987). Failure to address the underlying causes of maternal deaths, he warned, would mean that the problem would only increase in magnitude with population growth.

Formalising the right to safe motherhood

The decade following the SMI's launch was a period of intense activity by international agencies and NGOs on various aspects of women's health. By the mid-1990s, activism and research by women's rights organizations had contributed to growing global awareness that women's health needed to be understood and addressed within the economic, social and cultural context of individual women's lives (Gruskin *et al.* 2008: 591).

During this period, the women's health and human rights movement was instrumental in shaping several major UN-sponsored international conferences that culminated in formal international recognition of the importance of human rights to achieve women's health and well being (DeJong 2000; Gruskin *et al.* 2008). Despite being politically negotiated by governments, the outcome documents of the 1994 International Conference on Population and Development (ICPD) in Cairo and the 1995 Fourth World Conference on Women in Beijing stated explicitly that improving women's health would depend on promoting and protecting their rights, particularly in matters relating to reproduction and sexuality (Gruskin *et al.* 2008: 591). The Cairo document specifically recognized women's right to go through pregnancy and childbirth safely. It articulated this right in terms of access to appropriate health services (Yamin and Maine 2005). Likewise, the 10-year review of the SMI, published for a Technical Consultation in Colombo, Sri Lanka in 1997, framed women's lack of access to existing life-saving treatment as a violation of their human right to healthcare (Starrs 1997). As such, the document highlighted the responsibility of governments to ensure access to such services (Gruskin *et al.* 2008: 591).

The retraction of rights language in safe motherhood advocacy

Despite the lofty rights rhetoric in the policy documents of the 1990s, our interviews with key actors who were active in the safe motherhood field during this period suggest that the SMI did not uncritically embrace the use of human rights. On the contrary, many key safe motherhood advocates became progressively sceptical about the political and strategic value of invoking human rights in advocacy efforts.

A first reason for such scepticism was an emerging concern, evident from the mid-1990s onwards, that the SMI's original remit, which included women's social and economic rights, had proved to be too broad. Prominent Columbia University researchers Deborah Maine and Alan Rosenfield argued in an influential editorial in the *American Journal of Public Health* that because the term 'safe motherhood' encompassed a range of concepts and actions, it had created confusion about – and, in turn, neglect of – the 'priority actions' for reducing maternal mortality: namely, emergency obstetric care and professionalized delivery care (Maine and Rosenfield 1999: 481). Some policy-makers, they argued, had been discouraged from investing in maternal health because they perceived that it would require 'dauntingly vast efforts' (*ibid.*)

Policy-makers' confusion about and neglect of safe motherhood was also understood to result from conflation between safe motherhood and the concept of 'reproductive health rights', which was promoted at the ICPD in 1994 (Lush and Campbell 2001). 'Reproductive health' included, but was not limited to, concern about women's pregnancy-related health and survival. Controversially, it included demands for women's rights to abortion. The question of abortion was a difficult issue for the women's movement more generally and was contentious among many activists from the global south. At the global level, the controversy was enacted between women's health activists and the Catholic Church and many socially conservative national governments. This controversy came to a head at the ICPD in 1994 and was perceived to damage the SMI (DeJong 2000). By one account, after the ICPD, safe motherhood came to be seen as 'the Trojan horse for the introduction of legal abortion', with the consequence that some donors and governments who had initially been supportive of safe motherhood became wary and withdrew their support (AbouZahr 2003: 18).

These developments fed into emerging reticence about the use of rights as the basis for safe motherhood advocacy. After the ICPD, the Safe Motherhood Inter-Agency Group sought to distance the SMI from the politicized reproductive health agenda by promoting a much narrower, technical focus for advocacy and policy (Lush and Campbell 2001). A key policy document from this time continued to define safe motherhood as 'a right', but argued that, for strategic reasons, calls for action on social and economic determinants of health to improve women's survival, social justice and equity should *not* be at the core of the SMI's remit (Starrs 1997). Instead, the SMI should focus on promoting the reduction of maternal mortality through scientifically established technical-medical interventions (skilled birth attendance and emergency obstetric care) (*ibid.*). This strategic narrowing reflected that controversy around the ICPD had cemented the SMI's reputation within broader global health circles as an initiative driven by a 'bunch of feminists', guided by ideological conviction rather than science.

The perceived need to downplay rights-based language and focus on the technical aspects of safe motherhood was further reinforced by the continuing politicization of women's health in the decade after the ICPD, culminating in US President Bush's reinstatement in 2001 of Reagan's 1993 Mexico City Policy, which became known as the 'global gag rule'. Until President Obama rescinded it in 2009, the 'global gag rule' prohibited the use of US federal funds to support organizations that provide abortions or support abortion-related work. This had negative repercussions for the SMI, including withdrawal of US funding to key safe motherhood organizations including the UN's Population Fund (UNFPA). Several of our informants argued quite adamantly that, with time, having a feminist orientation had become a veritable liability. Within this fraught political climate, many safe motherhood advocates understandably sought to disassociate themselves from their feminist identity, despite their private convictions, and seek new sources of authority, particularly in science. As one Washington DC-based NGO representative explained, 'I think everybody's afraid of getting the feminist label because it turns so many people off' (13/3/07 I50).

The rise of evidence-based policy-making in global health

Safe motherhood advocates' emerging tendency to downplay their discredited feminist roots and rights-based language in favour of an appeal to the authority of science must also been seen in relation to the growing influence during the past decade or so of 'evidence-based' discourses within global health policy. Later, we contextualise this broader trend and then describe its specific impact on safe motherhood advocacy.

The evidence-based medicine framework aims to use 'clinical evidence [derived] from systematic research' (preferably experimental evidence from randomized controlled trails or RCTs) to guide and evaluate clinical practice (Sackett *et al.* 1996: 73). In global health, burden of disease and cost-effectiveness analysis were originally the two most prominent tools that enabled the expansion of an evidence-based medicine framework into the broader arenas of social welfare and health systems management (Lee and Goodman 2002: 109). These tools, and the economic logic for priority setting on which they are based, have become ubiquitous within global health policy, coupled with an increasing emphasis on monitoring and evaluation through quantitative performance indicators.

Characterized by a focus on quick, visible productivity, the current emphasis on evidence for accountability is driven by a demand for transparency. It is part of a type of 'audit culture' (Power 1997) that Marilyn Strathern (2000) has argued grows as trust in the authority of public sector institutions wanes. Cris Shore and Susan Wright (1999) claim that the expansion of audit tools from financial accountancy into multiple cultural domains such as education (and, we would argue, global health) has enabled the expansion of neoliberal forms of governance, in which professional relations are reduced to quantifiable and, above all, inspectable templates. Such governmentalizing tendencies demonstrate the broader historical growth during the twentieth century of the power of scientific authority and of a pervasive 'trust in numbers' (Porter 1995) and culture of objectivity that has come to characterize modern societies (Daston 1992; Nader 1996).

The diffusion of evidence-based tools in global health policy is also justified on rationalizing grounds; such tools are intended to ensure that health programmes are based on evidence of effectiveness and aim to instil 'accountability' between donors and recipients. However, they are clearly rationalizing gestures in a different sense, too, bound up as they are in the broader drive to economic efficiency. Within international health, this drive began almost immediately after the Alma-Ata Conference on Primary Healthcare in 1978, with the growth of a counter-movement for *selective* primary healthcare focused on reducing deaths from specific diseases through selective cost-effective interventions, rather than comprehensive approaches to realize health as a right (Irwin and Scali 2007). Proponents considered selective primary healthcare a more pragmatic, financially feasible and politically palatable alternative to the more idealistic comprehensive primary healthcare agenda, not least because it was consistent with the emerging neoliberal ideology in donor countries. The World

Bank and the other international agencies further entrenched an economic logic to health in the late 1980s and early 1990s. Ever since, evidence-based tools have been used to justify donor-driven health sector reforms in low-income countries, including the expansion of private sector involvement in healthcare (*ibid.*), despite what many argue has been the concomitant decimation of public health systems (Lakoff 2010).

During the past two decades, donors and policy-makers have increasingly started to demand scientific evidence in assigning priorities and evaluating the success of interventions. This reflects the intense competition between different global health priorities and subfields, a competition that results from major structural changes to global health governance. The past two decades have seen a major decline in the power of the intergovernmental structures established after the Second World War, which were dominated by the World Health Organization, in favour of an 'unruly mélange' (Buse and Walt 1997: 449) of disease-specific global health initiatives. The entry of private donors such as the Bill and Melinda Gates Foundation has contributed to a business-oriented approach and to intense competition between groups (Birn 2009). Two major global health initiatives dominate, namely the Global Fund to Fight HIV/AIDS, TB and Malaria and the GAVI Alliance, which funds vaccines for use in poor countries. Indeed, there is some evidence that donor investment in these entities has displaced funds and 'political priority' from other global health issues, including safe motherhood (Shiffman 2007).

The 'evidence problem'

Set against these broader changes in global health and their associated pressures for researchers, many of our informants suggested that the initiative's focus on rights and involvement in the politicized women's rights struggle had detracted from the production of convincing evidence about maternal health and thereby damaged the SMI's standing. Many echoed the claim, first expressed in the literature in the early 1990s, that the inadequate quality of maternal health-related data in low-income countries has produced a negative feedback loop or 'measurement trap', in which the lack of credible data has fed into the neglect of the maternal mortality in global policy (Graham and Campbell 1992: 967). Measurement problems were said to have led to difficulties establishing the levels and trends of specific maternal health outcomes, identifying the characteristics and determinants of maternal mortality, and monitoring and evaluating the effectiveness of programmes designed to reduce mortality (*ibid.*). This 'evidence problem' had put safe motherhood at a disadvantage relative to 'priority' global health issues such as HIV/AIDS and child survival, which, according to one European maternal health epidemiologist, have 'a better record of promoting evidence-based recommendations' (06/08/04 I48).

Even when statistics have been painstakingly produced, policy-makers and donors wedded to the burden of disease approach have often dismissed maternal mortality figures as not 'high enough' to warrant priority. As a communication specialist from a Washington DC-based international advocacy NGO specializing in the dissemination of research explained:

> The fact is you really have a struggle because if you compare the number of deaths there are half a million maternal deaths compared to 10 million infant and child deaths per year. You know, people say it's nothing compared to some of the other issues.
>
> (13/06/07 I05)

A campaigner from another US-based international NGO pointed to the logic of cost-effectiveness that underpins such attitudes:

> Donors always ask, 'How many maternal lives were saved? How many children were saved?' [But when they see that] for every million dollars [they can] reach 30 million children, but only affect the lives of maybe 50,000 mothers, well that's not very cost-effective, so [they say], 'let's go for the children [instead]'.
>
> (13/03/07 I50)

Our informants were adamant that within a global health culture obsessed with evidence, ideological justifications and appeals to intrinsic rights do not suffice to influence political opinion and donor behaviour, but can rather reduce the credibility of advocacy claims. In fact, by the mid-2000s, mainstream safe motherhood advocacy rarely referred explicitly to rights. Instead, the main international advocacy NGOs – sometimes aided by colleagues within UN agencies and by academics – actively promoted the adoption of a new approach to advocacy they referred as 'evidence-based advocacy'. As we discuss later, this approach is characterized by the use of scientific (primarily quantitative) evidence to influence donor priorities and policy endorsement. Although some of the NGOs promoting 'evidence-based advocacy' were original SMI partners, many were new entities sustained by the emerging emphasis on and funding for activities centred on 'knowledge translation' (making scientific evidence intelligible to policy-makers) and 'getting research into policy'. In the next sub-section, we describe the diverse manifestations of 'evidence-based advocacy' promoted by these actors.

Evidence for advocacy

Our observations show that 'evidence-based advocacy' encompasses a range of different practices, including direct interactions with policy-makers, presentations at conferences and policy meetings, written and web-based communication of evidence designed to persuade decision-makers. Advocacy materials our informants showed us, including policy briefs, leaflets and glossy reports, presented claims about the cost-effectiveness of interventions designed to save women's lives, favouring evidence on technical innovations where inputs could clearly be tied to reductions in the burden of maternal mortality.

Advocacy groups have become acutely aware of the political power of numbers. This includes the way in which numbers can help generate a political response where rhetoric alone is ineffective. Indeed, a main manifestation of evidence-based advocacy has been the use of statistics to demonstrate the significant 'burden of disease' resulting from pregnancy-related causes, in order to frame maternal mortality as a global health problem warranting priority. Often such work has relied on 'creative epidemiology', to use Daube's term (Wallack *et al.* 1993), whereby the presentation of statistics was manipulated depending on the target audience. According to one informant, such strategic use of numbers is particularly effective in many of the low-income countries that 'don't even have a word for feminism' (13/03/07 I50).

Informants had observed that the advocacy power of numbers applies even when their validity is contested. In fact, *controversy* over the validity of statistics can actually *help* to generate a political reaction. A UK-based maternal health researcher, for instance, had witnessed such a situation in a North African country, when the publication of a UN-produced maternal mortality estimate that was higher than the government's own census-based figure was taken by the political opposition to generate a parliamentary debate about the government's commitment to women's health. The opposition used the discrepancy between the two figures to raise questions about the government's 'accountability' and 'trustworthiness'. This occurred despite the fact that, at the technical level, the figures were not comparable because they derived from different statistical methods.

Maternal mortality league tables ranking countries' maternal mortality ratios (MMRs) have also proved to be particularly effective advocacy tools. A European epidemiologist who, in the late 1990s, contributed to such a table recalled how its publication sparked a major political response in one West African country that was ranked as having a higher MMR than its neighbour. 'For the politician, it is how he is judged. Because unconsciously people concentrate on the numbers', our informant explained, adding that the MDGs' emphasis on measurable results has enhanced this tendency (12/10/05 I68). The strong reaction to the league table was indicative of the fact that the MMR is not just an indicator of women's health, but also of a country's overall development. As he put it, 'maternal mortality has become sufficiently part of the collective conscience to appear as part of the MDGs' and is understood by policy-makers to be an important indicator of the performance of the health system and, in turn, the 'social performance of a country' (12/10/05 I68). A high MMR thus creates an incentive for a government to prioritize maternal health, even if only to avoid appearing less 'developed' than its neighbours.

Advocacy groups capitalized on such politics in their work. A good example is the Countdown to 2015 Initiative established in 2005, in which a number of our informants were involved. The Countdown's stated aim was to 'monitor and hold countries accountable' for their progress towards the MDGs on child and maternal health through collation and communication of statistics on the 'coverage of health interventions proven to reduce maternal, newborn and child mortality' (Countdown to 2015 2009). The Countdown's premise was that drawing attention to performance indicators would stimulate 'better and stronger efforts at the country level' by governments concerned with their image and with demonstrating the results of donors' investments (*ibid.*).

One of the most significant advances in evidence-based advocacy has been the use of economic rationales and evidence. The Women Deliver Conference in London in 2007, which brought together nearly 2000 delegates from 115 countries to mark the SMI's 20th anniversary, mobilized economic arguments in order to bring 'new ammunition to the case for investing in maternal and newborn health' (Women Deliver 2007). The conference slogan – 'invest in women – it pays' – was designed to convey the idea that investing in maternal health is a cost-effective way of achieving the MDGs. Authors of the conference press release claimed that 'maternal health ... is vital for families to survive' and, significantly, 'for economies to prosper' (The Lancet 2007). 'Women deliver so much more than babies', the head of the Women Deliver advocacy team often said, highlighting that the double meaning in the term *deliver* highlights women's combined reproductive and productive, or economic, contribution (14/06/07 I7).

In keeping with this economic 'rebranding' of the safe motherhood issue, Women Deliver also became a showcase for new economic estimates of productivity loss and impoverishment resulting from pregnancy-related mortality and morbidity. Moreover, at Women Deliver and similar events, advocacy specialists often argued that donors assessing the cost-effectiveness of investing in maternal health strategies should consider not only the potential benefits to *women's* survival, but also the benefits for children and newborns, and, in turn, the long-term positive impact on both household and national economic productivity.

Many advocacy specialists have progressively realized that engaging in technical debates enables them to influence high-level decision-making processes from which they would otherwise be excluded. An apt example is NGOs' engagement with the processes of defining target indicators for global-level monitoring and evaluation processes for the MDGs. In contrast to the important involvement of NGOs in the ICPD in 1994, NGOs were not invited to participate in the process of defining the MDGs. Although improving maternal health ended up being one of the eight goals (MDG 5), many of our informants felt that by defining the goal solely in terms of *maternal* health, the international community reneged on its broader commitment at the ICPD to improve sexual and reproductive health. According to these informants, this occurred because maternal health is less controversial than reproductive health. If their NGOs had been included in the MDG priority setting meetings, they could have fought to keep the previous commitments among the MDGs. However, they deemed it politically unwise to argue for an additional goal on reproductive health once the MDG agenda was set. Instead, key advocacy specialists began to demand NGO representation on the expert groups assigned to define targets and indicators for measuring progress towards MGD 5. Through this forum, they successfully argued that the existing target on maternal mortality reduction was too narrow to capture the broader goal of maternal *health*. In 2006 they finally achieved agreement on the inclusion of an additional target: universal access to reproductive healthcare.

Although this is clearly only a partial victory, many within the field nevertheless considered the inclusion of a new, measurable target as crucial, because it encouraged governments to adopt a wider set of health-promoting interventions in addition to those targeted at reducing maternal deaths. Indeed, they insisted that influencing the numerical targets and indicators used in global monitoring processes has become just as significant as defining overarching goals – if not more so – since, as several informants put it, in global health, 'what you measure is what you do'.

The reluctant displacement of rights language

On many levels, evidence-based advocacy has been successful. Along with other institutional and political strategies, it has doubtless contributed to a recent surge in donor interest in maternal health, exemplified by the growth of donor support for policy initiatives such as the recent Global Strategy for Women's and Children's Health (PMNCH 2011). Indeed, on the basis of their own experiences many advocacy specialists insisted that advocacy based on scientific evidence and numbers is much more effective than ideological claims and politically loaded notions of women's reproductive health rights. As the president of one New York-based international NGO concluded, 'our experience, we think, demonstrates that if you have solid scientific evidence and you communicate it very strategically to "change agencies", that you can over time have an impact on policies and programmes' (11/06/07 I63).

However, although advocacy groups have been shrewd at playing the 'numbers game' to increase their competitive edge in the global health market place, they have also done so with some hesitation and critical reflexivity. Such self-criticism reflects a deeper ambivalence about the benefits of the evidence-based movement and the ways it can also do a disservice to political commitment to equity and universal health rights. Later, we describe our informants' unsettled views of the unintended and unwanted consequences of evidence-based advocacy practices. We also consider how a sub-group of maternal health advocates have developed a new form of right-based approach to counter these unintended consequences and to continue advancing their own ideological vision of maternal health as a social justice, gender equality and rights issue.

Displacement of moral principles

While, on the one hand, the reticence to use rights-based language in global safe motherhood advocacy represents a strategic response to altered political-economic realities, it reflects developments, on the other, that many of our informants lamented. For one, many bemoaned that the emphasis on evidence in policy debates has become so intense that people are no longer willing or comfortable making statements about their principled convictions unless they have scientific evidence to back them up. As a result, ideological battles are increasingly couched in authoritative technocratic language for the sake of political expediency, but in ways that simply obscure – and make it more difficult to challenge – ideological principles.

The abortion debate provides a good example. One senior member of a prominent international NGO remarked that the US-dominated anti-abortion lobby – with its growing global ambitions – has partially replaced moral arguments about the sanctity of human life with scientific research demonstrating purported negative psychological and medical consequences of abortion. According to our informant, this research is often of poor quality, but the problem, she claimed, is that there is no shortage of conservative politicians who 'either unknowingly or quite willingly will use junk science to justify their political positions' (11/06/07 I63). Increasingly, the only option for rebutting these claims is also through the language of science. In response, her organization has established routine procedures to debunk the scientific merits of their opponents' evidence to 'smash it before it gets any traction'. As she explained:

> We have now had to set up a fire brigade, if you will, we call it a 'rapid response programme,' where we can very quickly take one of these questionable studies and deconstruct it and look at the methodology, look at the way the data has been handled, look at how the randomization ... you know, look at the science of it and critique it. And then [we] get that critique around to people who might otherwise be taken in by the studies ... before, we didn't use to have to worry about junk science.
>
> (11/06/07 I63)

Such responses are themselves indicative of how pervasive the competition between evidence-based claims has become in global health and of the extent to which evidence has become the only, or at the least the most legitimate, way to present an argument and achieve credibility in global-level spheres. As the informant cited above put it, 'I think it suggests the importance which policy-makers and the public attach to evidence-based policy, that people ... no longer feel that their moral position or an emotional position is sufficient to justify a particular policy' (11/06/07 I63).

Technocratic narrowing

Another common concern among our informants was that, by engaging in evidence-based advocacy, they were endorsing tools based in a priority setting logic of which they were, at heart, critical. For instance, while burden of disease data has provided important advocacy input, maternal health specialists have also been at the forefront of revealing how burden of disease analysis system- atically biases priority away from conditions suffered by poor women, including pregnancy-related conditions (e.g. Sundby 1999). Moreover, given that pregnancy and childbirth are not diseases, many were uncomfortable about buying into the notion that maternal mortality should be grouped with, and ranked for priority, against diseases (e.g. Fathalla 2006). Similarly, the idea that cost-effectiveness considerations should guide the allocation of resources is in irresolvable tension with many SMI actors' private conviction that intrinsic commitment to values such as social justice, equity and rights should drive policy.

In moments of private reflection, several of those who had participated in the Countdown to 2015 and similar 'accountability' projects also demonstrated discomfort and ambivalence about their contributions to the exportation of 'target culture' to low-income countries. They noted, for example, that the enforcement of accountability demands, especially onto those countries that are donor dependent, can encourage recipients to produce fake numbers and cer- tainly diverts attention from building sustainable and locally relevant health information systems.

One related worry was that the narrow hierarchy of evidence transposed from evidence-based medicine means that only certain forms of scientific authority achieve influence: 'It's all quantitative now', a communication spe- cialist working for a USAID-funded NGO commented (13/03/07 I50), echoing criticisms by anthropologists about the evidence-based medicine framework's marginalisation of plural forms of evidence (Lambert 2006).

Some of those involved in advocacy campaigns, particularly those pushing innovative cost-effective technical solutions directed at specific clinical causes of maternal mortality, were self-critical that their work was undermining the SMI's longstanding call for comprehensive health system development. An NGO-based researcher conceded that her involvement in a Gates-funded project to advocate for uptake of a drug that can prevent post-partum haemorrhage (one of the main causes of maternal death) contributes to narrowing of the bigger debate about public health, away from social and political solutions to purely technical ones:

> I'm actually doing something that philosophically I wouldn't have believed I would have done a few years ago because I *do* believe in holistic care and I *do* believe we need to address tackling the system. So what am I doing sitting here working on ... one of the few things that comes as close to a kind of silver bullet strategy as you might get?
>
> (12/03/07 I66)

Several others similarly admitted that restricting advocacy messages to those interventions that are measurable and for which there is evidence diverts attention from the SMI's original call for multi-sectoral action to improve women's health, survival *and* social status.

While recognizing the limitations of their approach, many informants insisted that they had little choice but to appeal to scientific evidence and an underlying economic logic if they want to engage global health decision-makers, who increasingly come from international financial institutions and private, business-oriented foundations. As a senior NGO associate and founding member of the SMI put it, 'You can mobilize a certain constituency group just by talking about the ethical and injustice issues, but for these hardcore decision-makers who look at economic factors, that kind of appeal doesn't necessarily carry the day' (13/06/07 I5). A senior UNFPA adviser who was involved in elaborating the Women Deliver advocacy strategy similarly insisted that 'economic rebranding' has become necessary to 'sell' safe motherhood. In her everyday work, she avidly endorsed activities that will be able, as she put it, 'to position this product as an opportunity of desire so people will want to invest in it' (14/06/07 I7).

Evidence and elitism

Informants were highly aware that a key negative consequence of evidence-based advocacy is to restrict political influence to members of the global health elite (including multilateral agency technical officials, global health initiative representatives and researchers) who are able to engage in highly sophisticated scientific debates about the validity of statistics or the technical aspects of economic evaluations. International advocacy groups have gained access to this elite precisely by recasting their approach to comply with the evidence-based framework. Ironically, however, those who may be best placed to represent the needs of women at risk of maternal mortality – women themselves of local government or civil society groups – have tended to be excluded from the debate because they lack the required scientific sophistication.

This is one of the reasons why a number of international NGOs have started to invest in 'capacity building' among their counterparts in low-income countries to instil skills in evidence-based advocacy. According to one American communication specialist involved in such work, capacity building involves 'flooding' local policy champions with evidence through workshops and other mechanisms. The aim is to improve their bargaining position vis-à-vis their governments and, especially, foreign donors. As she put it, 'I say [to them], "these are the talking points if you're going to go to USAID or if you're going to a safe motherhood meeting … this is why it's relevant to your country"' (13/03/07 I50). She admitted, however, that this approach addresses only part of the problem. Crucially, it does not ensure that local advocates have access to locally relevant evidence. Rather, it reinforces dominant models by teaching organizations how to participate in the donor-oriented strategic use of evidence-based claims and numbers, rather than to challenge donor priorities that may be at odds with local needs. It may also undermine international NGOs' potential to act as intermediaries between global elites and local actors in order to nurture, on the one hand, local rights consciousness, and, on the other, greater awareness of local issues among global-level donors and policy-makers (cf. Merry 2006: 134).

An unlikely marriage: the rise of 'evidence-based' rights

The power of scientific evidence, together with growing scepticism about evidence-based advocacy's reductionist tendencies, has fostered a trend in which commitment to ethical or moral reasoning and explicit recognition of rights is re-emerging among international maternal health advocates. However, this is not a return to the explicit feminist language used at the start of the SMI. Rather, in this new guise, the construction of maternal health as a rights issue is being rearticulated in terms of 'evidence-based' claims. That is, evidence-based advocacy has become, ironically perhaps, a means to get justice, equity and rights-based approaches accepted on more 'legitimate' scientific grounds by those who might otherwise oppose this.

As part of this trend, certain advocacy groups driven by human right lawyers (some with public health training) rely heavily on epidemiological evidence to advance a new type of 'rights-based approach' that brings together legal and scientific rationales to substantiate their claim that maternal mortality is a human rights issue. For instance, these groups argue that, since evidence-based medical interventions to reduce maternal mortality exist (notably skilled birth attendance and emergency obstetric care), a governments' failure to secure access to such care constitutes a violation of women's rights to life (e.g. Freedman 2003). Moreover, they make sophisticated use of statistics, for instance highlighting inequities in the realisation of health rights by disaggregating maternal health indicators according to socioeconomic, ethnic or geographic factors. Likewise, statistics on the provision of evidence-based medical interventions are used not only to identify inequities in access to care, but also to monitor governments' progressive realization of health rights.

The use of statistics has re-empowered these groups to engage governments in a discussion about their accountability to international human rights covenants and treaties that oblige states to address systemic discrimination and inequity through targeted policy action. According to a lawyer and advocacy specialist from one of the NGOs pushing this new evidence-based approach to rights advocacy, it is effective precisely because it avoids using 'off-putting rights language'; in many of the countries in which maternal mortality is highest, 'you take a rights-based approach and you speak into a desert'. Numbers, by contrast, are less likely to get 'lost in translation'. As she continued:

> If you look at a country where you have a middle class that's able to give birth safely but then you see very high rates of maternal mortality among minority groups, immigrant groups, then it is clear you have a discrimination issue and that's not a difficult rights argument to make.
>
> (15/06/07 I39)

Although the use of statistics in this way serves to identify rights violations and enforce accountability, proponents insisted that it is not intended to be punitive. 'It is not about banging on the table and fighting for your rights', said another proponents of the new rights-based approach (19/02/06 I25). By using statistics strategically, rights-based approaches are able to engage decision-makers in discussions about how public health systems are designed to address maternal health, and 'whether women's rights are front and centre in those systems'. In such ways, statistical indicators have become a tool for offering practical guidance to policy-makers about where they should direct policy efforts to redress rights violations.

While lauded by its proponents, this new rights-based approach deviates significantly from the original conceptualization of health rights espoused by the SMI in the 1980s. Whereas the SMI originally advanced a broad notion of women's right relating to social, economic, political *and* healthcare issues, this new approach reduces or distils the right to health to the right to health*care*. Thus, while impeding access to evidence-base healthcare interventions has been cast as a human rights violation, there is little explicit attention to the underlying social and economic determinants of health or to social welfare interventions to address these. The appeal is not so much to intrinsic ideals as to enshrined legal obligations to provide 'evidence-based' medical interventions. As such, these recent developments still resonate, at least partially, with the gradual dismantling of the Alma-Ata Declaration's Health for All strategy that has been occurring since the 1980s (Birn 2008: 37).

Conclusion

In tracing these shifts in discourse, we have sought to contribute to multidisciplinary understanding of the changing notion of rights in global health and to elucidate the social and political conditions under which rights can be usefully employed to advance different health issues. Our analysis of global-level safe motherhood advocacy approaches over two decades demonstrates just how contested the notion of rights has become. Key safe motherhood advocacy specialists have eschewed the language of rights for strategic ends, even as they remain personally committed to improving women's social rights – and not just their right to healthcare. Instead, they have adopted 'evidence-based advocacy'. We have argued that this shift responds to broader changes in the politics of global health, characterized by the growth of a market-based competitiveness between different global health initiatives and an intense emphasis on evidence and quantitative results to justify donor investment.

While the language of rights has remained important in safe motherhood advocacy, its very meaning has changed to bring it line with the evidence-based ethos. At the start of the Safe Motherhood Initiative, maternal health advocates operated with an informal notion of maternal health as a right rooted in feminist ideology and a commitment to health equity. Although many maternal health advocates retain these values, with the reconfiguration of rights through evidence-based advocacy discussed in the last section, the notion of maternal health as a right has taken on a more technical-legal and individualistic hue. It is focused on access to medical interventions more so than the realization of social rights and responsibilities through the welfare state and international solidarity. At the same time, the evidence-based turn to human rights not only displaces the old version by making it narrower and more technical, but also creates and produces something new, as numerical tools to make human rights claims more solid and persuasive within the global health sphere.

Advocacy specialists have become shrewd at conducting 'evidence-based advocacy' because they have recognized that, within global health, health statistics and other evidence have come to acquire a social life of their own and to constitute authoritative knowledge, despite the fact that the numbers are often fraught with technical difficulties (Kielmann 2002; Nichter and Kendall 1991). Their experience has shown, as Donna Haraway (1988) has pointed out, that claims for action gain more authority and legitimacy if they are dissociated from 'subjective' ideologies and linked to high-status social agents. However, even as the evidence-based framework purports to have banished subjective values from the decision-making scene, values are introduced in other ways that are more readily fungible with, or incorporated into, an evidence-based framework. In this sense, it becomes more accurate to say that values have not disappeared from safe motherhood, but have rather been re-encoded and reduced to that which can be statistically proven. Even the new 'rights-based approach' makes little explicit reference to rights, in favour of the strategic use of statistics.

Embracing evidence-based advocacy is clearly a pragmatic response to altered political realities in global health. Yet, fostering such a heavy reliance on purportedly objective claims, rather than explicitly challenging the basis on which global-level decision-making takes place through value-based and political arguments, may have negative consequences, as many of those contributing to these trends acknowledge.

Although the adoption of evidence-based advocacy aims to 'save' the SMI as well as the women on whose behalf it advocates, it also has the unintended effect of feeding into an unhealthy competition between global health initiatives, which engenders fragmentation within national health systems as each professional community advocates for the uptake of its own set of interventions. As a result, little attention is directed to cross-cutting issues central to the functioning of the overall health system or social and economic determinants of health (McCoy 2009).

Advocacy groups' engagement with technocratic priority-setting tools also sustains this narrow focus. Cost-effectiveness analysis, for instance, is not easily applied to the kind of health system developments maternal health specialists claim are essential for reducing maternal mortality. Crucially, evidence-based arguments articulated within a narrow economic ethos divert attention from the political changes needed to address the health inequities that maternal mortality illustrates so clearly. Thus, by pandering to the politics of global health, safe motherhood advocates may be extending the dominance of a technocratic approach to priority setting that is in many ways at odds with their underlying ideological commitment to the notion of health as a right.

Our observations highlight that health rights are part of changing arrangements and assemblages comprised of maternal health experts and advocacy specialists, organizational structures, knowledge production practice and political and donor-driven negotiations over the allocation of global health resources. Through the work of international maternal health advocates, health rights language has been transposed, adapted and altered to new cultural and political contexts characteristic of the global health field in ways that transform both health rights and the actors that deploy them for strategic ends.

Abbreviations

ICPD	International Conference on Population and Development
MDG	Millennium Development Goals
MMR	maternal mortality ratio
RCT	randomized controlled trial
SMI	Safe Motherhood Initiative
UNFPA	United Nations Population Fund
WHO	World Health Organization

Note

1 This chapter develops analyses presented in an article currently in press with *Medical Anthropology Quarterly* (Storeng and Béhague 2014) from a human rights perspective.

Bibliography

AbouZahr, C. (2003) 'Safe motherhood: a brief history of the global movement 1947–2002', *British Medical Bulletin* 67:13–25.

Adams, V. (2010) 'Against global health? Arbitrating science, non-science and nonsense through health' in J. Metzl and A. Kirkland (eds), *Against Health: How Health Became a New Morality*. New York: NYU Press.

Béhague, D. P. and K. T. Storeng (2008) 'Collapsing the vertical-horizontal divide: an ethnographic study of evidence-based policymaking in maternal health', *American Journal of Public Health* 98(4):644–49.

Birn, A. E. (2008) 'Special section: health and human rights: historical perspectives and political challenges', *Journal Public Health Policy* 29(1):32–41.

——(2009) 'The stages of international (global) health: histories of success or successes of history?', *Global Public Health* 4(1):50–68.

Buse, K. and G. Walt (1997) 'An unruly mélange? Coordinating external resources to the health sector: A review', *Social Science & Medicine* 45(3):449–63.

Collier, S. J. and A. Ong (2005) 'Global assemblages, anthropological problems', in A. Ong and S. J. Collier, eds., *Global Assemblages: Technology, Politics, and Ethics as Anthropological Problems*. Oxford: Blackwell Publishing.

Cottingham, J., E. Kismodi, A. M. Hilber, O. Lincetto, M. Stahlhofer and S. Gruskin (2010) 'Using human rights for sexual and reproductive health: improving legal and regulatory frameworks', *Bulletin World Health Organization* 88(7):551–55.

Countdown to 2015 (2009) *Tracking Progress in Maternal, Newborn and Child Health.* Available at: www.countdown2015mnch.org (accessed 4 October 2011).

Daston, L. (1992) 'Objectivity and the escape from perspective', *Social Studies of Science* 22:597–618.

DeJong, J. (2000) 'The role and limitations of the Cairo International Conference on Population and Development', *Social Science & Medicine* 51(6):941–53.

Fathalla, M. F. (2006) 'Human rights aspects of safe motherhood', *Best Practice and Research Clinical Obstetrics and Gynaecology* 20(3):409–19.

Freedman, L. P. (2003) 'Strategic advocacy and maternal mortality: moving targets and the Millennium Development Goals', *Gender and Development* 11(1):97–108.

Graham, W. J. and O. M. Campbell (1992) 'Maternal health and the measurement trap', *Social Science & Medicine* 35(8):967–77.

Gruskin, S., J. Cottingham, A. M. Hilber, E. Kismodi, O. Lincetto and M. J. Roseman (2008) 'Using human rights to improve maternal and neonatal health: history, connections and a proposed practical approach', *Bulletin of the World Health Organization* 86 (8):589–93.

Haraway, D. (1988) 'Situated knowledges: the science question in feminism and the privilege of partial perspective', *Feminist Studies* 14(5):575–99.

Irwin, A., and E. Scali, (2007) 'Action on the social determinants of health: a historical perspective', *Global Public Health* 2(3):235–56.

Janes, C. R. and K. K. Corbett (2009) 'Anthropology and global health', *Annual Review of Anthropology* 38(167–83).

Keck, M. E. and K. Sikkink (1998) *Activists Beyond Borders: Advocacy Networks in International Politics.* Ithaca, NY, and London: Cornell University Press.

Kielmann, K. (2002) 'Theorising health in the context of transition: the dynamics of perceived morbidity among women in peri-urban Maharashtra, India', *Medical Anthropology* 21(2):157–207.

Lakoff, A. (2010) 'Two regimes of global health', *Humanity: An International Journal of Human Rights, Humanitarianism and Development* 1(1):59–79.

Lambert, H. (2006) 'Accounting for EBM: notions of evidence in medicine', *Social Science & Medicine*, 62(11):2633–45.

Lancet, The (2007) *The Lancet: Women Deliver Press Conference and Press Release,* 12October, London.

Lee, K. and H. Goodman (2002) 'Global policy networks: the propagation of health care financing reform since the 1980s', in K. Lee, K. Buse and S. Fustukian (eds), *Health Policy in a Globalising World.* Cambridge: Cambridge University Press.

Loudon, I. (1992) *Death in Childbirth: An International Study of Maternal Care and Maternal Mortality, 1800–1950.* Oxford: Clarendon Press.

Lush, L. and O. Campbell (2001) 'International co-operation for reproductive health: too much ideology?', in M. McKee, P. Garner and R. Stott (eds), *International Co-operation in Health.* Oxford: Oxford University Press.

Mahler, H. (1987) Address to the Nairobi Safe Motherhood Conference. World Health Organization.

Maine, D. and A. Rosenfield (1999) 'The Safe Motherhood Initiative: why has it stalled?', *American Journal of Public Health* 89(4):480–82.

McCoy, D. (2009) 'Global health initiatives and country health systems', *The Lancet* 374 (9697):1237–1237.

Merry, S. E. (2006) *Human Rights and Gender Violence: TranslatingInternational Law into Local Justice.* Chicago: University of Chicago Press.

Mosse, D. (2011) (ed.) *Adventures in Aidland: The Anthropology of Professionals in International Development*. New York and Oxford: Berghahn Books.

Nader, L. (1996) (ed.) *Naked Science: Anthropological Inquiry into Boundaries, Power and Knowledge*. London: Routledge.

Nichter, M. and C. Kendall (1991) 'Beyond child survival: anthropology and international health in the 1990s', *Medical Anthropology Quarterly* 5(3):195–203.

Pfeiffer, J. and M. Nichter (2008) 'What can critical medical anthropology contribute to global health? A health systems perspective', *Medical Anthropology Quarterly* 22(4):410–15.

PMNCH (2011) *Analysing Commitment to Advance the Global Stratgey for Women's and Children's Health. The PMNCH 2011 Report*, The Partnership for Maternal, Newborn and Child Health.

Porter, T. M. (1995) *Trust in Numbers: The Pursuit of Objectivity in Science and Public Life*. Princeton, NJ: Princeton University Press.

Power, M. (1997) *The Audit Society: Rituals of Verification*. Oxford: Oxford University Press.

Rosenfield, A. and D. Maine
(1985) 'Maternal mortality – a neglected tragedy. Where is the M in MCH?', *The Lancet* 2(8446):83–85.

Sackett, D. L., W. M. Rosenberg, J. A. Gray, R. B. Haynes and W. S. Richardson (1996) 'Evidence-based medicine: what it is and what it isn't', *British Medical Journal* 312:71–72.

Shiffman, J. (2007) 'Has donor prioritization of HIV/AIDS displaced aid for other health issues?', *Health Policy and Planning* 23(2):95–1000.

Shore, C. and S. Wright (1999) 'Audit culture and anthropology: neo-liberalism in British higher education', *Journal of the Royal Anthropological Institute* 5(4):557–75.

Starrs, A. (1997) *The Safe Motherhood Action Agenda: Priorities for the next decade. Report on the Safe Motherhood Technical Consultation, 18–23 October 1997*. Colombo: Family Care International, Inter-Agency Group for Safe Motherhood.

——(1987) *Preventing the Tragedy of Maternal Deaths: Report of the Safe Motherhood Conference held in Nairobi, Kenya, February 1987*. Nairobi: Family Care International.

Storeng, K.T. (2010) *Safe Motherhood: The Making of a Global Health Initiative*, unpublished PhD thesis, University of London.

Storeng, K.T. and Béhague, D.P. (2014) '"Playing the numbers game": Evidence-based advocacy and the technocratic narrowing of the safe motherhood initiative', *Medical Anthropology Quarterly*, In press.

Strathern, M. (2000) (ed.) *Audit Cultures: Anthropological Studies in Accountability, Ethics, and the Academy*. New York: Routledge.

Sundby, J. (1999) 'Are women disfavoured in the estimation of disability adjusted life years and the global burden of disease?', *Scandinavian Journal of Public Health* 27(4):279–85.

Wallack, L., L. Dorfman, D. Jernigan and M. Themba (1993) *Media Advocacy and Public Health: Power for Prevention*. Newbury Park, CA: Sage Publications.

WHO and UNICEF (1978) *Declaration of Alma-Ata. International Conference on Primary Health Care*, Alma-Ata, USSR, 6–12 September 1978. Geneva: World Health Organization.

Women Deliver (2007) *2007 Conference*. Available at: www.womendeliver.org/conferences/2007-conference/ (accessed 10 January 2011).

Yamin, A. E. and D. P. Maine (2005) 'Maternal mortality as a human rights issue', in S. Gruskin, M. A. Grodin, G. J. Annas, and S. P. Marks (eds), *Perspectives on Health and Human Rights*. New York: Taylor & Francis.

9 State of exception, culture of medical police[1]

SARS and the law of no rights in the People's Republic of China

Christos Lynteris

The central thesis of this chapter is that, based on the Prussian model of *medizinalpolizei* (medical police) and on Confucian problematizations of flow, the biopolitical apparatus of China has placed migrant workers at the centre of the contradiction between China's economic and political regime, while simultaneously rendering health no longer a right but an obligation towards the Party–State. My study of this biopolitical relation focuses on the severe acute respiratory syndrome (SARS) outbreak of 2003 and the epidemiological subjectification of migrant labour since. My analysis draws on historical data, as well as on my own anthropological fieldwork in China, consisting of both non-structured interviews with members of the epidemiological community and day-to-day work as an intern at a major Centre of Disease Prevention and Control in the People's Republic of China in 2008.

The SARS outbreak of 2003 is regarded today as a twenty-first-century case study of containing an airborne epidemic in the contemporary world. From its imagined origin at the Metropole Hotel in Hong Kong in February 2003, to its international spread to Vietnam, Canada and Singapore and its final 'arrest' in July of the same year, SARS claimed a cumulative total of 8,422 probable cases, with 916 deaths from 29 countries and a case fatality ratio of 11 per cent (WHO 2003). In this chapter, I will examine how the means employed by the People's Republic of China for containing the epidemic amounted to the imposition of a 'state of exception', in Giorgio Agamben's sense of the word (Agamben 1998). My analysis will underline how this inclusive exclusion, implemented through measures of isolation and quarantine, reflected the re-emergence of a medical police culture in public health in China. Moreover, I will demonstrate how, reflecting the actual birth of Chinese biopolitics in 1911, the return of medical police was grounded in the pathologization of migrant workers and their conceptualization as a 'floating population'.

From this perspective, the contradiction between human rights and the resurfacing of Confucian notions of harmony in twenty-first-century China, as recently underlined by François Jullien (2012), will be demonstrated as rooted in the conjunction of biopolitics and the political economy, where discourses on 'flow' assume a central role in rendering the 'floating population' a foe of social harmony and humanness as sanctioned by the sovereign power of the Communist Party of China.

Immobilising the population

The main bulk of epidemiological containment in China after the belated public acknowledgement of the SARS outbreak in March 2003 revolved around the restriction of population movement. Blocking interregional and intercity passage was one of the main and more spectacular means of SARS control during spring 2003. Moore (2004: 7) claims that hotels authorized to house foreign guests during the SARS crisis had check-in desks installed at the reception, where a medical interrogation was performed for newcomers including temperature taking, sometimes on a daily basis. In areas of high SARS suspicion, admittance to a hotel even required a previous doctor's clearance, lung X-rays and blood tests. Of course, day-to-day reality was much harsher for locals than for foreign tourists or business travellers. Eckholm (2006: 127) describes the veritable state of siege imposed throughout coastal China at the time:

> At bus and train stations, airports, and even many building entrances, medical stations were set up to take temperatures of all who passed, or at least purported to do so, often with instruments of dubious value. It is unclear how many actual SARS carriers were detected with these procedures, but anyone with a visible cold or a high fever definitely got the message: stay at home or risk medical detention.

Eckholm (2006: 127) describes the state of emergency as involving the erection of barricades at the entrance of villages 'to prevent non-residents from entering and ensure a temperature check for residents as they came and went'. This containment tactic reached its apex during the weeklong 1 May celebrations, the single most important holiday in China and one of the rare chances on which students and workers get to visit their families. The holiday was officially cancelled in order to prevent intercity and interregional travel.

At the same time, population movement was also restricted within the confines of cities and towns, where the public health apparatus imposed its most daring and unprecedented measures of containment, with Beijing bearing the heaviest burden. Unsurprisingly, 'the first victims of the measure were the city's prisons where employees have been banned from leaving and family visits have been dropped' (Chetwynd 2003: 1). Then, according to a report from *Automotive News*, on 27 April 2003, the Chinese Party–State closed down all the city's primary and secondary schools in Beijing 'affecting some 2 million students'. Moreover, 'the Beijing government also instituted morning fever checks for all students and established fever clinics to isolate and observe febrile persons, students and otherwise. Beijing cancelled most public gatherings and closed elementary schools' (Kaufman 2006: 62). Soon, increasing numbers of students were brought under a regime of quarantine, with a portion of them trapped in buildings tagged as isolation premises that amounted to little more than medical detention centres, where SARS suspects were expected to prove their 'innocence' or succumb to the disease.

Isolation regime

While conducting interviews at a medical school in a major Chinese city, and during my participant observation internship at a neuralgic epidemiological station of the same city in 2008, the scale of quarantine and isolation measures during the course of the SARS outbreak was often talked about by students, trainees and professionals. In fact, only five out of 30 postgraduate students interviewed during my fieldwork had not been quarantined during the SARS outbreak, with the vast majority of the 25 being shut in campus where they were then reading medicine as undergraduates. One research student recounted how she was isolated in her dormitory initially. Twice daily for a fortnight she and her co-students had to take their temperature down and fill in a form with relevant data, on the weekly review of which depended the issuance of a health certificate bearing evidence that one 'was not suspicious' and could exit the hall of residence turned epidemic detention centre [17/03/08 I057].

This state of emergency, which lasted for almost three months, did not mean that anyone with a certificate could just roam about in the city. According to the same informant, 'only four [certified] people could go out of campus in one day in order to buy supplies, but most people opted to stay within the walls, as that made them feel more secure' [17/03/08 I057]. The fate of those diagnosed as 'suspicious' was far crueller. According to another research student, when he was diagnosed as 'suspicious' for harbouring SARS, due to a high temperature, he was isolated alone in a dormitory room with nobody allowed to go near him. Food and water would be left at his doorstep. During the two weeks of his medical solitary confinement, he was totally off limits, receiving no medical treatment other than anti-fever drugs until his temperature dropped and he was allowed to move out of isolation [05/05/08 I070].

A third research student was diagnosed as 'suspect' and isolated because she had visited a city in the south considered by medical authorities as a 'danger area'. She was kept in medical solitary confinement for 10 days in a room on campus designated an isolation zone. There, she was instructed to take her own temperature every day. Food and water in her case were left daily outside of the building. The 20 people who were isolated within it would never meet anyone from the outside, until their reported temperature met the norms. Students claimed that none of them received any debriefing or psychological support after their release.

This comes as no surprise, as the general attitude regarding epidemiological management in China is strictly disciplinarian, rather than cooperative with regard to the public. During a visit to a primary school in May 2008, the epidemiological task group with whom I was embedded as an intern held a meeting with teachers so as to discuss a recent suspected 'foot and mouth' disease outbreak. Rather than involving a discussion of the crisis or some kind of bilateral planning and decision making with the educational staff, the meeting had a thoroughly administrative character. Having discovered four new cases among the pupils, with two already in isolation, the headmaster was ordered simply to close down the school. Although teachers did their best to engage in some meaningful dialogue with our team, their efforts were rebuked by our leader in the following words: 'You don't need to understand, you just have to do what we tell you.' Our team then simply proceeded to visit suspect pupils at home, ordering them to stay indoors for seven to 10 days and charging parents to inform the local epidemiological station on the progress of their children on a daily basis.

This authoritarian attitude reflects a hierarchical structure of obedience at the top of which sits the Ministry of Health. One spring afternoon when, during a casual chat after work, I asked a leading epidemiologist how her team cooperates with the Ministry, she looked puzzled: 'Cooperate?' I tried to rephrase my Chinese, but to no avail. Finally, she took notice of my foolishness and scoffed, incredulous at my ignorance: 'But we do not cooperate, we just follow orders!' Echoing a recurring theme, when asked the same question, another epidemiologist confirmed: 'We do not decide, we merely follow Ministry guidelines', reassuring me that she would continue doing so even if she personally believed such guidelines to be mistaken or possibly harmful to the public [13/06/08 I089].

The result of this culture of obedience during the SARS outbreak of 2003 was a unique governmental ability to quarantine and isolate large numbers of the population with minimum resistance: by May 2003, in Beijing alone, up to 30,000 people were quarantined in their homes or specially designated sites. The 'Consensus for the Management of SARS', the leading blueprint of managing the epidemic crisis composed by the Chinese Medical Association (2003: 1633), is revealing:

> In principle, public places where patients were during the period from three days before the onset of illness to the date of isolation and treatment for patients, or where a patient stayed for more than half an hour in a small space with poor ventilation within ten days of the investigation, should be classified as an epidemic spot to be under management. An epidemic spot can be one household or a number of households, one office room or a number of office rooms, a railway carriage or car, an airplane, a ward, etc.

In fact, however, as a number of senior epidemiologists were ready to admit to me only under conditions of strictest confidentiality regarding their personal and institutional identity, quarantine was a purely 'administrative measure'. In the words of a leading epidemiologist: 'There was no science in it, it was all about following and implementing orders.' Asked to explain what he meant, the informant answered: 'The time duration and the form of the quarantine was not designed by scientists but by police and security cadres' [20/05/08 I080]. It was 'totally based on law, not scientifically designed'. The epidemiologist added: 'What people say about population cooperation is nonsense. It was police coercion that implemented SARS containment – the people were forced to obey' [20/05/08 I080]. Yet, this demand for obedience to political authority and *ad hoc* administrative decisions was not allocated equally as far as China's population is concerned. For, despite the governmental propaganda regarding a 'harmonious society', China retains a sharp social stratification with some of the harshest class divisions on the globe.

The confinement of migrant workers

During the SARS outbreak of 2003 the *ad hoc* containment measures described earlier targeted, above all, migrant workers. A *Zhongguan Network* report on 7 May 2003 formulated the problem paradigmatically:

> Henan province in China has over 5,000,000 people that work outside the province as migrant labourers. Because of SARS many of the migrant labourers went home in order to avoid infection in the cities where there are more cases. As of May 7, the number of returning workers was about to exceed 800,000 people. From May 1 to May 4 there were 290,000 people who had returned and 75 per cent of those that returned came from a SARS hotspot. This made the work of preventing and curing cases all the more difficult.
>
> (in Chino 2003: 9)

Titled *The Effect of SARS on Workers in China*, and published in the summer of 2003, a China Labour Watch report explained the situation further:

> Perhaps most emblematic of the powerlessness of the workers is that when a worker came down with a fever, regardless or not if it was SARS, the worker was without exception quarantined and was not paid or given any kind of allowance during this time. The corresponding loss of the right to leave their workplace for fellow workers placed a heavy burden and stress on those workers that were otherwise healthy. The workers for the most part were absolutely powerless and had to leave all decisions about their own lives, safety and health to the local authorities and the plant managers, without any means of having a voice in their own fate. No independent unions exist that can act on behalf of the rights of the labourers in these factories.
>
> (Chino 2003: 6)

The analysis of China Labour Watch's report is scathing: 'From a health perspective, migrant labour became the focus of concern for many in the government who were concerned that their movement may spread SARS to areas of the countryside previously unaffected by the epidemic' (Chino 2003: 7). Besides being conspicuous targets for isolation and quarantine during the outbreak, migrant workers were rendered an object of knowledge for local authorities through unprecedented census procedures, which as Foucault (2007) has demonstrated form the backbone of any biopolitical regime. Joan Kaufman (2006: 64–65) provides us with a case study of the way in which a rural county in South China set itself against the looming threat of SARS:

> Before the SARS epidemic, the county administration did not know how many migrants there were in the county. But one of the first actions after April 20 was the conduct of a complete county census to identify numbers of households with migrant workers. The county now has information on all of its 80,000 migrants.

In fact, the regime of mutual surveillance was so dense that:

> [V]illagers were also locally instructed to report any returning migrants to village and township authorities … Migrants returning from an infected area were required to quarantine themselves at home for twelve days. Health workers from township hospitals and health centres were dispatched to monitor the temperatures of all returned migrants on a daily basis. The health worker was required to notify the township health bureau of any febrile persons. The township would then dispatch a team to transfer the individual to Xiaotangshan for an additional twelve days of observation and quarantine.
>
> (Kaufman 2006: 64–65)

Besides such efforts of population mapping, controlling the movement of migrant workers during the SARS outbreak took the form of forceful confinement. Factories and construction sites were considered to be sites of pestilence *par excellence*. A detailed report by David W. Moore (2004) of the American Society of Safety Engineers provides us with some rare insights. In his *SARS: Preventive Plans Key to Managing Health Risk in a Construction Environment in China*, Moore outlined the prevention programme implemented by PetroChina, China's largest producer in crude oil and gas at the time, and one of the biggest corporations in the People's Republic of China, in the West-East Pipeline Project, which tried to connect Shanghai with the remote gas reserves of the Tarim Basin in the deserts of Xinjiang. The programme concerned the construction of the pipeline across the Gansu corridor in Northwest China. Following Moore (2004: 21): '[T]he first line of defence in keeping workers healthy was awareness training. Medical professionals from local clinics were brought in to describe SARS, its symptoms, identification methods, likely risk factors and first response practices.'

Moore (2004: 22) gives only five lines on this frontline approach. Yet, he dedicates a third of a page to outline what he calls 'the second line of defence', i.e. 'to isolate workers from the public to the greatest extent possible'. It is well worth recounting the nine measures here in detail (Moore 2004: 22):

[a] Entry gates or barriers, guards and signage were used to indicate that worksites and living quarters were not open to the general public. This included hotel floors occupied by contract personnel and other areas generally accessible by the public. Sign-in sheets and washbasins were provided for visitor's use. Some offices required that each visitor's temperature be recorded before entry was authorized; [b] Meals were provided in a controlled environment rather than allowing workers to dine in public restaurants; [c] Surgical-style facemasks were distributed to all workers along with instructions to wear the masks when in public areas; [d] All workers were required to stay in their assigned living areas and were discouraged from visiting public places. Some sites acquired additional entertainment equipment […] to make residences more accommodating; [e] Relatives and friends were forbidden from visiting worker housing; [f] Worker leave was suspended. The project owner agreed to accrue missed leave time so workers could use it when the epidemic passed or at the end of the project; [g] Outdoor worksites were isolated from public access via flagging. All worksite visitors were required to sign in and have their body temperature recorded prior to entry to the worksite; [h] All visitors and workers coming from cities where SARS cases had been confirmed were quarantined and monitored for two weeks before being allowed to mix with the local workforce. This requirement significantly reduced the number of visitors to the site and prevented workers from visiting areas where SARS had been confirmed; [i] Planned periodic meetings and audits were assessed to eliminate all but those absolutely necessary face-to-face interactions. Overall, physical meetings were minimized to the extent possible. Use of e-mail, phone, fax, and teleconferencing was encouraged to minimize exposure to the disease.

The first thing one notices in these nine measures is the prevalence of mobility prevention techniques. Yet, a closer look brings us towards a peculiar twist in this mode of confinement that we could have otherwise overlooked. It is not so much that movement was blocked *on the way to* the factory, but rather *on the way out of* it. China Labour Watch's report provides an illuminating account as regards this vital detail: 'As SARS developed into an epidemic, laws were put in place to prevent the spread of the disease and allegedly to protect the workers. This resulted in the temporary closing of factories and the quarantining of others while work continued' (Chino 2003: 5). On its fifth page, the China Labour Watch report clarified this statement in detail. The passage is worth quoting at length:

There have been two changes in the treatment of suspected SARS cases after April. Before April, factories would force workers suspected of having SARS to leave the factory and pay for medical attention themselves. Later on, the policy changed so that when a factory suspected a worker of having SARS, the local government would not permit factory workers to leave the factory, and would also not allow any of the workers of factories in the area to leave. For example, according to a China Labour Watch investigation, Shenzhen Nantain Electronics Factory on April 28th stopped letting its workers leave the factory because one worker was suspected of having SARS. The workers were forced to stay in the factory for 14 days, after which the workers in the area around this factory were quarantined in the same way and not permitted to leave their factories. The policy was strictly enforced for the average worker that had no way of having his or her voice being heard. This contrasted with some high level managers that did not have to abide by the quarantine and were able to leave the factories to go home to their families.

(Chino 2003: 7)

The conclusion of the report leaves no ambiguities:

The policy here was not to close the factory and cease operations, but rather prevent employees from leaving, as work at the factory continued normally with only those workers suspected of being sick not working. The rest of the workers continued to work as before. They were not permitted to leave, and were forced to remain in the factories.

(Chino 2003: 8)

By enclosing the migrant labour force as the Other to what Rogaski (2004) has called 'hygienic modernity', what the management of the SARS crisis produced was, following Giorgio Agamben (2004: 37), 'a kind of state of exception, a zone of indeterminacy in which the outside is nothing but the exclusion of an inside and the inside is in turn only the inclusion of an outside'. If the confinement of workers in the factories, where they were expected to continue producing goods for the Western markets until their final breath, is not enough to convince one of the exceptional nature of Chinese epidemiological measures during the SARS outbreak, the punishment decreed in May 2003 for anyone trying to violate quarantine restrictions or to 'intentionally spread the disease' is conclusive: execution or life imprisonment (Rawski 2006: 111).

Of course, one could claim that, in the case of SARS, confinement was a general principle aimed at containing the movement of Chinese subjects at large, and not a strategy directed primarily at migrant workers. Yet, I would argue for a reversal of this perspective: general confinement, as experienced during the SARS crisis, was an exception applied on the entire population to the degree that it reflected the confinement of migrant labour as a permanent political economic strategy in contemporary China.

The birth of biopolitics in China

Rather than being a panic move by the Chinese Party–State, attributable to the lack of proper legislative framework (Keith and Lin 2007), the 'law of no rights' imposed on large segments of Chinese society during the SARS outbreak of 2003, formed part of a biopolitical conceptualization of the population in general and its mobile labour force in particular with deep roots in Chinese governmentality and its reliance on the Prussian system of medical police [*medizinalpolizei*].

According to Rosen's classic work, the medical police arose within the context of a particular brand of Mercantilism known as Cameralism, and was introduced for the first time systematically by Johann Peter Frank (1791) in his monumental seven- volume work *System einer vollstandingen medicinishen Polizey*. Although Rosen's (1974) account is detailed, it nevertheless fails to problematize this mode of governmentality in terms elaborated by Foucault in his lectures to the Collège de France, *Security, Territory, Population*. According to Foucault (2007), the system of medical police did not simply try to regulate the population, its habits, movement and demography: it actually constituted the population as an object of governmental power knowledge. Medical police, as a generative technology of power, was institutionalized with the unification of the German states in the 1870s, when Bismarck sought to realize the late eighteenth-century ideal of rendering all activities, interactions, abilities and propensities, in other words any kind of sociality among the subjects of the Reich, beneficial to state power. This biopolitical subjectification and enclosure of the population was performed within the governmental confines of 'hygienic modernity', informed by eugenics and dynamic hybrids of miasmatic and germ theories in public health.

Similarly, in China the first systematic problematization of the population in terms of its health, reproduction, allocation and movement, circa 1910, was based on a system of knowledge preoccupied with issues of race extinction, eugenics, and a regulation of human reproduction (Dikötter 1998). It was actually Japanese colonialism that introduced the concept of medical police to China, with the chief evangelist of the new biopolitical doctrine being Gotô Shinpei, first colonial administrator of Taiwan, then director of the South Manchurian Railway. Gotô's doctoral studies under Max von Pettenkofer in Munich had equipped him with the lucidity to see that the implementation of medical police in Japan and its Asian colonies could not be a mechanical transplantation of the Prussian biopolitical model: one could not 'transplant the eyes of a flatfish into a sea bream' (Lynteris 2011: 347). Instead, both in his thesis and in practice, he engineered a marriage of medical police with the co-option of local systems of administration (Lynteris 2011). What was required for this was an in-depth study of the populations in place. Starting in Taiwan, and reaching its apex in Manchuria, Gotô's paradigm led to extensive ethnographic and sociological studies that rendered native and migrant populations legible for the Japanese colonial biopolitical machine (Katsumi 1999; Tsu 1999). The construction of a biopolitical net within which the population could be rendered legible and controllable was conditioned on the definition of ethnographic normalities that could be kept in check and regulated by the colonial forces through enclosing them within a model of what Rogaski (2004) has called 'hygienic modernity', aimed, among other things, at preventing two major irregularities threatening state power and its political economy: uprisings and epidemics.

Historians have largely neglected the importance of migrant workers in this governmental transformation. Still, it is certain that the great interest of the Japanese Empire in the traffic and labour of manual workers from mainland China, known in colonial parlance by the derogative term 'coolies', had significant biopolitical dimensions for both China and Japan. According to Drischoll (2010: 27–29), Japanese colonialists, although initially disturbed by the influx of poor labourers from adjacent Chinese provinces into Manchuria, soon came to see them as the very lifeline of their imperialist project. At the start of the twentieth century, 'coolies' were regarded as a naturally compliant and tireless labour force invested with a unique ability to toil without ever complaining. In this sense, Japanese colonialists constructed their very own 'coolie' anthropology, which 'strip[ed] coolie labour of all demands and nearly all human needs' (Drischoll 2010: 28).

The fascination of the Japanese colonial apparatus with 'coolies' was such that in 1908 the powerful South Manchurian Railway Company took the unprecedented step of laying off 2000 Japanese workers, replacing them with Chinese migrants (Drischoll 2010: 37). Such decisions rendered Chinese 'coolies' an indispensable pool of excess labour force in the hands of Japanese colonialism, given the fact that in 1910 alone Manchuria received 429,900 migrant workers from the Chinese provinces of Shandong and Hebei (Gottschang and Lary 2000).

The seasonal flow of these migrant workers constituted a major biopolitical challenge for both the Japanese and the Chinese Empire in their scramble for Manchuria's territories and living capital. Within this geopolitical context, the outbreak of the great Manchurian pneumonic plague of 1910–11, directly linked to marmot hunting and to the 'coolies' employed in it, constituted the event that brought about the birth of biopolitics in China proper. Chinese epidemiologists at the time claimed that plague, originally harboured by marmots, was spread across Northeast China through migrating 'coolies' employed in hunting and harvesting their fur for the international market (Nathan 1967). Talked about as 'roaming swarms' and 'hordes' (Strong 1911), but most often as a 'floating population', marmot-hunting migrant workers came under an extended state of exception, which saw their dwellings burnt, their passage forbidden and thousands of migrant workers isolated in immobilized train wagons under freezing conditions across the great Manchurian plains (Nathan 1967; Gamsa 2006; Lynteris 2012).

Migrant workers then, as today, were a labour force on the move, and thus provided a *locus classicus* for the exercise of medical police measures. The prevention of migrant worker mobility, and the pathologization of the 'coolie' body, both individual and collective, were central to the construction of the first large-scale biopolitical apparatus in China in 1911: the North Manchurian Plague Prevention Service. Instituted as a response to the great pneumonic plague of the previous year, the Service was instrumental in rendering the 'floating' of migrant workers a paradigmatic epidemiological problem in Republican China.

As I have demonstrated elsewhere, during the classic era of Chinese epidemiology (1911–35), roaming 'coolies' were imagined as the epitome of racial degeneration, resulting from lack of biopolitical control under the *ancien régime* (Lynteris 2012). In this way, the 'hygienic modernity' discourse of the Republic, imbued with Social Darwinist notions and Prussian medical police techniques, came in conjuncture with Confucian valorizations of flow and rootedness, which acquired a modern, biopolitical currency. The deplorable rootlessness of the migrant workers was associated with their equally imagined inability to heed to the signs of nature when hunting marmots, and thus contracting plague, in contrast to native Mongol and Buryat hunters, whose supposed 'roots' in the ancestral land allowed them to hunt harmlessly (Lynteris 2012). It is thus to the mobilization of this cultural matrix of meanings and values centred around the binary of flow and rootedness, in conjunction to the imposition of social exclusion and biopolitical exception on migrant workers by the Chinese state, that we must now turn our attention.

Flows of order and disorder

The fact that during the SARS crisis in 2003 it was the quality of the flow of migrant workers rather than the flow *per se* that rendered them pathological is testified by a sceptic comment made by a leading medical academic during my fieldwork: 'The President moves about China too, but he does not spread disease.' We thus stand before a fundamental biopolitical principle, which Michel Foucault (2007: 18) defined as the problem of circulation: 'organizing circulation, eliminating its dangerous elements, making a division between good and bad circulation, and maximizing the good circulation by diminishing the bad'; the institution of a 'security of circulations' (Thacker 2009: 143) as a form of fidelity towards the event of an epidemic (Badiou 2007), which creates subjects of decision (epidemiologists), but only on the condition of the subjectification of the 'floating population' as the object of that decision and its law of exception: the law of no rights.

Like 'coolies' at the beginning of the century, during the SARS crisis migrant workers were conceived as a 'floating population' with unique anthropological characteristics. Formally speaking, in today's China, the 'floating population' is defined in terms of the legal status suffered by migrant workers who remain *senso strictu* peasants ('farmers', in post-Marxist Chinese Communist Party discourse), in the sense that they have no right to welfare or to labour rights reserved for sedentary urban workers: 'They leave the land without leaving the countryside [*litu bu lixiang*] and enter the factory without entering the city [*jinchang bu jincheng*]' (O'Leary 1998: 55).

This state of inclusive exclusion, following Agamben (1998), urges one to agree with Li Zhang (2001: 23) that what renders migrant workers a 'floating population' today is not merely their legal standing with regards to the household residential system [*hukou*], but rather a complex power knowledge web of 'processes of naming, categorisation, and media representation; and the invention and implementation of new regulations that govern everyday migrant life'.

Following the so-called 'opening up' of China in the early 1980s, the mechanization and 'rationalization' of agricultural production produced some 200 million surplus rural workers, who started trickling into the labour-force hungry special economic areas of overseas industrial development and exploitation on China's coast (Li Zhang 2001: 27). After an initial knee-jerk response of the Chinese Communist Party to block and repress this wave of migration, regulations became more flexible and pragmatic. Thus, by the mid-1980s there were already a number of migrant workers who, being considered by local city authorities as a troublesome entity and category, were arbitrarily forced to move from city quarter to city quarter in search of work and housing (Li Zhang 2001: 27). The insufficiency of such *ad hoc* strategies was to be met by a legal enclosure of rural migrants at the end of the decade:

> Clearly, expelling [*pai*] does not work, and blocking [*du*] does not work either. The key is to pay special attention to regulation [*guan*] so as to establish an effective social control network, formulate proper rules and laws, and eventually make the floating population part of an efficient way of ordering our society.
>
> (Li Zhang 2001: 28)

In the course of the 1990s, migrant workers became the human locomotive of the new Chinese-led global economy, producing *en mass* the commodities consumed by a West cleansed of industrial production and its organized labour discontents. 'Floating' thus became a vital source of social and economic transformation in China, ushering in a constitutive governmental contradiction.

In the words of a senior epidemiologist, the Chinese Party–State 'cannot control population movement due to the mode of economic development, cannot restrict it, only monitor and provide health education to the migrant workers'. Echoing similar views among other public health experts and students, he described as inherently 'very difficult to control and track because they just float' [27/05/08 I081]. These words are strikingly similar to the Beijing West-District Government's opinions regarding internal migration, recorded by Li Zhang in the mid-1990s:

> The fundamental goal of making regulatory rules is not to clean up, drive away, or disperse migrant workers as before, but to guide, control and regulate them under the new condition of a socialist market economy – that is to transform a disorderly kind of floating into an orderly kind of floating.
>
> (Li Zhang 2001: 28)

What rendered this a truly biopolitical outlook was that it was based on technologies of regulation and normalization, aimed at imposing a state of inclusive exclusion on the migrant labour force via a manipulation of categories of orderly and disorderly circulation or 'population flow'.

The polar opposite of order/disorder has been pivotal in the biopolitical problematization of labour force mobility in China, which flourished first after the Tiananmen uprising of 1989 and once again as part of biopolitical reactions to SARS in 2003: 'It is said that rural migrants not only "float" from place to place; they also tend to "congregate in the rural-urban transitional zones" for extended periods' (Li Zhang 2001: 29). Just as they had been 100 years earlier, migrant workers are once again constructed as a pathogenic, virile mass whose movement and congregation cause crime, disease and disorder, reflecting an enduring Confucian ethico-juridical discourse on harmony and chaos as reflecting rootedness and rootlessness. The importance of this bipolarity becomes evident by a glance at a linguistic breakdown of the term 'floating population' put forward by Li Zhang (2001: 33):

> In Chinese the word *liudong* (floating) has two different meanings: one is to be lively and unencumbered; the other is to be rootless, unstable, and dangerous. This double meaning opens the image of floaters to multiple interpretations. The dominant discourse tends to invoke and overamplify the negative meanings by emphasising their relationship with related residual terms such as *liumin* (vagrants, homeless people), *liukou* (roving bandits), *liumang* (hooligans), *liucuan* (to flee), *liudu* (pernicious influence), *liuwang* or *liufang* (exiles), and mangliu (an unregulated flow of people, which is a transposition of the sounds in the derogatory term *liumang*-hooligans).

This chaos–rootlesness/harmony–rootedness binary structure reflected concrete political economic strategies on part of Han landowners throughout China's imperial history. Kuhn's (1990) study on the subject has elaborated on this juridical-spatial complex by portraying how 'itinerant people and wanderers in late-imperial China were widely perceived as ghostlike soul-stealers and were considered a potential threat to stable, rooted communities' (Li Zhang 2001: 34).

Confucian systems of knowledge have long been preoccupied with circulation and flow, a relation that retains to this day a social existence as a problem embedded in what Li Zhang (2001: 33) has called the 'metaphysics of sedentarism': 'Earth-bound sentiments are clearly expressed in a widely accepted Confucian saying, *antu zhongqian* (to be attached to one's native land and unwilling to leave it). Rootedness (not spatial mobility) is taken as the normal state of being in mainstream Confucian culture.'

A vital medico-juridical category, rootedness can thus be said to comprise the forming grounds of a pairing of bodily and spatial categories that reflects not simply a common problematization, but the constitution of a dialectical interphase of pestilence and hygienic backwardness, which pathologizes qualities of circulation and flow deemed disorderly and chaotic. In accordance to this paradigm, migrant workers are imagined as a highly mobile pestilent source that ravages its environs, reflecting the old Chinese proverb 'a rabbit never eats the grass around its nest' [*tuzi buchi wobiancao*], which according to Li Zhang (2001: 141) implies that '[S]ince migrants are not true members of any urban community, they are most likely to take advantage of it by committing crimes.'

Harmony's foe

By excluding migrant workers from the 'communion of life' and its Confucian attributes (ritual propriety, filial piety, etc.), the biopolitical apparatus of capture effectively subjectivates the 'floating population' in opposition to harmony as both the aim and guarantor of humanness (*ren*). As Choukroune (2012: 498) reminds us, harmonious society, the officially sanctioned goal of the Chinese Communist Party today, is 'a theoretical framework [that] turns law into a disciplinary principle given over to society's moral construction'; a political-theological principle that, by identifying the destiny of the state (*guo*) with the destiny of civilization (*tianxia*), renders humanness an aspect of the glory of the sovereign.

From this perspective, the 'floating population' is banished from the ontological sphere of humanness, and its modern juridical aspects (human/health rights), precisely because it is seen as a social category that cannot enact its duty to the sustenance of social harmony, the social reproductive apparatus of Communist Party sovereignty. What Thacker (2009: 149) has termed the 'topology of exclusive intervention of the sovereign' is thus articulated on the medico-juridical basis of rendering China's migrant labour force a figure of the inhuman.

Here we are not faced with the classic Euro-American biopolitical model of an exception imposed on 'external intruders', supposedly racial, ethnic or religious immigrant Others whose presence threatens and thus reproduces the most obscure foundations of the nation-state and its regime of sovereignty. On the contrary, we have Han Chinese workers moving within China proper being subjected to a regime of radical alterity that renders them beyond the very pale of Otherness as a system of normalized identity and difference. Consequently, migrant workers are a threat to social harmony, as defined by the biopolitical apparatus of capture, not because of some racial, ethnic or religious characteristic, not even because of their officially sanctioned class *per se*, but precisely because their 'flow' is imagined to render them categorically untraceable, illegible and unintelligible. It is precisely this imagined illegibility, and the medicalization of its imagining, that renders the 'floating population' the *cause célèbre* of Chinese biopolitics since its very inception in 1911. For it is not them, in and of themselves, that are pathologized, criminalized and stigmatized. It is rather their 'floating', the transgression of in-place categories, which amounts to no less than *their not being where they should have been by being where they must be*, that is imagined as disturbing the desired statist-Confucian 'harmonious society'.

Migrant workers thus embody a productive contradiction lying at the heart of the Chinese state of exception. In order for the Party–State to be reproduced as a social relation, everyone must remain at his or her post and all unsanctioned circulation must be banned. Yet, in order for the economy of the Party–State to flourish, a major deregulation of labour force mobility is required. If everyone stays in his or her prescribed place, as the doctrine of the 'harmonious society' dictates, the economy would stale, bringing the Party–State down with it. If, by the same token, everyone is allowed to move and seek residence and jobs where one pleases, then the Party–State itself collapses, losing control not simply over the value and distribution of living capital but over the overall discipline of its subjects. Only an inclusive exclusion in the form of a biopolitical enclosure of the internal flow of labour force can guarantee in a dialectical manner the perpetual gearing up of the biggest growing economy in the world and the totalizing power of the Party–State.

Migrant workers in China constitute a surplus humanity whose 'floating', both as a transregional work-seeking movement and as a medico-juridical category, is a necessary condition for the development of the wealth of the Party–State, to the extent that they are at the same time subjectificated as a threat to social harmony; a menace to the health and well-being of Chinese people as a void category signifying nothing else than the sovereign signature of the Communist Party on the vast heterogeneity of the nearly five million human beings trapped in the territory under its control.

It is a biopolitical axiom that the might of every modern state is predicated on the health of its population, yet, as the 2003 SARS crisis made more than clear, in the case of the People's Republic of China the latter, rather than being a right, constitutes no less than an objectification of social harmony as sanctioned by the Chinese Communist Party. Hence, health as a norm is conditioned on the suspension of health as a human right, in the sense that it is rendered an individual and collective obligation towards the state and its political economy. Under the current regime of medical police, health in China constitutes an enduring debt, which encloses an ever expanding range of social and individual activities, behaviours and relations in a biopolitical regime of exception whose role is to guarantee the perpetuation of the Party–State and its 'harmonious society'.

Notes

1 The field research leading to this chapter was funded by the Carnegie Trust for the Universities of Scotland and was sponsored by a scholarship of the Department of Social Anthropology of the University of St Andrews. I would like to thank the participants of the Health Rights Conference at the London School of Hygiene and Tropical Medicine for their feedback to my chapter. I would also like to thank David Napier, Roy Dilley, Tristan Platt and Nikolai Ssorin-Chaikov for their insightful comments and anthropological discussion on the subject. I am most grateful to all informants who placed their trust in me during my fieldwork. In accordance to anthropological ethics, this chapter preserves in full my informants' anonymity, as

well as the anonymity of their respective institutions and their location. The analysis of Chinese governmental policies with regard to SARS and to migrant workers is exclusively mine and neither it nor any of its parts is shared by or expresses the opinions of my supervisors, co-workers and informants in the field.

Bibliography

Agamben, G. (1998) *Homo Sacer: On Sovereign Power and Bare Life*, Stanford, NJ: Stanford University Press.

——(2004) *The Open, Man and Animal*, Stanford, NJ: Stanford University Press.

Badiou, A. (2007) *Being and Event*, London: Continuum.

Chetwynd, P. (2003) 'Huge Quarantine in Beijing after WHO Advisory Hits China', *Sun. Star News*, April 24, 2003.

Chinese Medical Association (2003) 'Consensus for the Management of Severe Acute Respiratory Syndrome', *Chinese Medical Journal* 116 (11) (November 2003): 1603–35.

Chino, A. B. (2003) *The Effect of SARS on Workers in China*, China Labour Watch, Hong Kong.

Choukroune, L. (2012) 'Global "Harmonious Society" and the Law: China's Legal Vision in Perspective', *German Law Journal* 13 (5): 497–510.

Dikötter, F. (1998) *Imperfect Conceptions: Medical Knowledge, Birth Defects and Eugenics in China*, New York: Columbia University Press.

Drischoll, M. (2010) *Absolute Erotic, Absolute Grotesque; The Living, Dead and Undead in Japan's Imperialism, 1895–1945*, Durham, NC: Duke University Press.

Eckholm, E. (2006) 'SARS in Beijing: The Unravelling of a Cover-Up', in A. Kleinman and J. L. Watson (eds) *SARS in China, Prelude to Pandemic?*, Stanford, NJ: Stanford University Press.

Foucault, M. (2007) *Security, Territory, Population, Lectures at the Collège de France 1977–1978*, London: Palgrave.

Frank, J. P. (1791) *System einer vollständigen medicinischen Polizey*, Vienna: J.T. Edlen von Trattnern.

Gamsa, M. (2006) 'The Epidemic of Pneumonic Plague in Manchuria 1910–11', *Past & Present* 190: 147–84.

Gottschang, T. R. and Lary, D. (2000) *Swallows and Settlers: The Great Migration from North China to Manchuria*, Ann Arbor: University of Michigan Center for Chinese Studies.

Jullien, F. (2012) 'Droits humains contre harmonie', *Manière de voir – Chine, état critique* 123 (June–July): 95–97.

Katsumi Nakao (1999) 'Japanese Colonial Policy and Anthropology in Manchuria', in J. van Bremen and Akitoshi Shimizu (eds) *Anthropology and colonialism in Asia and Oceania*, London: Routledge.

Kaufman, J. (2006) 'SARS and China's Health-Care Response: Better to Be Both Red and Expert!', in A. Kleinman and J. L. Watson (eds) *SARS in China, Prelude to Pandemic?*, Stanford, NJ: Stanford University Press.

Keith, R. and Zhiqiu Lin (2007) 'SARS in Chinese Law and Politics', *China Information* 21: 403–25.

Kuhn, P. A. (1990) *Soulstealers: The Chinese Sorcery Scare of 1768*, Cambridge: Cambridge University Press.

Li Zhang (2001) *Strangers in the City; Reconfiguration of Space, Power, and Social Networks within China's Floating Population*, Stanford, NJ: Stanford University Press.

Lynteris, C. (2011) 'From Prussia to China; Japanese Colonial Medicine and Gotô Shin-pei's Combination of Medical Police and Local Self-administration', *Medical History* 55: 343–47

——(2012) 'Skilled Natives, Inept Coolies; Marmot Hunting and the Great Manchurian Pneumonic Plague (1910–11)', *History and Anthropology* 23 (3): 453–71.

Moore, D. W. (2004) 'SARS: Preventive Plans Key to Managing Health Risk in a Construction Environment in China', *Professional Safety* (March): 18–24.

Nathan, C. F. (1967) *Plague Prevention and Politics in Manchuria 1910–1931*, Cambridge, MA: Harvard East Asian Monographs.

O'Leary, G. (1998) *Adjusting to Capitalism: Chinese Workers and the State*, New York: M. E. Sharpe.

Rawski, T. G. (2006) 'SARS and China's Economy', in A. Kleinman and J. L. Watson (eds) *SARS in China, Prelude to Pandemic?*, Stanford, NJ: Stanford University Press.

Rogaski, R. (2004) *Hygienic Modernity, Meaning of Health and Disease in Treaty-Port China*, Berkeley: University of California Press.

Rosen, G. (1974) *From Medical Police to Social Medicine: Essays on the History of Modern Health*, New York: Science Publications.

Strong, R. (ed.) (1911) *Report of the International Plague Conference (held at Mukden in April 1911)*, Manila: Bureau of Printing.

Thacker, E. (2009) 'The Shadows of Atheology: Epidemics, Power and Life after Foucault', *Theory, Culture & Society* 26 (6): 134–52.

Tsu, T. Y. (1999) 'Japanese Colonialism and the Investigation of Taiwanese "Old Customs"', in J. van Bremen and Akitoshi Shimizu (eds) *Anthropology and Colonialism in Asia and Oceania*, London: Routledge.

WHO Department of Communicable Disease Surveillance and Response (2003) *Consensus Document on the Epidemiology of Severe Acute Respiratory Syndrome (SARS)* (produced by the Severe Acute Respiratory Syndrome (SARS) Epidemiology Working Group and the participants at the Global Meeting on the Epidemiology of SARS, 16–17 May 2003). Available at: www.who.int/csr/sars/WHOconsensus.pdf (accessed 20 December 2010).

Index